יום תרועה

YOM TERUAH
THE DAY OF SOUNDING THE SHOFAR

Rabbi Jim Appel

OlivePress
צהר זית
Messianic & Christian Publisher

יוֹם תְּרוּעָה

YOM TERUAH, The Day of Sounding the Shofar
Appointed Times Series - Rosh Hashanah
Copyright © 2011 by Rabbi James Appel

Printed in the USA

ISBN 978-0-9790873-5-6

1. Jewish Holidays 2. Messianic Judaism 3. Spiritual Growth

Cover photo and photos on pages 91 and 131 copyright © 2011 by Allan Miller, Rochester, NY, amille2@rochester.rr.com

All pencil drawings of Shofars copyright © 2011 by Artist, Karen Van Lieu, kavanlieu@gmail.com

Karen A. Van Lieu
Turin, NY 13473

Photo on page 227 copyright © 2011 by David Bowling, m16m.com/photogallery.html

Photos on pages 113 and 215 copyright © 2011 by David Adams, Jerusalem, Israel

Photos on pages 23, 41, 57, and 121 copyright © 2011 by Elisabeth Adams, Jerusalem, Israel

Cover design copyright © 2011 Cheryl Zehr, Olive Press

Published by

Olive Press Messianic and Christian Publisher   צהר זית
www.olivepresspublisher.org   P.O. Box 163
olivepressbooks@gmail.com   Copenhagen, NY 13626

Our prayer at Olive Press is that we may help make the Word of Adonai fully known, that it spread rapidly and be glorified everywhere. We hope our books help open people's eyes so they will turn from darkness to Light and from the power of the adversary to God and to trust in יֵשׁוּעַ Yeshua (Jesus). (From II Thess. 3:1; Col. 1:25; Acts 26:18,15 NRSV *New Revised Standard Version* and CJB) May this book in particular reveal more deep meaning in the Jewish roots of our faith.

To honor Him, all pronouns referring to the Lord are capitalized, satan's names are not. Scriptures quotes are left as they are.

Blessed are the people who know the joyful sound (the Teruah)!
They walk, O LORD, in the light of Your countenance.
Psalms 89:15 (NKJV)

I dedicate this book to

יֵשׁוּעַ

Yeshua
who saved me.

Acknowledgements

Special thanks to the Ruakh HaKodesh (the Holy Spirit) who will "*guide you into all the truth; for He will not speak on His own initiative but will say only what He hears*" (John 16:13).

Also thanks to all the people in Congregation Shema Yisrael, and at other venues, who have encouraged me with their feedback and comments on my teachings.

And special thanks to my publisher, Cheryl Zehr, who valued these teachings enough to convince me that they should be made more widely available in a book, who spent many hours transcribing the messages, and who had great patience with my slow responses to her e-mails.

Table of Contents

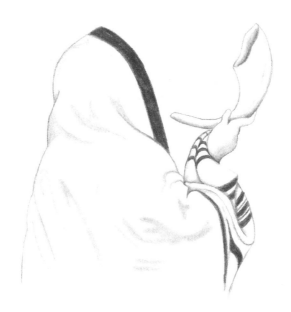

CHAPTER 1

WHAT ARE WE TO REMEMBER?

In this book, we are going to study a Biblical holiday. But before we get to that specific holiday, let's discuss what Biblical holidays are called in general. In Leviticus 23, where all the holidays are mentioned, they are called, in Hebrew, "Moadim." There are many different translations for the word "Moadim." The common ones you might have in your Bibles are "designated feasts" or "feasts of the Lord." But it really doesn't make any sense to call them "feasts" because one of them is Yom Kippur (Day of Atonement). Is it a feast? No, it's a fast! So, if one of the holidays is a fast, how can you call all of them feasts?

The New American Standard translation calls these days "Appointed Times." I like that term because these are times that God has appointed. They are specific times that He has decided we are to meet with Him. *He* has made the appointment.

When we make an appointment with somebody, we set the agenda. So these are days when God has set the agenda. The Moad (singular for one "Appointed Time")* we'll study in this book is known as Rosh Hashanah to Jewish people and as the Feast of Trumpets to church people.

So, what is God's agenda for this Appointed Time? Well, to find out let's look at what the Scripture says about it.

Leviticus 23:24-25 *Tell the people of Isra'el, "In the seventh month, the first of the month is to be for you a day of complete rest for remembering, a holy convocation announced with blasts on the shofar* (ram's horn). *25 Do not do any kind of ordinary work, and bring an offering made by fire to ADONAI* (the Lord)."

Notice there are five commands given here:
1.   Have a day of rest (a Shabbat).
2.   Hold a holy convocation or assembly.
3.   Blow the Shofar (ram's horn).
4.   Make offerings.
5.   And it also tells exactly on which day it is to be celebrated.

That seems clear enough. But we'd like to know a little more, wouldn't we? So, let's look at what some other Scriptures say about it. But, you know what? We can't do that. You know why? Those are the only verses in the whole Bible that give the instructions for Rosh Hashanah!

So, in looking at these five Scriptural commands for Rosh Hashanah, we find ourselves in a quandary over how to celebrate it. Why? Well, first because we can't make offerings anymore. God commanded in Leviticus 17:8-9 that sacrifices can only be made at the Temple, so ever since the Temple was destroyed in 70 CE, Jewish people have not been able to make sacrifices to the Lord.

We have no problem obeying the other four commands. We like making this day a Shabbat (Sabbath) because a day of rest is always nice. We have no problem with assembling together because we like fellowship. We definitely have no trouble with blowing the Shofar. We love doing that. And the date? That command has always been followed. Rosh Hashanah is always held on the first day of Tishri, the seventh month of the Jewish calendar.

So we do all those things, but then we kind of scratch our heads and wonder why? What is the meaning of it all? What exactly are we supposed to do when we meet and blow the Shofar? And is there anything else we should be doing?

* The glossary (p. 267) contains most of the Hebrew used in this book.

So, in preparing for Rosh Hashanah I have
"Lord what did You intend for this day? Is it v
Traditional Judaism? Is that what You had in m
HaKodesh (Holy Spirit) gave me a first insight f
Hebrew words that are translated "announced w

The Hebrew words are "zih-kh'ron teruah"
memorial of blowing the Shofar and shouting for joy." Yes, those
little words really do mean all that! And, you know what? To be Biblical,
we could call this holiday "Yom Zih-kh'ron Teruah" or "Yom Teruah."
("Yom" is Hebrew for "day.") Thus the title of this book!

"Zih-kh'ron" means *a memorial to bring to memory for the purpose
of keeping it fresh in our minds.* [See Strong's H2146.] We have lots
of other memorials in our culture. A bridge can be a memorial. Take
the Veteran's Memorial Bridge where I live in Rochester, NY, for
example. A building can be a memorial. The War Memorial building
here in Rochester is a building named to remind us of World War II. It
is important to us to keep reminding ourselves of that war. That's why
there was so much objection several years ago to renaming it "The Blue
Cross Arena." The city officials compromised by naming it "The Blue
Cross Arena at the War Memorial."

A day can be a memorial. We have Memorial Day when we remember
those who lost their lives defending our nation. Yom HaShoah, the
Holocaust Remembrance Day, is an important memorial day to us
as Jewish people. We want to remember those who perished and to
continue to commit ourselves to our motto, "Never again." Those are all
solemn or sorrowful memorials, but memorials can also be joyous, for
example, the Fourth of July.

Now, can you think of another Biblical Appointed Time, besides
Rosh Hashanah, that is a memorial? Actually, all the Biblical Appointed
Times except for Yom Kippur (Day of Atonement) are memorials of
something. Pesakh (Passover), Firstfruits, Shavuot (Feast of Weeks
or Pentecost), and Sukkot (Feast of Tabernacles) are all memorials
of important events in Israel's history and of Messianic events: The
Crucifixion, the Resurrection, the coming of the Ruakh HaKodesh (Holy
Spirit), and the future Millennial reign.

Can you think of any other events that have been memorialized
in Judaism? Khanukah (also spelled Hanukkah), Purim (celebrating
Queen Esther), and Yom HaShoah (Holocaust Remembrance Day) are
a few of them.

Can you think of some events memorialized in Christianity? Of
course! There's Easter, Christmas, and Pentecost.

in order to have a memorial, there has to be something to ...ber, right? But Scripture doesn't say what we are to remember ...osh Hashanah. That's why we're back to scratching our heads. ...hat are we to be remembering?

Well, to find out, let's look at the other word in that Hebrew phrase in Leviticus 23:24 *zih-kh'ron teruah*. We just looked at "zih-kh'ron." Now lets look at "teruah" *blowing the Shofar and shouting for joy.* Yes, that whole phrase is all wrapped up in that one little Hebrew word, "teruah." (See Strong's H8643.)

So, what does this word tell us about the thing we're supposed to remember? Well, since it says "shouting for joy," it must be for something good. So, this day is a memorial of shouting for joy over something good.

Now, let's look further at the word "memorial." A memorial serves two purposes. First, it causes us to remember an event that we should be thankful for, or sad about. Second, it reminds us to be committed to the cause of what we're remembering! For example, on Yom HaShoah (Holocaust Memorial Day), we re-commit ourselves to never letting a Holocaust happen again. On July 4th we re-dedicate ourselves to our country.

So, there are two questions we need to answer concerning this day of Rosh Hashanah. What event are we to remember? And to what cause are we to renew our commitment?

Well, traditional Judaism has an answer to each of these questions. We're going to look at those answers. Then we'll find answers in the prophetic Scriptures. Lastly, we'll look at the Scriptural instructions for the use of the Shofar.

In Traditional Judaism, Rosh Hashanah is the day we celebrate the New Year. The words "Rosh Hashanah" mean Head (or start) of the Year. Now, before I go any further, I need to untangle for you the confusion surrounding this tradition. Rosh Hashanah is on the first day of Tishri which is the seventh month, as I told you. Why would we celebrate New Years Day on the first day of the seventh month? That would be like celebrating the Fourth of July on January 4th or New Years Day on July 1st. Yet the Jewish community really does celebrate Rosh Hashanah as New Year's Day. Our Jewish calendar year actually changes number on this date.

This is especially strange since God specifically commands in Exodus 12:2 that the first month of the year must be Nisan, the month of Pesakh. So why didn't our forefathers obey that command? Well, there is an archaeological justification to this. We learn from archeologists and scholars that this day was the head of the civil year which they say pre-dated the Biblical year commanded by God.

So, it might seem that we Jewish people were once again just too stubborn to obey God. I was thinking that was maybe the case, but then I found two Scriptural justifications.

1. Exodus 34:22 *"Observe the festival of Shavu'ot* (Feast of Weeks, known as Pentecost) *with the first-gathered produce of the wheat harvest, and the festival of ingathering at the turn of the year. "* The Feast of Ingathering or Sukkot, also called the Feast of Booths or Tabernacles, is two weeks after Rosh Hashanah and in this verse, Scripture calls that time the "turn of the year." At this season, in the seventh month, the year has revolved, and is beginning anew.

2. Creation is described in Job 38:7. *"Where were you when I founded the earth ... when the morning stars sang together, and all the sons of God shouted for joy...?"* Because this last phrase "shouted for joy" is identical to the Scriptural command for Rosh Hashanah, the ancient rabbis taught that creation was finished on this day.

The Jewish calendar years date from creation which we just noted apparently happened at Rosh Hashanah. Although the first month changed when God told Moses to change it, the counting of years didn't change. So, because of those two Scriptures, we will be lenient with our Jewish ancestors and agree there is a reason to celebrate the New Year at this time.

Now, in America we have New Year's Day on January 1. Then we have a new year for school and businesses have their fiscal new years which start at varying times. Well, we Jews have several new years, too. We have the Biblical New Year in the spring on Nisan 1 as I just mentioned. (Passover is on Nisan 14.) In the month of Elul in August or September (depending on how long it's been since the leap year lunar month has been added), we have the New Year for the tithing of animals. Tu B'Shevat in mid January to February is the New Year for trees for determining tithes of fruit. And as we just learned, Rosh Hashanah has always been our New Year for counting our years.

Culturally and traditionally New Year Days are joyous occasions all around the world. It is the same for the Jewish people. For us, Rosh Hashanah is a time for remembering the good things from the past year. Therefore, we are already obeying God's commandment to have a "memorial of shouting for joy" on this day. We rejoice over what the Lord has done in the past year and over all the blessings we have received. This is similar to what many believers do on December 31st—New Year's Eve on the Gregorian calendar. Jewish people also celebrate Rosh Hashanah as a day to remember and be thankful for the creation of the world because of that verse in Job.

We get the second part of the Jewish answer to what we are to remember on this day from our traditional "Happy New Year" greeting, "L'Shanah Tovah." The full, traditional Jewish greeting is "L'Shanah Tovah Tikkah Tevu" which together means, "May your name be inscribed for a good year." What we are saying is "May your named be inscribed in God's Book of Life to live another year." There is very much a memorializing or awakening of memory in this traditional greeting. It reminds us that our future is in God's hands. Traditional Judaism focuses on this theme, believing that God decides our fate for the next year between Rosh Hashanah and Yom Kippur (the Day of Atonement). Therefore, since Yom Kippur comes ten days after Rosh Hashanah, Rosh Hashanah begins Ten Days of personal introspection and repentance.

Rosh Hashanah itself is not actually a day for repenting but it is the *start* of the ten days of repenting. It is a day for remembering and appreciating the sovereignty and awesomeness of God as a first step toward repenting. Being in awe of God is a very fitting thing to do before repenting. These Ten Days are thus called "Yomim Norim" which means "Days of Awe."

So Rosh Hashanah, as the traditional Jewish New Year, memorializes, not an event, but the awesomeness of our God and our need to turn to Him. It is a time to remember His sovereignty over our lives and His blessings over the past year. It is a time to renew our commitment to walk with Him.

That is well and good, but what has the Shofar got to do with all this? Well, the traditional, Jewish teaching on the use of the Shofar is that its powerful, loud sound wakes us up and makes us remember how awesome our God is. The Shofar sound helps us concentrate on His might, His love, and His sovereignty. It gives us an appreciation of His awesomeness which causes us to see our need to change. It reminds us of our need to repent and turn toward God.

In traditional Judaism, these Ten Days are set aside for repentance—for examining our deeds and attitudes. It's a time to turn from evil, to devote more time to Torah (Bible) study, to performance of its precepts, and to giving to charity. And also, most importantly, it's a time to make amends for misdeeds against others.

This time is very similar to the Christian tradition of Lent. The similarity becomes especially marked when you realize that for the whole month before Rosh Hashanah, the month of Elul, the Shofar is blown every morning to remind people of the upcoming Days of Awe, and to remind them to begin to make their hearts ready for repentance.

Maimonides, the great Jewish scholar from the Middle Ages who wrote the Mishna, wrote this prayer for these days:

Awake you that are sleepy, and you that slumber awake from your slumber, and ponder your deeds, remember your Creator, and go back to Him in penitence. You who miss the truth in your hunt after vanities, and waste your years in seeking after vain things that can neither profit nor deliver, look after your own souls, and improve your ways and your deeds. Let everyone of you abandon his evil ways and thoughts and return to God that He may have mercy on you."

This prayer is part of a forty-five minute group of prayers for repentance and forgiveness, called the Slikhot, that are recited daily starting at midnight after the Shabbat before Rosh Hashanah and continuing through the Ten Days of Awe. If Rosh Hashanah falls on a Monday or a Tuesday, these prayers are started two Shabbats before Rosh Hashanah.

This time surrounding Rosh Hashanah is a time to call the whole nation to repent as we see here in Isaiah 58:1 *"Shout out loud! Don't hold back! Raise your voice like a shofar! Proclaim to my people what rebels they are, to the house of Ya'akov* (Jacob) *their sins".*

Now let's look at the answers in Prophetic Scriptures. As Messianic Jews, we believe that we have some additional reasons to have a Zih-kh'ron Teruah: A memorial of shouting for joy. To us, it is a day when we memorialize or bring to remembrance, not an event of the past, but a promise for the future!

The first three Moadim ("Appointed Times") in the Biblical year have all had great Messianic events occur on them. The Crucifixion took place on Pesakh (Passover), the Resurrection on Firstfruits, and the coming of the Ruakh HaKodesh (Holy Spirit) happened on Shavuot (Pentecost). These "coincidences" cause us to believe that the rest of the Biblical Moadim (Appointed Times) will have significant things happen on them, too. We get a clue of what Messianic event will occur on Rosh Hashanah from what the Torah (Bible) commands to be done on it, namely, that there should be Shofar blasts.

In the Scriptures, one of the reasons for the blowing of the Shofar was to assemble the people to meet with God. Well, three times in the B'rit Hadashah (New Covenant) the blowing of a Shofar is described as a call to gather God's people to go to be with the Lord. Let's look at what Rabbi Sha'ul, (Paul) had to say about the blowing of the greatest Shofar and the greatest gathering together of the people of God.

1 Thessalonians 4:16-17 *For the Lord himself will come down from heaven with a rousing cry, with a call from one of the ruling angels, and with God's shofar; those who died united with the Messiah will be the first to rise; then we who are left still alive will be caught up with them in the clouds to meet the Lord in the air; and thus we will always be with the Lord.*

This event is widely known as the "Rapture" even though the word "Rapture" is not found in the Bible. We use the word "Rapture" because it best describes the event.

There are two reasons I believe this event will occur on Rosh Hashanah. One reason is because it involves the Shofar. The other reason is because Rosh Hashanah is the next Moad (Appointed Time) to be fulfilled in the yearly cycle of Moadim (plural: Appointed Times) commanded by the Torah (the Bible—specifically, the first five books of Moses).

So, we Messianic Jews have something special to celebrate with a Zih-kh'ron Teruah (memorial of sounding of the Shofar and shouts of joy). It's not an event that already happened, but a promise of what is to come, the return of the Lord and our departure to be with Him. We remember the promise and we renew our commitment to walking in the hope of its fulfillment.

There are other Biblical passages with instructions for use of the trumpet. We can see an application to our lives today in each one.

Numbers 10:2 *"Make two trumpets; make them of hammered silver. Use them for summoning the community and for sounding the call to break camp and move on."*

We no longer have these two special, silver trumpets so we use the ram's horns.

Numbers 10:3 *"When they are sounded, the entire community is to assemble before you at the entrance to the tent of meeting."*

They were to sound both of the silver trumpets to assemble the people. Notice where they were to assemble. They were to assemble at the entrance to the Tabernacle. This is the place where they met with God!

We can have a Zih-kh'ron Teruah and rejoice because through Yeshua's sacrifice on the cross, we can come into the presence of the Lord at any time. We can shout for joy remembering His work on the cross which opened the door to God's throne-room for us. We can renew our commitment to come before Him often. Or you can come before Him for the first time if you never have before.

Numbers 10:4 *"If only one is sounded, then just the leaders, the heads of the clans of Isra'el, are to assemble before you."*

Only one trumpet was sounded to assemble the leaders. Who is a leader? A leader is anyone leading people in the congregation, for example, Khavarah (Fellowship) Group leaders, Ministry Heads, Shabbat School teachers, etc., and anyone leading people to the Lord.

So this is a Zih-kh'ron Teruah to remember to be thankful for those who serve by leading. It's also a call to commitment to being faithful in the leadership God has called you to.

Numbers 10:5-7 *"When you sound an alarm, the camps to the east will commence traveling. 6 When you sound a second alarm, the camps to the south will set out; they will sound alarms to announce when to travel. 7 However, when the community is to be assembled, you are to sound; but don't sound an alarm."*

This passage shows that trumpets were used to start the people on their journeys. It's a call to set out to do the work of the Kingdom. So this is a Zih-kh'ron Teruah to remember the work God has called us to do. We renew our commitment to stay the course, to keep our hands on the plow, to walk the straight and narrow.

Numbers 10:8 *"It will be the sons of Aharon* (Aaron), *the cohanim* (Priests), *who are to sound the trumpets; this will be a permanent regulation for you through all your generations."*

This is a Zih-kh'ron Teruah to remember that we are entrusted to be cohanim (priests). We renew our commitment to fulfilling our priestly role as intercessors and as leaders.

Numbers 10:9 *"When you go to war in your land against an adversary who is oppressing you, you are to sound an alarm with the trumpets; then you will be remembered before ADONAI your God, and you will be saved from your enemies."*

This is a Zih-kh'ron Teruah for remembering that the battle belongs to the Lord. It is a reminder for us to prepare for battle against an oppressing enemy in our own land. It is a call to ask for God's help against the oppressor.

I first studied this verse just after the missile strikes that President Clinton launched against the terrorists in Somalia. This is a call to pray for protection against terror in the US. Let's also apply this call to pray for Israel, since we are part of Israel. Let this remind us to pray for protection against terrorism around the world and in Israel, too.

Numbers 10:10 *"Also on your days of rejoicing, at your designated times and on Rosh-Hodesh* (New Moon), *you are to sound the trumpets over your burnt offerings and over the sacrifices of your peace offerings; these will be your reminder before your God. I am ADONAI your God."*

This is talking about a Zih-kh'ron Teruah to remember that our God is a God who calls us to rejoice. This is a call to those who are willing to lead us in shouting for joy. And as we do that, remember that this is also a call to come before Him for the first time if you never have before.

*   *   *

Why We Celebrate the Biblical Feasts

Some people say that we are no longer under the Law. They ask, "Why should we, as New Covenant believers, celebrate the Jewish holidays? Didn't Yeshua bring in a New Covenant with a new set of rules to live by? Aren't we saved by grace, and not by keeping festivals?" Yes, we are saved by grace. But, let's look at what Yeshua said about the Law.

Matthew 5:17 *"Don't think that I have come to abolish the Torah* (Law) *or the Prophets. I have come not to abolish but to complete. 18 Yes indeed! I tell you that until heaven and earth pass away, not so much as a yud* (Hebrew "y" which looks like an apostrophe) *or a stroke will pass from the Torah—not until everything that must happen has happened. 19 So whoever disobeys the least of these mitzvot* (commandments) *and teaches others to do so will be called the least in the Kingdom of Heaven. But whoever obeys them and so teaches will be called great in the Kingdom of Heaven. 20 For I tell you that unless your righteousness is far greater than that of the Torah-teachers* (Scribes) *and P'rushim* (Pharisees), *you will certainly not enter the Kingdom of Heaven!"*

Yeshua spoke this to Jewish people in the context of a culture that observed the Law. Now let's look at what the Book of Acts shows us about the Law.

Acts 21:20 *On hearing it, they praised God; but they also said to him, "You see, brother, how many tens of thousands of believers there are among the Judeans, and they are all zealots for the Torah* (Law).

In some translations Acts 21:20 says *"many myriads of Jews believed and were all zealous for the law"* Myriads = ten thousands. Many myriads = many ten thousands. That's a lot of people!!

Acts 21:21 *Now what they have been told about you is that you are teaching all the Jews living among the Goyim* (Gentiles) *to apostatize* from Moshe (Moses), *telling them not to have a b'rit-milah* (circumcision) *for their sons and not to follow the traditions.*

Sha'ul (Paul) was accused before the leaders of the Messianic Jewish community in Jerusalem by Messianic Jews who kept the Law that he was teaching the Jewish people who were living in the Diaspora (dispersion of the Jewish people among the nations) to forsake the Laws of Moses. But it is very clear that this was a false accusation.

Acts 21:22-24 *What, then, is to be done? They will certainly hear that you have come. 23 So do what we tell you. We have four men who are under a vow. 24 Take them with you, be purified with them, and pay the expenses connected with having their heads shaved. Then everyone will know that there is nothing to these rumors which they have heard about you; but that, on the contrary, you yourself stay in line and keep the Torah.*

The community leaders instructed Sha'ul to participate with four other men in a traditional purification ceremony. Sha'ul was willing to do what they asked him to do, in order to prove the accusation was untrue.

And listen to what Sha'ul says when he journeyed to Rome.

Acts 28:17 *After three days Sha'ul* (Paul) *called a meeting of the local Jewish leaders. When they had gathered, he said to them: "Brothers, although I have done nothing against either our people or the traditions of our fathers, I was made a prisoner in Yerushalayim* (Jerusalem) *and handed over to the Romans.*

Sha'ul denied he ever broke any of the laws or even the customs of the Jewish people

Here's another story in Acts concerning the Law.

Acts 15:23-29 *...with the following letter: From: The emissaries and the elders, your brothers To: The brothers from among the Gentiles throughout Antioch, Syria and Cilicia: Greetings! 24 We have heard that some people went out from among us without our authorization, and that they have upset you with their talk, unsettling your minds. 25 So we have decided unanimously to select men and send them to you with our dear friends Bar-Nabba* (Barnabas) *and Sha'ul, 26 who have dedicated their lives to upholding the name of our Lord, Yeshua the Messiah. 27 So we have sent Y'hudah* (Judas) *and Sila* (Silas), *and they will confirm in person what we are writing. 28 For it seemed good to the Ruach HaKodesh and to us not to lay any heavier burden on you than the following requirements: 29 to abstain from what has been sacrificed to idols, from blood, from things strangled, and from fornication. If you keep yourselves from these, you will be doing the right thing. Shalom* (Peace)!

This council in Jerusalem declared that Gentiles (not using the word in a derogatory way but meaning non-Jewish people) did not have to keep the Law, but they didn't say that the Jewish people didn't have to!

It's important to understand that this declaration applied only to the Jewish Laws of the Bible. These are those laws that were given by God specifically to the Jewish people to keep us a distinct people. They include the Moadim or Biblical Holidays, circumcision, and the food laws. The council were not saying that the Gerim Mishikhim (Gentile believers) did not have to obey God's moral or spiritual laws. His moral laws concern relations between human beings, like Exodus 20:13 *Do not murder.* His spiritual laws concern relations between people and God, like Proverbs 3:5-6 *Trust in ADONAI with all your heart; do not rely on your own understanding. In all your ways acknowledge him; then he will level your paths.*

In Acts, the headquarters of the whole new Messianic faith was in Jerusalem. Years later, all Jews, including the Y'hudim Mishikhim (Messianic Jews) were scattered by the Romans. The first time was after the destruction of the Temple in 70 CE. The second was after the destruction of Jerusalem in 135 CE. Many from among the believers went out and spread the Good News to the Jewish and Gentile peoples throughout the Roman Empire. The early congregations started and led by these Y'hudim Mishikhim would have been much like Messianic congregations today. It would have been Y'hudim Mishikhim keeping the laws, traditions, and customs of Judaism with Gerim Mishikhim (Gentile believers who join with Messianic Jews) participating in as much of these as they were led by the Ruakh HaKodesh (Holy Spirit) to do so.

With Jerusalem destroyed and Jewish people forbidden by the Roman government to re-enter the area for a hundred years, the Messianics, both Jewish and Gentile, began to believe that traditional Judaism was about to become extinct. But, what about all God's promises to Israel in the Scriptures that had not yet been fulfilled? They rationally concluded that the Body of Messiah would receive those promises instead of traditional Jewish people whose religion seemed to be about to disappear from the face of the Earth. This rational conclusion led to the rise of Replacement Theology which holds that the Body of Messiah has replaced the Jewish people in God's plan, claiming all the wonderful promises of the Bible for the Body, while allocating all the curses to the traditional, Jewish people.

But, then a surprising thing happened. Rather than disappearing when Jerusalem was destroyed, non-Messianic Judaism began to thrive and grow along side Messianic Judaism in the cities of the

Roman Empire. This flourishing of non-Messianic Judaism contradicted the theology of the Messianics.

Over the early centuries, the Gerim Mishikhim (Gentile Believers) began to outnumber the Y'hudim Mishikhim (Messianic Jews) in the Body of Messiah. Because the non-Messianic Jewish people refused to acknowledge Yeshua as Messiah and were a living testimony that Replacement Theology was not correct, the theologians and leaders of the Body of Messiah began to hate them and see them as a people cursed by God.

Since Jerusalem was no longer the headquarters, the leaders all got together in the year 325 CE (Common Era) in what is called the Council of Nicea. They were convened by Constantine to unify the faith. The terrible new rules that came out of that meeting were this.

- Sunday was substituted for Shabbat
- The Holy Week was substituted for the Moadim (Biblical Feasts) of Pesakh and Firstfruits
- Keeping of Shabbat and the Moadim was forbidden.

It was now a crime to practice Jewish customs or traditions.

So, now the Christian faith that started among Jewish people who had decided not to burden Gentiles with Jewish rules, had turned completely against Biblical, Jewish customs, and was completely unfriendly to Jewish Believers. Very soon Jewish Believers who continued the "crime" of practicing any form of Judaism were being punished with the death penalty.

Another question people often ask is "Why do Gentiles celebrate these Jewish holidays? Are they trying to be Jewish?" There are three answers.

First, they have an understanding that because Yeshua was Jewish and lived in a Jewish culture they can understand Him better when they understand His culture better. Understanding a culture is best accomplished by living within it. Thus, they are enriching their faith by learning to understand the Jewish roots of their faith.

Second, they have a love for the Jewish people so they love being around Y'hudim Mishikhim (Messianic Jews), worshipping with them, and celebrating with them.

Third, some of them want to distance themselves from the history of those in centuries past, who, in the name of "Christianity," persecuted the Jewish people.

CHAPTER 2

THE RAPTURE

Jews all over the world celebrate Rosh Hashanah for two days. Why two days when the Bible speaks of only one day? Well, the reason is that the Jewish calendar is based on the first appearance of the first sliver of the moon each month. In ancient times this was based on actual sightings, so people were never quite sure when it was going to appear.

After 70 CE (Common Era) after the Diaspora when the Jewish people were scattered all over the world, the news of the new moon sightings could not get to all of them in time. So Rabbi Yochanan ben Zakkai (circa 1 CE- 80 CE) started the custom of celebrating the feasts for two days to make sure all those in the Diaspora would be celebrating them on the actual day. So, again, I think the Rabbis did the safe thing.

"Let's figure out the day and then let's back it up a day to make sure that we don't miss the right day." Centuries later when the rabbis began to understand that we have a round earth and that different time zones exist, they began to realize this meant that people would not be celebrating the day at the same time and that people scattered too far away would even be celebrating at the wrong time! So they continued the two day custom so that all around the world Jews would be celebrating together for some part of the day, and they would be sure to be celebrating at the correct time.

The important question for us to continue to ask, though, is not about getting the date correct, but, about how we are supposed to be celebrating this holiday. To answer that, let's look again at what God commanded in the Torah.

Leviticus 23:24-25 *Tell the people of Isra'el, "In the seventh month, the first of the month is to be for you a day of complete rest for remembering, a holy convocation announced with blasts on the shofar. 25 Do not do any kind of ordinary work, and bring an offering made by fire to ADONAI."*

Note the command to commemorate this holiday with Shofar (ram's horn trumpet) blasts. In all the traditional English Bibles, like the King James and the NIV, it says "a memorial of blowing of trumpets" or "commemorated with trumpet blasts." This is why this holiday is called the Feast of Trumpets. In the Scriptures, the blowing of Shofarot (plural of Shofar) has four main purposes, as we noted before: To call to battle, to warn of danger or attack, to call to begin a march, and to gather the people. We will now delve deeper on that last one: The blowing of the Shofar to assemble the people.

There are four traditional passages that are read over the two days of Rosh Hashanah in traditional synagogues. They are Numbers 29 which gives the commandment for Shofarot and all the offerings, and Genesis 22 which tells about the sacrifice of Isaac. The Genesis passage is read because of God supplying a ram. A Shofar is made from a ram's horn, so that's where the connection is for choosing that passage. 1 Samuel 1:1-2:10 is also read which speaks of the giving up of Samuel to the Lord, a similar incident as the sacrifice of Isaac. The last traditional passage is Jeremiah 31:2-20 which speaks of the gathering of Israel to God.

Jeremiah 31:10 *Nations, hear the word of ADONAI! Proclaim it in the coastlands far away. Say: "He who scattered Isra'el is gathering him, guarding him like a shepherd his flock."*

There are several passages associating the Shofar with the gathering of the people. The first one is in Exodus 19 when the people were called to meet with God at Mt. Sinai. Three times in the B'rit Hadashah (The New Covenant), it talks about how the blowing of a trumpet will be used as a call to gather all believers to meet with God. Let's look at what Yeshua had to say about this blowing of the greatest Shofar for the greatest gathering together of the people to God. As we go through what He said together, let's see if we can get a sense of the future timing of the events predicted. Let's begin in Matthew where Yeshua first starts talking about it.

Matthew 24:14 *And this Good News about the Kingdom will be announced throughout the whole world as a witness to all the Goyim. It is then that the end will come.*

"Goyim" here is a Hebrew translation of the Greek word "ethnos" which means "political entities" or "ethnic groups." Has this happened yet? Yes, it has happened already if you interpret "ethnos" to mean "political entities." But the answer is "no," if you interpret "ethnos" to mean "ethnic groups." Wycliffe Bible Translators believe it means all language groups and therefore they are working toward the translation and production of the Scriptures into every language.

Matthew 24:15 *"So when you see the abomination that causes devastation spoken about through the prophet Dani'el standing in the Holy Place" (let the reader understand the allusion) ....*

Yeshua was predicting a future event, and it is still a future event today. You might be thinking that it was fulfilled by the Greeks at the time of the Maccabees, but it couldn't be that event. Let me explain why it couldn't be. At the time of Yeshua, Antiochus Epiphanes, the Greek leader, had already desecrated the Temple. It happened in about 150 BCE which is 150 years before Yeshua! So that "desolation" was in the past already in Yeshua's day. In 70 CE, forty years after Yeshua, the Romans did not desecrate the Temple. They just burned it to the ground. So this passage has to refer to the Third Temple, yet to be built, which will be desecrated by the Anti-Messiah (Anti-Christ) ("Christ" is Greek for "Messiah.")

Matthew 24:16-21 *"... that will be the time for those in Y'hudah (Judah) to escape to the hills. 17 If someone is on the roof, he must not go down to gather his belongings from his house; 18 if someone is in the field, he must not turn back to get his coat. 19 What a terrible time it will be for pregnant women and nursing mothers! 20 Pray that you will not have to escape in winter or on Shabbat. 21 For there will be trouble then worse than there has ever been from the beginning of the world until now, and there will be nothing like it again!*

This period of time is called the "Days of Jacob's Trouble." You might know it by the more familiar term used in Christian circles, "The Great Tribulation."

Matthew 24:22 *Indeed, if the length of this time had not been limited, no one would survive; but for the sake of those who have been chosen, its length will be limited.*

Note the phrase "those who have been chosen" here. It is the Greek word "eklectos" which could also be translated "favored."

Matthew 24:23-27 *At that time, if someone says to you, "Look! Here's the Messiah!" or, "There he is!" don't believe him. 24 For there will appear false Messiahs and false prophets performing great miracles—amazing things!—so as to fool even the chosen, if possible. 25 There! I have told you in advance! 26 So if people say to you, "Listen! He's out in the desert!" don't go; or, "Look! He's hidden away in a secret room!" don't believe it. 27 For when the Son of Man does come, it will be like lightning that flashes out of the east and fills the sky to the western horizon.*

Who will know it when the Son of Man comes back? Everybody! That's right! So, when He comes no one will be ignorant of the fact. All will know it. People won't have to tell each other where He is.

Matthew 24:28 *Wherever there's a dead body, that's where you find the vultures.*

This is an idiom meaning "where there's smoke there's fire."

Matthew 24:29 *But immediately following the trouble of those times, the sun will grow dark, the moon will stop shining, the stars will fall from the sky, and the powers in heaven will be shaken. 30 Then the sign of the Son of Man will appear in the sky, all the tribes of the Land will mourn, and they will see the Son of Man coming on the clouds of heaven with tremendous power and glory.*

Why will the tribes of the Land mourn? Yes, you're right, because they have rejected Him. What does this passage describe? It describes the Second Coming of the Messiah.

The ancient Rabbis thought there would be two Messiahs:
- Mashiach ben Yosef (Messiah son of Joseph)
  - the suffering servant
- Mashiach ben David - the reigning king

The B'rit Hadashah (New Covenant or New Testament) teaches that there is one Messiah who will come twice:

- First coming – as the suffering servant
- Second coming – as the reigning king

Yeshua already came as the suffering servant. Now we are waiting for His return as the reigning King of Kings!!

Matthew 24:31 *He will send out his angels with a great shofar; and they will gather together his chosen people from the four winds, from one end of heaven to the other.*

Here we find Yeshua associating His Second Coming with the gathering of "His chosen people" which will be heralded with "a great Shofar."

Now, the way Yeshua words this *"from the four winds, from one end of heaven to the other"* made me wonder whether He is talking about His chosen (or "elect" in other translations) in heaven or on earth. Look down at verse 40.

Matthew 24:40 *Then there will be two men in a field—one will be taken and the other left behind.*

Here we learn that He is talking about people still on earth, not those in heaven. The most important question however is, who are His chosen? Let's hold this question for a few minutes while we read on.

Matthew 24:32-33 *Now let the fig tree teach you its lesson: when its branches begin to sprout and leaves appear, you know that summer is approaching. 33 In the same way, when you see all these things, you are to know that the time is near, right at the door.*

I believe that the "fig tree" here refers to the Nation of Israel which blossomed in 1948. We saw the re-birth of Israel as a nation in 1948. So I believe we can conclude that the Second Coming and the Rapture are "near, right at the door."

Matthew 24:34 *Yes! I tell you that this people will certainly not pass away before all these things happen.*

I believe this means the generation that sees the fig tree blossom. Who is that? Well, who saw this great event of the birth of the Nation of Israel? It's those of us with white hair! We are that generation! Isn't that exciting?!

Let's look again at what Paul or Rabbi Sha'ul had to say about these events.

1 Thessalonians 4:14-15 *We believe that in the same way God, through Yeshua, will take with Him those who have fallen asleep in Him. According to the Lord's own word, we tell you that we who are still alive, who are left till the coming of the Lord, will certainly not precede those who have fallen asleep.*

What will happen to those already dead and buried, those "who have fallen asleep in Him"? Yes, it says in the next verse. They will rise from their graves!

1 Thess. 4:16-17 *For the Lord himself will come down from heaven with a rousing cry, with a call from one of the ruling angels, and with God's shofar; those who died united with the Messiah will be the first to rise; 17 then we who are left still alive will be caught up with them in the clouds to meet the Lord in the air; and thus we will always be with the Lord.*

Here's another reference to the Shofar. Did you notice that? So, how will His chosen be gathered? With the sound of the Shofar!! The Shofar will call them to meet Him in the clouds of the air!

What will be the effect on the earth when this event occurs? His chosen or elect will suddenly disappear. They will all disappear at exactly the same time! I believe there will be millions of them, though not a majority of the people on the earth. So, there could be massive traffic jams, plane crashes, and disruption of vital services like hospitals, food distribution, power, water, communications, defense, and transportation. Those left behind who had heard the predictions of the Rapture and the Second Coming and did not become "chosen" will know that the predictions were true and some will turn to the Lord. But they will go through the terrible period of tribulation described in the Book of Revelation. This will be when God's judgment will be poured out upon the earth.

Let's look at another passage.

1 Cor. 15: 51-53 *Look, I will tell you a secret—not all of us will die! But we will all be changed! 52 It will take but a moment, the blink of an eye, at the final shofar. For the shofar will sound, and the dead will be raised to live forever, and we too will be changed. 53 For this material which can decay must be clothed with imperishability, this which is mortal must be clothed with immortality.*

Here again, another reference to the Shofar or trumpet call! Now, according to this passage, how will His chosen be able to float in the air with the Lord? Will they get onto airplanes and rendezvous in the sky? No? Then how? They will have transformed, imperishable bodies. Are you getting excited?

Now, you might be wondering how soon this is going to happen. We are all wondering about that. So, let's look at what Yeshua said about that.

Matthew 24:36 *"But when that day and hour will come, no one knows —not the angels in heaven, not the Son, only the Father.* So, can we know when it will happen? No, we can't. So, if we don't know, then how are we to make it through to that day? Well, Yeshua talks about that.

Matthew 24:42 *So stay alert, because you don't know on what day your Lord will come.*

Matthew 24:44 *Therefore you too must always be ready, for the Son of Man will come when you are not expecting Him.*

This is the beginning of one of the longest sections of the B'rit Hadashah (the New Testament). It consists of four parables. All four exhort us to live in expectancy as if He were returning today.

Matthew 24:45-51 is about the Faithful Servant who keeps doing his master's will until he returns.

Matthew 25:1-13 is about the Ten Bridesmaids, five who were ready and five who weren't. Again, it is exhorting us to be ready for His return.

Matthew 25:14-30 is the parable of the Ten Talents. It tells us to use what He has given us, while He is away, to advance His Kingdom.

Matthew 25:31-46 is the parable of The Sheep and the Goats which instructs us to reach out in love to the sick, the poor, and those in jail because He will return to judge.

Why do we need to live as if His return was going to happen today? I believe it is because it is vitally important to help us have a Godly attitude through these times of tribulation. We need to be people of hope. It makes the struggles we are going through seem less important, and then we are better able to handle them.

I know I struggle to live each day in that expectation of readiness. How about you? Can you honestly say you are living in expectation of His return today?

Well, God knew we would struggle with persevering in that state of expectation. That's why He gave us Rosh Hashanah! The point of Rosh Hashanah is to remind us of His soon return and to awaken us and inspire us to get excited about it as we are stirred by the Shofar blasts and we join in with shouts of joy! It renews our enthusiasm and our sense of alertness and great anticipation. So, keep that in mind as you celebrate Rosh Hashanah this year.

Now let's get back to the earlier vital question: When that Greatest Shofar blows, who will be His chosen that we read about in Matthew 24 whom His angels *"will gather ... from the four winds, from one end of heaven to the other"*? When that Greatest Shofar blows, who will be His elect who will be *"caught up with them in the clouds to meet the Lord in the air"? And so ... will be with the Lord forever*? When that Greatest Shofar blows, who will be His elect who *will all be changed—in a flash, in the blink of an eye, at the final shofar*? Who will receive an immortal body? Well, to find the answer, let's look at what the word "chosen" or "elect" means.

In the Greek dictionary it says "eklektos," means *select; by implication, favorite—chosen, elect.* So, the "elect" are His chosen ones. Well, then we have to ask, "Who can become chosen?" All of us can! And God wants you to know for sure that you ARE chosen!

1 John 5:13 *I have written you these things so that you may know that you have eternal life —you who keep trusting in the person and power of the Son of God.*

We can infer from this verse that the entire Bible was written so that we can know for sure if we are chosen. How can you know if you are one of His chosen? Here's the amazing answer to that question. If you want the assurance that you've been chosen, and you are willing to simply obey the teaching of the Scriptures, you will have that assurance!! God wants you to have it!!

Some people think they are already one of His chosen:

- Because they try hard to obey His laws
- Because they were born Jewish
- Because they belong to some religious organization
- Because their parents belong to some religious organization
- Because they've never done anything wrong intentionally
- Because they've asked God to forgive them

That's not the kind of assurance that I'm talking about. Real assurance—deep down inside assurance—is a supernatural work of the Ruakh HaKodesh or Holy Spirit of God. You've heard of flight insurance which you can purchase at the airport before you board an airplane. Well, there are six steps to Yeshua's flight assurance which will give you assurance that you'll rise to meet Him in the air when that Greatest Shofar sounds.

The assurance comes:

1. When you admit to God that you are a sinner who has fallen short of the requirements for Holy living which He requires in His Tanakh, the Bible.

2. When you understand that you, as a sinner, can't come into God's Holy presence, even if you have sinned just once, because He is a Holy God, and will not allow sin in His presence.

3. When you understand according to the Torah in Lev 17:11 (...*it is the blood that makes atonement*) that without the shedding of blood there can be no forgiveness for sin.

4. When you believe that God made a way for you to come into His presence by coming to earth as a man, the Messiah, to shed His Blood to pay the penalty for your sins.

5. When you put your trust in His shed Blood to pay the price for your sins.

6. When you ask and receive His forgiveness, invite Him into your heart, and make Him Lord of your life.

These six steps lead to true t'shuvah or repentance and bring with them true, deep down assurance that you are now one of His chosen ones.

The next time you listen to the sound of the Shofar, hear it as a call to start the New Year in true T'shuvah that leads to this glorious assurance! If you already have the assurance that, if He comes back today, you will rise to meet the Lord in the air. Then let the Shofar's blast be a call to rejoice in that coming day! What a marvelous day it will be. It is truly something to shout about!

CHAPTER 3

Intercession

Rosh Hashanah is an ancient holiday, given to us by God thousands of years ago. So, we might wonder if it has significance anymore. We might ask ourselves, "What should Rosh Hashanah mean to us today?" Well, we've learned that someday our Lord will come to gather all His chosen ones with the sound of the Shofar on a Rosh Hashanah day. And we will all be "raptured" up to meet Him in the air! We can certainly hope that this glorious Rapture will be this Rosh Hashanah, can't we?! Amen! So, go ahead and shout. It is something to rejoice about.

We can also enjoy the stirring sound of the Shofar and obey its call to worship. But, should we, as forgiven believers in Messiah, make this a time of repentance as Traditional Jews do? Well, I believe the B'rit Hadashah teaches us to live lives of continual, personal repentance as believers in the Messiah. Yeshua told us to participate in the S'udat Adonai (the Lord's Supper) periodically and Paul tells us this is a time to examine ourselves. We don't believe that our repentance and good works will influence God to make our fate better for the coming year, as the traditional Jewish people teach, but we certainly do focus on having a repentant attitude. Our purpose is not to better our fate, but to grow closer to Yeshua.

But I believe that we as Y'hudim Mishikhim (Messianic Jews) and Gerim Mishikhim (Messianic Gentiles) have more to do than personal repentance during the coming Ten Days of Awe. In the book of 1 Peter it says that we have been chosen to be royal cohanim or priests.

1 Peter 2:9 *But you are a chosen people, the King's cohanim (priests), a holy nation, a people for God to possess! Why? In order for you to declare the praises of the One who called you out of darkness into his wonderful light.*

The idea of being a priest is foreign to Jewish people who think only of Catholic priests when we hear the English word "priest." But a cohane (singular for cohanim) is a very Jewish concept. In the Laws of Moses the Bible says God established one clan of the tribe of Levi, the descendants of Aaron, as the cohanim. We call them the Levitical Cohanim. So, if Messianic Believers are cohanim we need to understand the Biblical role of the Levitical cohane.

First the Levitical Cohanim made sacrifices and repented for their own sins. Then they made atonement for the people's sins. They served as intercessors for the nation of Israel, their community.

The priestly role is to repent and intercede for the community or nation we are a part of. Most people are part of at least four communities. Some of you are part of a fifth.

1. We are either Gentile or Jewish. If we are Jewish, we need to repent for the Jewish community turning away from God, for accepting humanist philosophies, becoming legalistic, inventing its own religion, and rejecting Yeshua as Messiah.

Psalm 81:10-16 *I am ADONAI your God, who brought you up from the land of Egypt. Open your mouth, and I will fill it. 11 But My people did not listen to My voice; Isra'el would have none of me. 12 So I gave them over to their stubborn hearts, to live by their own plans. 13 How I wish My people would listen to Me, that Isra'el would live by My ways! 14 I would quickly subdue their enemies and turn My hand against their foes. 15 Those who hate ADONAI would cringe before Him, while [Israel's] time would last forever. 16 They would be fed with the finest wheat, and I would satisfy you with honey from the rocks.*

We can repent for Israel's turning away and pray for the promise of provision and for the returning to Him to come to pass.

Take special notice of verses 10 and 16: *Open wide your mouth and I will fill it. … They would be fed with the finest of wheat; with honey from the rock I would satisfy you.* [This is where we get the tradition of eating honey on Rosh Hashanah.]

2. We are also Americans. As Americans, we need to repent for America turning away from Godliness, for not standing against abortion, for political corruption and taking bribes, for materialism, for sexual sin, for not caring for our poor, etc.

3. We are also Messianic Believers. As such we should repent for the divisions among us.

4. We are members of the Body of Messiah which needs to repent for not standing against evil, for persecution of both Traditional Jewish people and Messianic Jewish people, and for turning Christianity away from its Jewish roots, among other things.

5. Some of you are part of other minority communities. Are there things in those communities you could be repenting for?

So, we've got a lot of work to do during the next ten days, right? Do you feel tired already?

There's been a lot of talk in the Body of Messiah about intercession. We have many intercessors in our Messianic congregations and many intercessors outside who are praying for us and for the whole Messianic Movement. As His Royal Cohanim we are called to be intercessors and this is an Appointed Time—appointed by God—for intercession.

The dictionary definition of "intercede" is *to plead or make a request on behalf of another or others, to intervene for the purpose of producing agreement, mediate.*

Let's see what we can learn about intercession from a few Biblical examples. All of these examples relate to praying for people who have sinned and are in danger of God's judgment. As we look at these and study these together, I hope you will find some help for your prayer assignment for these Ten Days of Awe. I want you to use what we learn here in your private prayer time and as you meet in groups.

First, let's look at Moses' intercession when the people made the Golden Calf and God was about to destroy them.

Exodus 32:11-14 Moshe (Moses) pleaded with ADONAI his God. He said, "ADONAI, why must your anger blaze against your own people, whom you brought out of the land of Egypt with great power and a strong hand? 12 Why let the Egyptians say, 'It was with evil intentions that he led them out, to slaughter them in the hills and wipe them off the face of the earth'? Turn from your fierce anger! Relent! Don't bring such disaster on your people! 13 Remember Avraham (Abraham), Yitz'chak (Isaac) and Isra'el, your servants, to whom you swore by your very self. You promised them, 'I will make your descendants as many as the stars in the sky; and I will give all this land I have spoken about to your descendants; and they will possess it forever.'" 14 ADONAI then changed his mind about the disaster he had planned for his people.

What arguments did Moses use to try to convince God to spare the Israelites? He reminded God of how His reputation would suffer. And then he reminded Him of His promises. And he was calling on God to fulfill those promises, wasn't he?

Now let's see how Moses prayed later in the same chapter after he had actually seen the Golden Calf.

Exodus 32:31-32 Moshe went back to ADONAI and said, "Please! These people have committed a terrible sin: they have made themselves a god out of gold. 32 Now, if you will just forgive their sin! But if you won't, then, I beg you, blot me out of your book which you have written!"

What did Moses offer God in return for sparing the Israelites? Yes! Isn't that amazing?!! He was offering himself, his own life, as atonement for the people! This was true intercession! He was putting himself between those who deserved punishment and God who should have punished them!! Wow! That is something to ponder, isn't it? What true selflessness, true self-sacrifice.

We will come back to Moses, but right now let's move on and look at Daniel and how he prayed during the Babylonian captivity.

Daniel 9:2-3 in the first year of his reign, I, Dani'el, was reading the Scriptures and thinking about the number of years which ADONAI had told Yirmeyah (Jeremiah) the prophet would be the period of Yerushalayim's (Jerusalem's) desolation, seventy years. 3 I turned to Adonai, God, to seek an answer, pleading with him in prayer, with fasting, sackcloth and ashes.

Daniel understood that God had spoken through Jeremiah that the Babylonian captivity would last seventy years. Fifty years had already passed. So Daniel began to pray that what God had promised would happen.

What did Daniel do along with prayer and supplication? He interceded with fasting, sackcloth, and ashes. He was very serious and sincere about his intercession.

Now, if we want to be like Daniel, what promises of God for the Jewish people can we pray to be fulfilled? Can you think of some? I'm sure you can. Let's read on to see how we should proceed with those prayers.

Daniel 9:4-6 *I prayed to ADONAI my God and made this confession: "Please, Adonai, great and fearsome God, who keeps His covenant and extends grace to those who love Him and observe His mitzvot* (commandments)*! 5 We have sinned, done wrong, acted wickedly, rebelled and turned away from Your mitzvot and rulings. 6 We have not listened to Your servants the prophets, who spoke in Your Name to our kings, our leaders, our ancestors and to all the people of the land.*

Did you notice that he used the pronoun "we" even though the sins were not his? Had Daniel participated in the sin he is referring to? No! In fact the people who had committed these sins were dead. But, in this way, he identified with the sin of his people. In the spirit he was taking these sins upon himself. He spoke of himself as if he had committed these sins.

Let's look at another interceder, Ezra. This period of time was after the return of the Jewish people to the land of Israel, and after the rebuilding of the Temple.

Ezra 9:1-3 *After these things had been done, the leaders approached me and said, "The people of Isra'el, the cohanim and the L'vi'im* (Levites) *have not separated themselves from the peoples of the lands and their disgusting practices—the Kena'ani* (Canaanites)*, Hitti, P'rizi, Y'vusi* (Jebusites)*, 'Amoni, Mo'avi, Egyptians and Emori. 2 They have taken some of the women from these nations as wives for themselves and their sons, so that the holy seed has assimilated to the peoples of the lands; moreover, the officials and leaders have been the main offenders in this treachery." 3 When I heard this, I tore my robe and tunic, pulled hair from my head and beard, and sat down in shock.*

He tore his clothes and pulled his hair out! Even from his beard! Ouch! That had to hurt! And he sat appalled (it says in another translation), in shock and tore his clothes. Did you notice all those things? This was real, personal remorse by Ezra for the sins of his people. Again, these were sins not committed by him. Yet, in the spirit, he took them upon himself.

Ezra 9:4 *All who trembled at the words of the God of Isra'el assembled around me when confronted with the treachery of these exiles; and I sat there in shock until the evening offering.*

What effect did Ezra's intercession have on those around him? His intercession inspired others to intercede. And they remained remorseful for a long time.

Ezra 9:5-6 *At the evening offering, with my cloak and tunic torn, I got up from afflicting myself, fell on my knees, spread out my hands to ADONAI my God, 6 and said, "My God, I am ashamed. I blush to lift my face to you, my God! For our sins tower over our heads; our guilt reaches up to heaven."*

His remorse and shame was so great, he was unable to even pray! Ezra had the same identification with his people as Daniel.

Now let's talk about our sins and our guilt. Who did what Ezra and Daniel did for us? Who interceded for us? Yeshua did! Now, as I was studying this, I thought, Yeshua didn't identify with Israel's or the world's sin by saying "we have sinned" like Daniel and Ezra did because He had never sinned!

Then I asked myself, "What is the real meaning of intercession?" The word "intercession" literally means putting yourself between the one about to receive punishment and the punisher! Daniel and Ezra identified with Israel's sin by confessing "we have sinned" even though they had not personally sinned. They experienced the remorse and shame of the sin of the nation of Israel as their own. But a higher level of intercession than identifying with the sin of those you are interceding for is to offer yourself as a substitute for receiving the punishment for the sin! Moses did this when he pleaded with God to blot his name out of the Book of Life rather than blotting out the Israelites who had made the Golden Calf. God did not accept Moses' offer. But let's read a passage in Isaiah to learn about what Yeshua did for us.

Isaiah 53:12 *"Therefore I will assign him a share with the great, he will divide the spoil with the mighty, for having exposed himself to death and being counted among the sinners, while actually bearing the sin of many and interceding for the offenders."*

God did receive Yeshua's offer to take on our punishment. Yeshua put Himself between God and us whom God should punish. He offered Himself in our place and God accepted. His sacrificial death was the ultimate act of intercession as a cohane (priest). He gave His own life to save His people. That is the absolute, ultimate form of intercession. Yeshua is our ultimate example.

Now, I'm not saying we are all called to physically lay down our lives for other people, although during times of danger many have actually done that—given their lives. But I am saying that we are called to be laying down our lives in doing God's will instead of our own. Being daily in the service of God is one way of interceding. Those who live their lives close to the heart of God will have a desire to intercede. Yeshua is always interceding. He is making intercession for us right now.

Hebrews 7:25 (NKJV) *Therefore He is also able to save to the uttermost those who come to God through Him, since He always lives to make intercession for them.*

This means that whenever we are in danger of God's judgment, He is still pleading our case before the Father, still identifying with our sin. It also means He is still experiencing our remorse, our pain, and our shame.

Romans 8:26 *Similarly, the Spirit helps us in our weakness; for we don't know how to pray the way we should. But the Spirit himself pleads on our behalf with groanings too deep for words;*

We can actually experience what His heart is enduring. The Ruakh HaKodesh causes us to groan as we intercede, as He is identifying with the plight of those we are praying for.

This happened to me one day when I was praying for my parents who were Communist atheists. I started to really get into my praying. I was lying on the floor crying out to God. Then I found myself groaning. No words were coming out, just groaning. I began to realize that it was probably the Ruakh HaKodesh guiding me to pray like that.

As we are praying in intercession, God Himself is groaning as He identifies with the people we are praying for. He feels their remorse, shame, guilt, and pain.

Let's spend some time right now to pray for our four communities. And I want you to continue to spend time interceding for them in these next Ten Days of Awe.

<u>CHAPTER 4</u>

THE PROMISED LAND

Let me start this chapter with a little bit of a quiz. When you think about the blowing of the Shofar and the shouting, what is the first Biblical incident that comes to your mind? There are several such events, but Jericho is the one that comes to my mind first. That's the one that just seems to jump out at me. Was it Jericho for you, too?

The sounding of the Shofar and shouting is such a big part of the falling of the walls of Jericho. But if you think about that for a little bit, Jericho could not have been something that Moses would've thought of in connection to Shofar blowing. Why not? It hadn't happened yet! It happened in the next generation! Perhaps Moses thought it meant Sinai—to remember the loud Shofar that sounded at Mount Sinai.

Nevertheless, in this chapter, I'd like to focus on the story of Jericho and Joshua. It's a wonderful piece of history. Everyone remembers the tremendous climax of the blowing of the Shofars and the falling down of the walls. But as I studied it this time, I decided to go back and look at it all again. And it just jumped out at me that this story can be seen as an allegory, an allegory for each one of us in our spiritual development of growing closer to God each day. And as we look at what happened in the first six chapters of the book of Joshua, you will see this allegory.

You know, this story surprised me again because I hadn't read it in awhile. Sometimes you think you know those stories and then you go back and read them and you say, "Oh yea, I forgot about this and I never noticed this!" There's so much in the Jericho story, but I'm going to just highlight certain parts of it and point out how they have a parallel in our own lives. Each parallel has something for us to learn.

First Allegory

Joshua 1:1-2   *After the death of Moshe* (Moses) *the servant of ADONAI, ADONAI said to Y'hoshua* (Joshua) *the son of Nun, Moshe's* (Moses') *assistant, 2 "Moshe my servant is dead. So now, get up and cross over this Yarden* (Jordan), *you and all the people, to the land I am giving to them, the people of Isra'el.*

Now if you think about this a minute, this was a turning point in the life of Joshua. Moses, remember, was a great leader. He had brought the Israelites out of slavery, parted the Red Sea, led them in the desert for forty years, given them the Law, and built the tabernacle—all these incredible things!! And Joshua's relationship with God, of course, would've been greatly influenced by Moses. But I think this is the start of Joshua having his own relationship with God as the leader—as being the man that God had called to lead.

There's a parallel here in our own lives. I saw it in my children, and in the youth in my congregation, that generally young people grow up with the beliefs of their parents. Then at some point in their life, usually in their late teens or early twenties, they have to decide if they are going to continue in their parents' belief system. And sometimes parents get very shook up when this starts happening because the kids start testing their beliefs, and it looks like a lot of rebellion at times. But I believe it's something that very often needs to happen. Being a parent myself who has gone through it, I can sympathize with those of you who are still going through it. Many young people have to test and say, "Well, this is what my parents taught me, but is it really true?" Sometimes they try another belief system which is very unsettling to their mom and dad.

I think this is kind of what was happening in Joshua's life. It was time for him to stand on his own feet before God. It was time to not just be Moses' assistant, but to be the leader. It was the time to test and see what his relationship with God was going to be like. And God understands this. God does not deal with us only through what our parents taught us. He deals with us as individuals.

Joshua 1:3-4 *" I am giving you every place you will step on with the sole of your foot, as I said to Moshe* (Moses). *4 All the land from the desert and the L'vanon* (Lebanon) *to the great river, the Euphrates River—all the land of the Hitti—and on to the Great Sea in the west will be your territory."*

Let me point out to those who have an understanding of geography. That's a whole lot bigger than present day Israel. The Euphrates River is over in Iraq somewhere. So whenever somebody tells me they're worried about what's happening in Israel and this and that, I always think, you know, God's got a lot more coming. We don't know what's going to happen because somehow, I believe, it's going to be all the way to the Euphrates some day. Who knows how that's going to happen!

Joshua 1:5 *"No one will be able to withstand you as long as you live. Just as I was with Moshe* (Moses), *so I will be with you. I will neither fail you nor abandon you."*

I think that this promise made directly to Joshua—instead of through Moses—was a new point in Joshua's life. God said it to him directly so that he didn't have to just depend on promises made to Moses anymore—even though they were written down and he had read them. Now God was giving him what we call rhema. He was giving him a personal word, "This promise is for you, Joshua, and you are to lead the people in." The allegory for us is that we should also expect to receive personal words (rhema) from the Lord that help us mature in our spiritual development.

There are many other places in Scripture where people received a rhema, some from angels, some directly from God Himself. Abraham, Isaac, and Jacob each heard directly from the Lord. Elijah received a word of encouragement when he was feeling very down. King David wrote what he heard in the Psalms. The Lord spoke to Samson's parents, King Solomon, Balaam, all the prophets, and many more. In the New Covenant He gave rhema messages to Zechariah, Mary, Apostle Paul, Philip, Cornelius, Peter, and others. So, there is no reason, we should not expect to receive a personal Word ourselves.

Second Allegory

So, what was Joshua promised? What did we just read? Yes, the Land! He was promised the Land. That's why it's called the Promised Land! This was God's promise. And this was a wonderful Land! God describes this Land as ...*a good and spacious land, a land flowing with milk and honey* (Exodus 3:8). That was the promise to Joshua. You're going to have this Land.

Joshua 1:6 (NIV) *"Be strong and courageous, because you will lead these people to inherit the land I swore to their forefathers to give them."*

So, now we see here that the promise wasn't just given to Joshua, right? Who else was it for? Yes, for all the people! For all of the Israelites! And there's an analogy of this in our own lives. Just as the Children of Israel were promised a Land, we are promised a Land—each one of us! Now, you may be thinking, "It's not a piece of Israel!" No, it's not. It's a spiritual Promised Land. I believe what it really is, is the Kingdom of God! That's the Land that we are promised. And that Promised Land is a place that is like it was described here! *"A good and spacious land, a land flowing with milk and honey."* It's a Land that is a wonderful place.

You may be thinking right now, "He's got to be kidding! Does anyone possess that Promised Land in this lifetime? I mean that's something that's for the next life if we're lucky, but in this life?" Well, you may find this hard to believe, but I can testify that I've lived in a spiritual place called the Kingdom of God. And it is a wonderful place! It's a good and spacious Land, and it flows with milk and honey! Now, it's not a physical place. But I believe that this physical place that is being talked of here was like an example—an allegory—for us, to show us that we would have a spiritual place.

And what is it like? Well, to me it represents all the things that we would like the land that we live in to be. What do I mean by that? It's a place where we want to live our lives! It's a place of peace; a place where there's fulfillment. It's a place where there's satisfaction; a place where there is provision; where we know that we're going to have what we need. It's a place where there's love! Both received and given. It's a place where there's joy! It's a place where there's a connection with God. Those are just some of the things that come to my mind. That's the place where I live! I know that some of you live in that place, too, but sometimes we forget that it's a different place than where many people in this world live. They don't know yet about this Promised Land.

Those who know me personally might say, "I can't believe he's living in a Promised Land. I know the struggles that he's going through!" And it's true! We can live in that Promised Land and still go through a lot of struggles. But my life changed when I entered this Promised Land. It changed radically! I experienced, for the first time, a relationship with God and peace and purpose and all the things I just mentioned. Yeshua has said this to us.

John 16:33 *"I have said these things to you so that, united with me, you may have shalom. In the world, you have tsuris* (tribulation, "tsuris" is what we say in Yiddish). *But be brave! I have conquered the world!"*

So, this Promised Land is a mystery. It's a paradox. We can live in this Promised Land, but we still have to deal with this life and with this world. There's still "tsuris." There are still troubles. But the Lord is with us in those trials. His presence turns it into a luscious Promised Land.

Third Allegory

Now, how do you get there? Let's look at what Joshua needed to do to posses the Promised Land.

Joshua 1:7 *"Only be strong and very bold in taking care to follow all the Torah which Moshe my servant ordered you to follow; do not turn from it either to the right or to the left; then you will succeed wherever you go."*

By the way, the word "Law" used in most English translations here is the Hebrew word "Torah" used here in the *Complete Jewish Bible* and it doesn't just mean the first five books of Moses. It means the "instruction"—"God's instruction." So He's saying, "Be careful to obey My instruction—My instruction given through Moses."

Joshua 1:8 *Yes, keep this book of the Torah on your lips, and meditate on it day and night, so that you will take care to act according to everything written in it. Then your undertakings will prosper, and you will succeed.*

Now, why does it say to "keep the Torah on your lips"? Well, I think God was telling Joshua to read it aloud to himself. He was to take the Bible and read it to himself so that it would be not only in his eyes, but in his mouth, that he would hear himself say it.

Now, what qualities did Joshua need, that we just read about, to possess the Promised Land? Strength! Courage! And what else? Leadership qualities. Boldness and one more: Obedience! Yes, obedience. Those are the things that Joshua needed. Now, it doesn't sound easy, does it? You've got to be strong. You've got to be courageous. You've got to be bold. You've got to be obedient. That sounds pretty tough! And it **IS** tough! It is **VERY** tough to enter the Promised Land. But the good news is, it's possible! It is possible to enter the Promised Land and to possess it. It wasn't easy for Joshua, and I'm not going to say it's easy for me! And I don't suppose it's easy for you either. But it's possible. It **IS** possible.

Fourth Allegory

Now, to possess this Promised Land, Joshua and the people needed to conquer a city called Jericho. It was a fortified, walled city with an army. And the reason it was so important is that it guarded the fords of the Jordan River. There was no way to get across that river except through these fords (the shallow place where you could cross), and this city guarded that place. That's why it was so significant. The Israelites had already conquered the east side of the Jordan. But if they wanted to possess the rest of the Land, to advance into that Land and possess it, they had to conquer Jericho. Otherwise, if they got across some other way, they would be cut off from their brothers possessing this side of the river.

So there's a lesson for us here. And that lesson is that there are walled cities that will oppose us possessing the Promised Land—that will resist us. And what do I mean by "walled cities"? The forces of darkness that are arrayed against us, that resist us possessing the Promised Land. And we need to strive—to make a forward effort against them! It isn't easy to move against those forces of darkness. We need to be strong and courageous and obedient to overcome!

Fifth Allegory

So, what was Joshua's first tactic? Well, the first thing that Joshua did was to send two spies into the Land. I believe he wanted to find out what the cost was going to be. What was the city like? What was it going to require to take this city?

Now, how does this apply to us? Well, the allegory to me is explained in what Yeshua says here.

Mark 8:34-37 (NIV) *"If anyone would come after Me, he must deny himself and take up his cross and follow Me. For whoever wants to save his life will lose it, but whoever loses his life for Me and for the Gospel will save it. What good is it for a man to gain the whole world, yet forfeit his soul? Or what can a man give in exchange for his soul?"*

So Yeshua tells us that in order to enter the Promised Land, to follow Him, we need to count the cost. And so that's a question to you right now. Are you willing to pay the price to enter the Promised Land? The cost that was stated here is denying yourself! Not being selfish basically—giving yourself to the Lord, picking up your cross daily for His sake and the Gospel. But the alternative question is what price could you pay for your soul? What is your soul worth? Ponder that a minute.

Sixth Allegory

These spies came back after a lot of adventures that I'm not going to go into right now—some really exciting adventures, actually.

Joshua 2:24 (NIV) *They said to Joshua, "The LORD has surely given the whole land into our hands; all the people are melting in fear because of us."*

So, here Joshua learned that this enemy that they were facing had no confidence. They were afraid. They heard what Joshua had done to the kings on the other side of the river and what Moses had done!

I see an allegory in that for our lives, too, at least for me. I have learned that the enemy that I'm facing is dangerous, but that he *will* yield, and I *can* overcome him. I think that's what Joshua has learned here. I also think the people were learning that by obeying the Lord, by being ready to give up their lives—actually risking their lives—to do what God told them to do, they were actually saving their lives.

Seventh Allegory

So how did Joshua actually enter the Land? Well, we're up to chapter three now.

Joshua 3:6 *Then Y'hoshua (Joshua) said to the cohanim (priests), "Take the ark for the covenant, and go on ahead of the people." They took the ark for the covenant and went ahead of the people.*

So, let me give you a chance to figure out this allegory. What do we learn about our spiritual journey from how Joshua entered the Land? Any ideas? The cohanim (priests) went before them. Yes. Who is our cohane (priest) who went before us? Yes. Yeshua is our Great High Priest that went before us. What's another way to look at it? God went before them! So they went into the Land, but they didn't try to go without the presence of God leading them. And, of course, you can see what that means to us. God has to lead us into our Promised Land. We can't get in there on our own.

Eighth Allegory

Now, the first place God led them was to a place where there was a significant barrier! They came to the Jordan River and it says this.

Joshua 3:15 ... *for throughout harvest season the Yarden* (Jordan) *overflows its banks*....

So the first barrier that they encounter is this river at flood stage. There were fords in the Jordan during some parts of the year, but now it was flooded! You could not walk across that river! So, God is leading and hey! What is this? I thought it was going to be easy when God leads! Well, God led them first to a barrier that was impossible to cross. But then it says:

Joshua 3:15-17 *When those carrying the ark had come to the Yarden* (Jordan)*, and the cohanim* (priests) *carrying the ark had waded into the water (for throughout harvest season the Yarden* (Jordan) *overflows its banks), 16 the water upstream stood piled up like an embankment for a great distance at Adam, the city next to Tzartan; so that the water flowing downstream toward the Sea of the 'Aravah, the Dead Sea, was completely cut off; and the people crossed over right by Yericho* (Jericho)*. The cohanim carrying the ark for the covenant of ADONAI stood fast on* dry ground *in the middle of the Yarden* (Jordan)*, while all Isra'el crossed on* dry ground*, until the entire nation had finished crossing the Yarden.*

So, God brought them to a barrier and then told Joshua, "Just tell the cohanim to put their feet in the water and I'm going to overcome that barrier." So, they did this. And, of course, you know, they might have been thinking that they were going to look foolish. But this incident teaches us that there is a fruit of the Spirit we need to possess in order to come into the Promised Land. Do you know what it is? What fruit did they have when they put their feet in the water? Faith! Absolutely! They had faith.

God had a purpose for them in having them cross this barrier. That purpose was to increase their faith. And in verse ten it actually says that.

Joshua 3:10 [This] *"is how you will know that the living God is here with you and that, without fail, he will drive out from before you the Kena'ani* (Canaanites)*, [etc].*

So this was kind of a confirmation to the people. By stopping the water, God was saying to them, "Here, I'm going to do a miracle for you so you know that when you get into that Land, you're going to be able to conquer it."

That passage through the water strengthened their faith. And there's a tremendous parallel that I've experienced and you have also. As you step out in faith and you see God move and the thing that He's told you to do happens *because* you stepped out, your faith grows. You risked looking foolish. You risked losing money. You risked a lot of things. You stepped out in that faith and He did a miracle for you. Then what happens the next time you step out in faith? You have more faith! So God was building their faith in this. He did that for them and He does it for us!

Ninth Allegory

Now, going through these waters of the Jordan also represents something very interesting. Many people, when they go to Israel, do something in the waters of the Jordan. And what is that? Yea, they are immersed (baptized) in the Jordan for repentance. And I believe that this is another one of those stages in our lives. We talked about having to hear directly from God and be strong and courageous and obedient and able to give up things. Well, one of the other stages in our spiritual development, I believe, is to have a contrite heart. What that means is to get to the place where you recognize that in God's eyes you can't be good enough to meet His standards. You realize you need His forgiveness.

Psalms 51:17 (NIV) *The sacrifices of God are a broken spirit; a broken and contrite heart, O God, you will not despise.*

This is talking about the brokenness of repentance. *The Complete Jewish Bible* puts it this way:

Psalms 51:17 *My sacrifice to God is a broken spirit; God, You won't spurn a broken, chastened heart.*

This is another step in our lives. And it's interesting that He took the Israelites through the water. In the New Covenant it talks about going through the Red Sea being like an immersion or a baptism—a time of cleansing. In Judaism, we have a mikveh, which is a ritual bath for sin. So, symbolically, they cleansed themselves from sin before going into the Promised Land.

What's the analogy for our lives? We need to be cleansed. Right? And it's from sin. And, of course, we know that the way is no longer by the animal sacrifices that were available back in the times of the Temple. The only way is by the Blood of the perfect Lamb of God—of Yeshua. By His Blood, we can be cleansed of that sin.

Rosh Hashanah traditionally is a time of repenting. And that attitude is very important. It's important to be saying, "I'm open to you, O Ruakh HaKodesh (Holy Spirit). Show me if I'm doing anything wrong." There's a song I remember. It talked about the Ruakh HaKodesh (Holy Spirit) as a search light. "Shine your light on me." And what it is talking about is, "Shine your light on my darkness, and on those places where I don't even realize that I'm doing things that are displeasing to You; or where I have a wrong attitude." Have you ever had an attitude about something? You know, you have an attitude, but you just can't see that it is an ungodly attitude. Well, those are the kinds of things the Ruakh HaKodesh (Holy Spirit) wants to reveal to you.

Let's ponder that a minute. I suggest you stop reading for awhile and allow the Ruakh HaKodesh to speak to you.

*   *   *

Tenth Allegory

After they successfully crossed the Jordan, they set up a memorial in chapter four. And this is also another step in our spiritual development.

Joshua 4:5-7 *"Go on ahead of the ark of ADONAI your God into the riverbed of the Yarden (Jordan). Then, each of you take a stone on his shoulder, corresponding to the number of tribes of the people of Isra'el. 6 This will be a sign for you. In the future, when your children ask, 'What do you mean by these stones?' 7 you will answer them, 'It's because the water in the Yarden (Jordan) was cut off before the ark for the covenant of ADONAI; when it crossed the Yarden, the water in the Yarden was cut off; and these stones are to be a reminder for the people of Isra'el forever.' "*

Now, maybe you can answer this. Why did the Lord instruct them to set up a memorial? What is His purpose in making memorials like this? Do you know? Yes! To cause people to not forget! For what reason? Right! To remember what God has done. Which increases their what? Yes, their faith!

See, memorials are necessary so that we will have increased faith. And the analogy to our own lives is that when God says something or does something in our lives—when we step out in faith and God does a miracle, we should remember that! We should tell somebody about it. We should write it down! We should give a testimony about it. That's a memorial of God working in our lives.

I can remember when my wife and I were relatively new believers, we had not bought a house yet. When we were finally able to buy a house there had been lots of miracles that had happened. I remember every time I came home to that house, it was like a memorial! God had gotten us that house because it was impossible for us to do it on our own strength. The whole idea of memorials ties in with Rosh Hashanah. Remember Rosh Hashanah is to be a day of remembrance and of giving thanks for the things God has done.

Eleventh Allegory

Okay, we've passed the river. We're in chapter 5 now, and we have a very interesting incident here.

Joshua 5:13-15 *One day, when Y'hoshua (Joshua) was there by Yericho (Jericho), he raised his eyes and looked; and in front of him stood a man with his drawn sword in his hand. Y'hoshua went over to him and asked him, "Are you on our side or on the side of our enemies?" 14 "No," he replied, "but I am the commander of ADONAI's army; I have come just now." Y'hoshua fell down with his face to the ground and worshiped him, then asked, "What does my Lord have to say to His servant?" 15 The commander of ADONAI's army answered Y'hoshua, "Take your sandals off your feet, because the place where you are standing is holy." And Y'hoshua did so.*

Now, my belief is that this is what we call a Theophany. This was an appearance of God in physical form. The reason why I believe this is because this Being encouraged Joshua to worship Him. An angel wouldn't do that because God had given commandments that said don't worship anybody else. Don't worship anything that you make. Don't even worship angels. Worship only the one true God. And so this was an appearance of God in the form of a man. It's amazing that many people, especially Jewish people, say God could never come as a man, like Yeshua did. But here it is right here—God in the form of a man. He even told him to take his shoes off. It was holy ground because He was there.

There's a message in here for us. By striving for the Land—being obedient, having faith, counting the cost and being willing to pay it, Joshua entered into something that was very precious—a greater revelation of God. He got to know God in a new way—as the Commander of the Lord's army. He got to see God! I mean that's really something. And that's something that we can also expect, something we can look forward to. As we strive to enter our Promised Land, as we count the cost, as we lose our lives, as we do all these things, we can expect to draw closer to the Living God—to a greater revelation of Him.

The Battle Plan

Then the Commander gave Joshua his battle plans. These are strange battle plans, let me tell you.

Joshua 6:2-5 *ADONAI said to Y'hoshua* (Joshua), *"I have handed Yericho* (Jericho) *over to you, including its king and his warriors. 3 You are to encircle the city with all your soldiers and march around it once. Do this for six days. 4 Seven cohanim are to carry seven shofars in front of the ark. On the seventh day you are to march around the city seven times, and the cohanim will blow the shofars. 5 Then they are to blow a long blast on the shofar. On hearing the sound of the shofar, all the people are to shout as loudly as they can; and the wall of the city will fall down flat. Then the people are to go up into the city, each one straight from where he stands."*

Don't you agree those are strange battle plans? Notice in verse 5, it was a long blast that was to be blown on the Shofar. This is an incredible promise that God is giving here. But I want you to see that there was a cost to this promise. Just imagine it for a moment. You are an army and you go out and march around this city. You're not protected. You've got all these cohanim (priests) with you. The enemy could come charging out the gates of that city at any time. They most likely had weapons that could reach you from the walls of the city. So, there was a cost—a great risk—to this. They were risking everyone's lives, yet they were willing to do it.

You've got to think about Joshua's soldiers. They might have been shaking their heads saying, "Really, Joshua? This is what we're supposed to do? We're not supposed to have an ambush or trick them or build a siege work or start a fire or something? We're just supposed to march around the city with Shofars blowing? And on the seventh day the walls are going to come down when we shout? Okay, sure!" I mean this would've been hard for a soldier to handle. They had fought already. It wasn't like they hadn't been fighting. They had conquered several cities on the other side of the Jordan. They knew what warfare was. And they had been successful at it, too. So, why this?

Joshua 6:16 *The seventh time, when the cohanim* (priests) *blew on their shofars, Y'hoshua* (Joshua) *said to the people, "Shout! because ADONAI has given you the city!"*

Joshua 6:20 *So the people shouted, with the shofars blowing.*
When the people heard the sound of the shofars, the people let out a
great shout; and the wall fell down flat; so that the people went up into
the city, each one straight ahead of him; and they captured the city.

Of course, once they took that city, they were in possession of the
first part of their Promised Land. This was really possessing it. They
now had access to all the rest of the Promised Land. They had that
beach head established, if you will. They were going to have to fight for
the rest of the Promised Land, but they had that foothold.

Now, I've seen studies by archeologists that say they can tell that
those walls of Jericho collapsed outward. Outward! They would've fallen
inward if they had done it by their own strength. But they collapsed
outward because God did it.

There's something we need to understand about this battle plan.
This was a faith battle plan. It was all faith. This battle plan had nothing
to it but faith. There was nothing natural in any sense that could've
caused this to happen. They walked around the city blowing Shofars
for seven days. Then they walked around the city seven times and blew
those Shofars. And they shouted! Notice that they didn't shout for the
six days. They only shouted on that seventh day for the first time.

Now, I thought about this for awhile. I've been wondering what
they shouted. What words would they have yelled? What came to me,
and I don't know if this is right or not, but I believe they started with a
shout of command—commanding those walls to collapse. "Collapse,
walls!" "Fall down, walls!" And remember. Think about this a minute.
When we shout, we breathe out, right? And when we sound Shofars
we are blowing breath through them, right? If you know a little bit of
Hebrew, I have a quiz question for you. What's the word in Hebrew for
that breath? Do you know? Ruakh! Yes! That same word also means
"wind" and "spirit." So, I believe that when they blew their Shofars and
shouted, the Spirit of God, the Ruakh HaKodesh (the Holy Spirit), the
Breath of God became active and began to crumble those walls.

Then I believe (this is just my belief of what happened) that faith
took hold of them and their shout changed from a shout of command
to a shout of faith. What's a shout of faith? What do I mean by that? I
believe that before it happened, they began to shout, "Thank you, Lord,
these walls are falling down!" By faith they were seeing, in the Spirit,
those walls crumbling. And then when it actually started happening,
their shouts turned into another kind of shout. What kind of shout do
you think it was then? Joy! Right! They went to shouts of joy, of victory.
"Hallelujah!"

Remember the song that says, "Joshua fought the battle of Jericho and the walls came tumbling down." We want to see this happen to the Jerichos in our lives.

Well, that's kind of the end of the story, but I want to challenge you a little bit and ask you where you are on the road to possessing the Promised Land. I think we're each in a little bit of a different place on that road. Are you ready to take another step along that road?

I'm going to do something now and invite you to participate. I'm going lead in some prayers that will be steps along that road. And I want you to pray along with me. Not that you have to recite it, but just pray along with me as I pray—agree with it for yourself. You may not be able to agree with every step. You may not be ready for those steps, but pray along with the steps that you can agree with. Okay?

So let's just come before the Lord and pray.

Lord, I receive the promise that You give us of a spiritual Promised Land—the Kingdom of God. I receive that as personally for me, not just for all of Your people, Lord, but personally for me.

Lord, I realize that I need to be strong, courageous, and obedient so that I may possess this Promised Land. And Lord, I confess that I need Your help to be that. Help me to be strong, to be courageous, and to be obedient.

Lord, I count the cost of possessing the Land. It requires effort. It requires risk. And You said it requires me giving my life to You. And I declare that I'm willing to make that effort, to take that risk, and to give my life to You.

Lord, I also realize that You must lead me in, and I'm prone to trying to do it my way. And so I ask You to keep me from that. Keep me from trying to go in my own strength—in my own wisdom. Cause me, Lord, to follow You again.

Lord, I recognize that I need faith to enter into the Promised Land. And I ask You to help me to step out on Your promises, and to trust You and the direction that You give.

Lord, I realize that I could look foolish! I could lose things! I could be humiliated! But Lord, I believe it's worth it to receive that Promised Land. So, I pray that You would increase my faith.

And, Lord, I realize that it's necessary to be cleansed to come into Your Presence. And so I ask Your Spirit to cleanse me from sin. I accept the Blood that You shed for my atonement—Your sacrifice for me.

Then, Lord, I read about how Joshua saw You face to face. And Lord, that's my heart's desire. I want to know You better. I pray that You would reveal Yourself to me in whatever form You choose. Reveal Yourself to me as the One True Living God.

Thank You, Lord. Thank You, Lord.

*   *   *

I'd like to end this chapter by executing Joshua's battle plan in our own lives. Rosh Hashanah is the Sabbath of Remembrance—Shabbat Zih-kh'ron Teruah which, as we have learned, means all that. So, we're going to sound the Shofar and shout! We're going to shout a command and shout in faith. Then we're going to shout for joy. What are we remembering that we are shouting for joy about? Well, I would like us to remember God's promises. God has promised us this good Land, this Promised Land, this Kingdom of God. So we're going to shout for joy that we can enter this Land.

There are spiritual walls, fortified cities, and enemies trying to prevent you from entering into this Promised Land. I believe that as we blow the Shofar and shout in faith, those walls are going to crumble and you're going to be able to enter into the Promised Land. There may be some of you readers who are not quite ready to cross the Jordan and enter into the Promised Land. There may be a wall somewhere back along the trail that I talked about. But, I believe that if you will shout as you listen to Shofar blowing or blow a Shofar yourself, that those walls can come down and you can move ahead in this journey of coming to the Promised Land.

If you have a Shofar, please get it out now and be ready to blow it. Or you can get a recording or video of Shofar blasts and be ready to play them. Before we start, let's say the blessing over the Shofar.

Blessed are You, Lord our God, Ruler of the universe, who has sanctified us with Your commandments and commanded us to hear the sound of the Shofar.

Okay, now this is what we're going to shout. We're going to shout at the walls, "Come down!" That's a shout of command. Then we're going to shout in faith, "Thank you, Lord, that the walls are coming down." Then we're going to shout in joy that the walls have come down.

Instead of doing the traditional order of Shofar blasts for Rosh Hashanah, I'd like to have seven shorter blasts because they went around seven times. Remain silent during those blasts.

Then I'd like to have a really long blast. As that blast is sounding, we're going to command those walls to come down—those walls that are blocking us from coming into the fullness of possessing the Land. Or, as I said, if you're farther back—if you haven't crossed the Jordan River yet; if you haven't been washed; if you haven't had faith to do that yet; or if you haven't personally heard that there's a Promised Land for you—then there's a wall that's preventing you from receiving all that.

If you're in that place, you can command those walls that are stopping you from receiving those things to come down.

Are you ready? Alright, let's hear the Shofars!

(Seven short blasts.)

(Long blast.)

"Collapse, walls!" "Come down, walls." "Collapse!"

Now, shouts of faith, "Thank You, Lord, You're breaking those walls down."

Now shouts of Joy! "Thank You, Lord, for bringing them down!!!"

CHAPTER 5

SHOUT FOR JOY
FOR PAST EVENTS

I have been involved in the Messianic Movement now for more than twenty-five years. It seems like every year the Lord gives me a little bit more revelation of what these Appointed Times are all about. Every year around this time, I always think, well, what more can I say than I said last year? And I get a little anxious about it. But there's always something new. So I'm thankful for that. I guess when I run out of new things to say, it'll be time to retire.

This is an interesting Appointed Time, as I said before, because there isn't a lot said about it—only two or three verses in the whole Bible refer to it. Yet there has been a lot of Jewish tradition that has developed around it. Let's look at one of those Bible verses again.

Leviticus 23:24 *"Tell the people of Isra'el, 'In the seventh month, the first of the month is to be for you a day of complete rest for remembering, a holy convocation announced with blasts on the shofar.'"*

If you could hear it read in Hebrew, you would pick up on the three words we've been emphasizing, Shabbaton Zih-kh'ron Teruah. Can you recall what they mean?

"Shabbaton" means a Sabbath, a day of rest (Strong's H7677)

"Zih-kh'ron" means a day of remembrance or a memorial—a day of remembering what the Lord has done (Strong's H2146)

"Teruah" means with blowing of Shofars and shouting for joy. I continue to find it amazing that all that is in that one little Hebrew word! (Strong's H8643)

So, what are we to remember? Well, if it's in God's instructions, one would think it has something to do with the mighty acts of God—what God has done. But why? Why have this memorial—this remembrance day once a year like this? Is it so we can have another holiday? Visit our relatives? But, we don't really need another holiday, especially this time of year when there are three in a row.

I believe it's because God knows us. He made us, so He knows that periodically we need certain kinds of refreshing. We need certain kinds of things to happen in our lives to enable us to walk with Him. And so one of the things that this day is for is to remember the things God has done to strengthen our faith!

There's a Psalm—Psalm 136. You probably remember it. It's the one that says about twenty times, "He is good and His mercy endures forever." And each time it says this it talks about one of the great deeds of God. He brought us out of Egypt. He had us cross the Red Sea. He defeated Pharaoh. It lists all the great miracles. The purpose of that Psalm is to strengthen the readers' faith as they remember what God has done.

But why at this time of year would there be a day of remembrance? I believe it's because we are to prepare ourselves for what comes ten days from this holiday—to actually humble ourselves—in preparation for Yom Kippur, the Day of Atonement.

Now, back in the days of the Tabernacle and the Temple, God appointed this Day of Atonement (Yom Kippur) annually to make a sacrifice for the whole nation. If you read it carefully you'll see that it was a sacrifice for un-confessed sin. There are other sacrifices throughout the year that dealt with sins that people knew about, that they confessed, that they wanted to make atonement for. But God knew the people so well. He knew that they would do lots of things that would be sin, and they wouldn't even realize it. And I think we're still like that. Right? Did you ever find out that you did something you didn't even realize was wrong when you did it? Then later someone tells you that what you did was wrong. So God knew that about us. And that's why He set into place this Appointed Time of Yom Kippur. In those days He wanted to dwell amongst His people. But, in order for Him to dwell amongst His people, Israel, they had to have this atonement covering. Otherwise, the Scriptures say He would have consumed them. The Glory of God would have been so powerful that it would have burned them up.

Exodus 33:3 (NKJV) *Go up to a land flowing with milk and honey; for I will not go up in your midst, lest I consume you on the way, for you are a stiff-necked people.*

So, He knew, because He created us, that we needed this annual cleansing. And He didn't say to do it just once, but every year! Every year there was to be this Yom Kippur sacrifice—every year for hundreds of years.

Now, we know, and we're going to talk a lot about this later, that He brought to us something called the B'rit Hadashah, the New Covenant. And with that New Covenant there is no need for the Yom Kippur sacrifices to be made every year because we have had the one sacrifice of the Messiah done once and for all.

However, if you go back and look at Leviticus 23, it doesn't say anywhere in there that at any point the keeping of Yom Kippur is to stop. In fact, it says it's to be repeated yearly forever.

Leviticus 23:31 (NKJV) *You shall do no manner of work* (referring to Yom Kippur). *It shall be a statute _forever_ throughout your generations in all your dwellings."*

So, God didn't say to stop keeping this day—at least for us Messianic Jews. In verse 32 it tells about what is done on this day, even if there's no Temple.

Leviticus 23:32 (NKJV) *It shall be to you a Sabbath of _solemn_ rest, and you shall _afflict_ your souls.*

Rosh Hashanah is the beginning of the Ten Days of preparation, called the Yomim Norim (Days of Awe), leading up to this day of *afflicting our souls.* Now what does it mean to afflict our souls? If you look it up, the word in Hebrew is "anah" and it means: *to afflict, to chasten one's self, to deal hardly with one's self, to humble one's self.*

So, to do that a person needs to have a contrite heart. I can think of several places in Scripture where it talks about a "contrite heart."

Isaiah 66:2 *The kind of person on whom I look with favor is one with a poor and humble spirit, who* <u>*trembles*</u> *at my word.*

The Hebrew word for "trembles" is "Kha-rad." It means *to tremble, to be fearful, to be reverent, to be afraid.*

Now, I don't know about you. Maybe you're not at a place of admitting this about yourself, but I know about *me.* Every once in awhile, I need to humble myself. What happens if I don't? The Lord humbles me. And it's much better to humble yourself than to have God humble you. I know that for sure! So, I think God put this in place to be a yearly time of humbling ourselves. But, if we're not in a place of being willing to humble ourselves—to "afflict our souls"—then Yom Kippur is really of no value to us.

So, what does it mean to humble yourself? Well, to *me*, it simply means to open myself up to the Ruakh HaKodesh—the Holy Spirit— and say, "Is there something in me that is not pleasing to You, God? Is there some change You want to make, Lord? Is there something You want to convict me about? I just want to open myself up to You."

To have a day to focus on that, I believe, is important. It's important for *me!* It's certainly important to God since He set up an Appointed Time for it.

Now Rosh Hashanah is the beginning of these Ten Days of preparation for this. That's why it's a day of "remembrance with the sounding of the Shofar and shouting for joy."

Now why joy? Well, because what's supposed to happen on Rosh Hashanah is we're supposed to be restored to that sense of gratitude for and awe of who God is. That's where we start. We don't just start out saying, "O Lord, I'm humbling myself." We start out by grasping who God is and then we are naturally humbled—or *supernaturally* humbled. We don't have to work at it. It's what happens when we really get a handle on who our God is.

The purpose for all this, again, is to restore that sense of awe and wonder. I don't know if you can recall, maybe when you first came to know the Lord, that sense of awe you had of knowing the Creator of the universe. I know for me it wears off after awhile. You have to renew that. That's why David prayed, "Restore to me—renew in me—the joy of Your salvation." (See Psalms 51:12.)

So, how do we do this? Well, there's much in the Scriptures we could look at to do this, but at this time I felt led to look specifically at times that are associated with "shouting for joy and blowing of the Shofar," and to just grasp and appreciate the greatness of our God in doing this.

Where do we start with our remembrances? Let's start by looking at things of the past. In a later chapter we will look at things in the present and the future. We'll talk about how you can remember the future. It's kind of an oxymoron, but what it really means is we're going to remember and rejoice that God predicted that these things would happen. And they *are* happening! To me that is awesome! When I see the fulfillment of prophesy, it just strengthens my faith so much. So, that's what we're going to do later, but right now we're going to look at some of these things in the past.

Let's start way back in the beginning. We have a very interesting passage here where God was speaking to Job:

Job 38:4-7(NIV) *"Where were you when I laid the earth's foundation? Tell me, if you understand. Who marked off its dimensions? Surely you know! Who stretched a measuring line across it? On what were its footings set, or who laid its cornerstone—while the morning stars sang together and all the angels shouted for joy?"*

Because of this passage and because Rosh Hashanah is a day we're supposed to shout for joy, the Jewish Rabbis saw it as saying that God finished His Creation on this day and that Rosh Hashanah is a day to remember Creation. This is the teaching that has gone around in Judaism for literally thousands of years which is kind of awesome.

If we think about God and His Creation, what comes to my mind is a verse in Romans that tells us the value of appreciating God's creation.

Romans 1:20 *For ever since the creation of the universe His invisible qualities—both His eternal power and His divine nature—have been clearly seen, because they can be understood from what He has made.*

So, we can see His eternal power and divine nature in creation as we look around. It's especially beautiful this time of year when we're coming into the fall season and for no apparent reason, other than God has this incredible sense of beauty, trees change color. Can you think of any Darwinian reason for the trees to change color? I mean, does that help the birds somehow? Why does He do that? Just because He is an awesome God! He created beauty! And He created it for us to enjoy. As we see creation we begin to grasp His awesomeness.

So, the first thing we shout for joy for is creation.

Get your Shofar out again or your recording of Shofar blasts. And let's say the blessing over Shofar blowing again before we start.

Blessed are You, Lord our God, Ruler of the universe, who has sanctified us with His commandments and commanded us to hear the sound of the Shofar.

Now, let's sound the Shofar and shout for joy over the wonder of His creation like the angels did.

(Shofar blasts.)

HALLELUJAH!! Thank You, Lord. Thank You for your creation. Thank You, Lord. Thank You for creating this world! Thank You for the beauty we're about to see as the trees change color! Thank You for the bounty of the harvest, Lord God. Thank You for this summer and the pleasant weather, Lord. Thank You for all the things—for the rain that You bring down on us. Thank You for creating us wondrously and amazingly, Lord. Thank You, Lord! We shout for joy!

*   *   *

The Lord himself sounded the first Shofar mentioned in the Bible and that happened in the Book of Exodus on Mt. Sinai. The Children of Israel were encamped before the mountain.

Exodus 19:18-19 *Mount Sinai was covered with smoke, because the LORD descended on it in fire. The smoke billowed up from it like smoke from a furnace, the whole mountain trembled violently, and the sound of the shofar grew louder and louder. Then Moses spoke and the voice of God answered him.*

If you know the rest of the story, you know that God gave the Ten Commandments and what we call the Mosaic Covenant to the Israelites at this time. And this was such an awesome sight.

Exodus 20:18-19 *All the people experienced the thunder, the lightning, the sound of the shofar, and the mountain smoking. When the people saw it, they trembled. Standing at a distance, 19 they said to Moshe, "You, speak with us; and we will listen. But don't let God speak with us, or we will die."*

This sight was so awe-inspiring that they were trembling. They reacted in fear of dying, and drew back. More than that, how awesome it was that the Creator would come down to visit His people in a visible presence and speak to them from this mountain and give them Words— Words to live by—His instruction. Remember that the word for what God gave us in Hebrew is "Torah," and it doesn't just mean "Bible" or "Law" it means "instruction."

His instruction is the thing that gives us Life. And, of course, the Torah has several purposes. One of them is it enables us to live together! I mean, we barely manage to live together without killing each other in this world *with* the law! Right? Could you imagine what it would be like if there was no law? There are places in this world where there is no law and it is not easy to live there. And there was a time before the flood when there was no law and everybody just did what was right in their own eyes. They were just out for themselves, and it was murderous! So that's one of the purposes.

Another purpose of the Torah or the Law is to convict us of our own sin.

Romans 7:7 *...the function of the Torah was that without it, I would not have known what sin is. For example, I would not have become conscious of what greed is if the Torah had not said, "Thou shalt not covet."*

So the Word makes us aware of our sinfulness. During the Ten Days of Awe, as is done in Traditional Judaism, I urge *you* to seek the Lord and let His Spirit show you where He wants to make changes in you.

The rabbis teach that the day God came down on Mt. Sinai and gave the Law was actually on Shavuot, the day the church has celebrated as Pentecost. So here's an amazing thing that people don't realize. The Word and the Spirit were both given on the same day. The Word was given on Shavuot at Mt. Sinai. Then the Ruakh HaKodesh was given on Shavuot 1500 years later. So we have the Spirit, and we know that without the Spirit, the Law—the Word—is empty. They both are needed. In fact, Yeshua is quoted as saying:

John 6:63 *It is the Spirit who gives life, the flesh is no help. The words I have spoken to you are Spirit and life.*

So, it's His Spirit that makes the Word have Life. So, we have something to shout for joy about. He has given us His Word. He's given us the Mosaic Covenant. And He's given us His Spirit to make the Word come alive and to convict us of sin so that we can change.

So, let's sound the Shofar now, and let's shout for joy for the Word. (Shofar blast.)

Thank You, Lord! Thank You for Your Word! Thank You Lord! Your Word is a lamp to our feet and a light to our eyes. Thank You for giving it, Lord God. Thank You that Your Word is Life to us. It is our very life, our nourishment. It's like our Bread, Lord God. Thank You for wisdom in Your Word. Thank You that Your Word brings revelation of who You are, that it brings conviction of sin, that it brings us to You. Thank You for Your Word! Thank You for the Covenant that You gave on Mt. Sinai. Thank You, Lord. We shout for joy for Your Word.

*   *   *

*   *   *

Well, we talked about the Mosaic Covenant that was given on Mt. Sinai. But in Jeremiah 31 it says something very interesting.

Jeremiah 31:31-34 *"Here, the days are coming,"* says ADONAI, *"when I will make a new covenant with the house of Isra'el and with the house of Y'hudah* (Judah). *32 It will not be like the covenant I made with their fathers on the day I took them by their hand and brought them out of the land of Egypt; because they, for their part, violated my covenant, even though I, for my part, was a husband to them,"* says ADONAI. *33 "For this is the covenant I will make with the house of Isra'el after those days,"* says ADONAI: *"I will put my Torah within them and write it on their hearts; I will be their God, and they will be my people. 34 No longer will any of them teach his fellow community member or his brother, 'Know ADONAI'; for all will know me, from the least of them to the greatest; because I will forgive their wickednesses and remember their sins no more."*

Now there's something to shout about—a New Covenant! Now let me just explain to some of you who maybe aren't aware of what a covenant is. A covenant is like a contract. It's a contract between man and God. And when we talk about our relationship with the covenant we speak about entering into a covenant as one would enter into a contract by signing it. For those who enter into this New Covenant, He says that He:

- Puts the Law in our minds and writes it on our hearts
- Enables us to *know* Him
- Forgives us our iniquity
- Does not remember our sin

But if you don't *have* that New Covenant—if you haven't entered into it or if you're not *sure* that you *have* entered into it, there's no reason to shout for joy about it. How do you know if you've entered into it? Well, have you ever signed a contract? For a house? For a car? Did you know you signed it? Yes, you knew you signed it. Well, in the same way, I know personally, when I entered into that New Covenant with the Lord. I *knew* I was entering it! There wasn't any question in my mind. You know!

So, if you are not sure if you've entered that Covenant, it's probably because you never *have* entered into it. But you can enter into that Covenant now, because God wants all people to enter in. I'm going to explain it further later, but for now if you are sure you've entered into the New Covenant, let's sound the Shofar and give thanks for that

New Covenant—that we are alive in a time when we have that New Covenant.
(Shofar blasts.)
Hallelujah! Thank You, Lord! Thank You for the New Covenant. Thank You that You brought that New Covenant. We shout for joy!! Thank You, Lord, that You are the one who initiated this Covenant. It wasn't us. It was You! Thank You that You promised it through Jeremiah so many hundred years before it even came—six hundred years before the Messiah. You predicted it would come and it came just like You said it would with all those benefits, Lord. Thank You for enabling us to know You. Thank You for forgiving us our iniquities and remembering our sins no more. Thank You for placing Your Law in our minds and in our hearts, for being our God and for calling us to be Your people. Thank You, Lord.

*   *   *

How did the Lord bring us this New Covenant? It's actually a very surprising way, if you step back and think about it. If God was going to bring it like He did with the Mosaic Covenant when He just came down and said, "Here it is!" —wrote it on tablets and gave it to the people, that would be awesome enough. But for the New Covenant, He did it in such a different way.

First of all, He came to earth in the form of a man. Now if you think that's strange, just study the Book of Genesis and you'll find about four or five incidents where He came to earth in the form of a man. For example, He came to Jacob and wrestled with him; and He appeared to Abraham as a man to tell him about Sodom. So, He came to earth as a man. But then again, this was also strange because He didn't come as a full grown man, like he did when he visited Jacob and Abraham. Instead he came as an infant—which is mind-boggling! He created the universe. I think sometimes we get so used to this story that we don't realize how amazing this is—that He would come down, not as a mighty warrior with a sword, like He did for Joshua, as the captain of the Lord of Hosts, but as an infant.

I was looking through these things and I was saying, "I wonder if there's anything that connects this with shouting for joy." And you know what I found? I found out that the conception of the Messiah was greeted with shouts of joy. You probably never heard that, but let me show you. There weren't any Shofars blown, but somebody shouted for joy! This is when Yeshua's mother, Miryam (Hebrew for Mary), became pregnant and she went to visit her cousin, Elizabeth.

Luke 1:41-42 *When Elisheva* (Elizabeth) *heard Miryam's* (Mary's) *greeting, the baby in her womb stirred* (or jumped). *Elisheva was filled with the Ruach HaKodesh and spoke up in* <u>a loud voice</u>,...

(What's that? A shout! She shouted!)

..."How blessed are you among women! And how blessed is the child in your womb!"

She was shouting for joy! For joy that the Messiah had been conceived! Isn't that wonderful? Now not only was His conception greeted with shouts of joy, but in Luke 2, we have another incident where after He was born, angels appeared to shepherds out in a field and spoke to them, probably very familiar to some of you:

Luke 2:11-14 *"This very day, in the town of David, there was born for you a Deliverer who is the Messiah, the Lord. Here is how you will know: you will find a baby wrapped in cloth and lying in a feeding trough." Suddenly, along with the angel was a vast army from heaven praising God: "In the highest heaven, glory to God! And on earth, peace among people of good will!"*

Now, what do you think—when this "vast army" appeared, do you think they whispered? *"In the highest heaven, glory to God."* No, I think they shouted for JOY that the MESSIAH WAS BORN! **"IN THE HIGHEST HEAVEN, GLORY TO GOD!!!!"**

Let's blow the Shofar and give a shout that the Messiah was born and that we're alive to know about it.

(Shofar blast.)

Thank You, Lord! Thank You for sending the Messiah. Thank You for sending the Deliverer, O God. We shout for joy! Thank You, Lord!

*   *   *

Now this Messiah was an infant. He grew up the same way all of us grew up—slowly. He lived among the people of Israel. He lived there for thirty-three years. The Scriptures say He was without sin and that He was a Torah-observant Jew. He taught the Word of God and performed many miracles. And then, at the appointed time—God's Appointed Time—He was unjustly accused by jealous men, and was sentenced to be executed on a cross—a criminal's death—a Roman cross. But, His death on that cross was part of God's plan. He died as a sacrificial offering to pay the price for our sin. Six hundred years before He was born, one of the Hebrew prophets, Isaiah, said this:

Isaiah 53:12 (NIV) *...He poured out his life unto death, and was numbered with the transgressors; for he bore the sin of many, and made intercession for the transgressors.*

You know what? There were no shouts of joy or sounding of Shofars when that happened. None. Because all of those who had followed Him, and His mother and brothers thought that He was being smitten by God, that maybe how He had handled His ministry was wrong. Maybe because He had said the things He had said, He messed things up with the Jewish leaders, getting Himself killed.

Isaiah predicted this.

Isaiah 53:4 (NKJV) ...Yet we esteemed Him stricken, smitten by God, and afflicted.

So they buried Him in a tomb and His body spent three days and three nights in it. This happened on the Day of Pesakh (Passover) at the time when the Passover lambs were being sacrificed. There's another Appointed Time on Sunday during Passover week that is called First Fruits. On that day, God raised Him from the dead. The purpose of that raising was to confirm that the death that He died was part of God's plan. It was God's plan that His death would be like a sacrifice—like the sacrifices made in the Temple. But His sacrifice is greater than any other sacrifice that had ever been made.

His first appearance to His followers was to Miryam of Magdala (Mary Magdalene) who didn't recognize Him. And once again we have a shout.

John 20:14-16 ...she turned around and saw Yeshua standing there, but she didn't know it was He. Yeshua said to her, "Lady, why are you crying? Whom are you looking for?" Thinking He was the gardener, she said to him, "Sir, if you're the one who carried Him away, just tell me where you put Him; and I'll go and get Him myself." Yeshua said to her, "Miryam!" Turning, she cried out to Him in Hebrew, "Rabbani!" (that is, "Teacher!")

Did you see that? She cried out! She shouted. She shouted for joy!

Then He appeared alive to the rest of His followers that same day. And you know what happened there? They experienced something that was so moving that it was beyond shouting for joy. You know, you can get to that place where something is so incredible, so amazing, so wonderful you feel overwhelmed.

Luke 24: 36-41 ...there He was, standing among them! Startled and terrified, they thought they were seeing a ghost. But He said to them, "Why are you so upset? Why are these doubts welling up inside you? Look at My hands and My feet—it is I, Myself! Touch Me and see—a ghost doesn't have flesh and bones, as you can see I do." As He said this, He showed them His hands and feet. ... they were still unable to believe it for joy and stood there dumbfounded.

Do you know what "dumbfounded" means? It means they couldn't say anything! They couldn't shout. It was so joyous. It was overload—overload of joy.

Try to put yourself in their place. These men and women had walked with Him every day for three years. They had seen the miracles that He did. They had heard the wisdom that flowed from His lips. They had heard Him preach from the Scriptures.

But then they thought that He had blown it—that it was all over. They thought He had let Himself be taken captive and He shouldn't have. They thought He should've gone on and made Himself king. They thought all those things because they still didn't know God's plan. And they were crushed. They felt hopeless. They were in despair for three days!

Then on that third day, suddenly He appears. Can you imagine the joy? The person that you had put all your hope in was destroyed—all your hopes were destroyed along with Him, but He is now come back. This is what happens—dumbfounded—unable to speak.

His resurrection confirmed that His death on the cross was the plan of God—that by His sacrificial death, He offers us this New Covenant:
- To enable us to be forgiven of all the things we've ever done that were against His Law.
- To have our iniquity remembered no more.

Now, you may not know what iniquity is. Iniquity is different from sin. Iniquity is our inclination toward evil. In other words, it's the thing in us that we all suffer from, which is, that if we don't control ourselves we tend to do what's wrong. We have to make an effort to do what's right. Even that is remembered no more when we enter into the New Covenant.

His Law is written on our minds and in our hearts so that it doesn't become a burden to keep the Law anymore. It becomes a pleasure. I can testify to that.

And we are enabled to know Him personally. This is, I think, the most important part that Jeremiah said—*"that they will all know Me, from the least to the greatest"* because He's alive. And He's still alive today.

Well, I can personally testify of the joy of entering into this New Covenant—of signing on—a joy that it is beyond shouting. It really is. I wasn't able to shout. I don't know if others were able to shout when it happened to them, but I wasn't able to. I was just too dumbfounded. The grace of God was there.

Now when we shouted for joy for the giving of the Covenant, perhaps you weren't able to shout for joy because you're not sure you've entered into the New Covenant. You can enter into it now. If you want to enter into the New Covenant just wait a minute and I will tell you how you can enter into it.

Now, let's shout for joy and sound the Shofar because Messiah was raised from the dead. Let's stand up and shout for joy that God has given us in this New Covenant; that He has invited us to enter in; that we know we have entered in; that we're living in this life with the knowledge that we're His Covenant people; that we have a relationship with Him. And we didn't even add that He gives us an assurance of eternal Life; that we'll go to be with Him. What a joy! So, let's blow the Shofar and just give thanks.

(Shofar blasts)

Thank You, Lord. Hallelujah! Thank You, Lord. Thank You for Your Covenant, Lord God. Thank You that You freely give this New Covenant. O Lord, thank You. It is the thing that has changed all of our lives, God. You turned us away from darkness with this New Covenant. Thank You. We thank You that it was promised by Jeremiah hundreds of years before it came. Thank You, Lord, that You fulfilled that promise. Thank You that You paid a terrible price of suffering and separation and humiliation. You paid that terrible price while You hung on that cross to give us that New Covenant. Thank You that You did it because You love us so much. We thank You, Lord. Thank You for revealing to us that we need to enter into it, Lord. Thank You, Lord.

*   *   *

Now, I want you to tell you how you can enter into the New Covenant—how you can know for sure that you are a part of it—how you can be sure that your name is written in the Lamb's Book of Life. (See Revelations 21:27.)

Do you believe that Yeshua is the Messiah and that His sacrificial blood atones for your sins? If so, then tell this to Yeshua right now in prayer.

Now tell Him that you know you are a sinner and that you are sorry for your sins. Ask Him to wash away your sins and iniquity with His Blood.

Now ask Him to come into your heart and be Lord of your life.

If you have done that then you have now entered into the New Covenant!!

Praise the Lord!! Now you have something new to sound the Shofar and shout for joy about!!

Hallelujah!!

CHAPTER 6

The Shofar

In traditional synagogues, Jewish leaders sound the Shofar each Shabbat for a month leading up to Rosh Hashanah. When we started our congregation in 1984, most of us had never heard a Shofar blown. Only those who attended traditional Rosh Hashanah services had ever heard one. For the last 1700 years the body of the Messiah has not known about Shofars. Who knows the reason for that? Yes, the church separated itself from its Jewish roots about 1700 years ago.

So, the Shofar was hidden from the church for close to 2000 years due to this intentional cutting off of its Jewish roots. But now, since the early 1990's, suddenly it is becoming very popular in Messianic congregations and churches. The nations—the Gentiles—are beginning to realize that there is an important spiritual significance to the Shofar—even in India. A Shofar player, Jonathan Cahn, from New Jersey was invited in 2001 to go to India to come up to the mountain where their history says Apostle Thomas was martyred. They asked him to come and be on that mountain as a Jewish believer—the first Jewish believer to be there since the time of Thomas, but mostly to blow the Shofar over the nation of India. They grasp something about the importance of the Shofar. And that's what we're going to do.

Shofars are usually made of ram's horns, but actually horns from other kosher animals, such as goats, antelopes, gazelles, big horned sheep, etc., can also be used. However, because of the golden calf the Israelites made, a cow's horn cannot be used even though it is a kosher animal. The larger Shofars called Kudu Shofars are made from an African antelope. I wish that when I first saw one of them I had taken my money and invested it in raising Kudu antelope or in a Shofar manufacturing company. They can't keep up with the demand! I would be very rich today.

Different things come and go. Is the fascination with the Shofar one of them? Is this just a fad in the church? It could be, but I don't believe it is. I think it is part of the End Time revival that God is bringing! We'll learn about that in this chapter.

Many people are now blowing the Shofar or listening to it blown, but they don't really understand what it actually is. They don't understand its power and its importance.

The Shofar is not a musical instrument. Have you noticed that? It can be played in such a wonderful worshipful way or in a loud, dramatic blast. I love it when it has a mournful, deep sound during worship. But it's not playing the melody. Right? You aren't musically challenged enough to not catch that, are you? The Shofar simply makes a sound. It doesn't follow the melody or the harmony or anything like that. It is different.

So, the Shofar is a special instrument and it shouldn't really be used by a person unless they know what it is all about. The enemy can really confound us if we take things that are special to God and use them in just any ordinary, frivolous way we want. That opens a door to the enemy. It's good to use one, but we need to use it with respect as a holy instrument.

We're going to learn about its importance. The Shofar is a tool chosen by God for certain uses or functions. We're going to look into those uses. There are actually six of them.

First Function

Let's start at Mt. Sinai when God was about to give the Ten Commandments and the rest of the Torah to Moshe (Moses). We find here that the Shofar is associated with the voice of God.

Exodus 19:19 *When the voice of the Shofar sounded long and waxed louder and louder, Moses spoke, and God answered him by a voice.*

Now, first of all, in your Bible it probably says, "the voice of the trumpet." There are two Hebrew words that are translated "trumpet." This one is the word "Shofar." We'll talk about the other one later. Shofar is the ram's horn. Shofar comes from the root that means *to incise, or to cut (as giving a cutting sound—a clear sound).* Most of the places where you find the word "trumpet" in the Books of Moses, except in Numbers 10, you will find that it is the word "Shofar."

Now, also notice that it said "God answered him with a voice" and that the "voice of the Shofar sounded." There's a play on words here that is very, very important. The Shofar is referred to as having a voice. The Hebrew here is "kol haShofar" which is literally "voice of the Shofar." It ends with God answering him by a voice – "b'kol." Notice the same Hebrew word is used here—"kol." It's a poetic play on words—the voice of the Shofar and the voice of God. The Shofar voice grew louder and louder—very strong.

Exodus 20:18 *Now all the people witnessed the thunderings, the lightning flashes, the sound of the Shofar, and the mountain smoking; and when the people saw it, they trembled and stood afar off.*

Who made the thunderings, lightning flashes, and mountain smoke? God was doing that. Right? Now, included in that was the "kol ha-Shofar." Who was blowing on the Shofar? God! Yes, it was not Moses blowing the Shofar, nor the people. God was making this sound of the Shofar. This is something I want you to grasp now. This instrument is created by God. It's an animal horn. Man does not make this instrument. God does. And God sounds this instrument. This is the only instrument recorded in the Scriptures that God makes or uses. He sounded it on Mt. Sinai. And the people heard it. For confirmation of God using it, let's look in Zechariah.

Zechariah 9:14 *The Lord GOD will blow the Shofar.*

Now, to get a little deeper into this and to understand it, let's go to Revelations. We're going to look at John who was in the Spirit and saw these visions of heaven. The "voice of the Shofar" is not only associated with the voice of God. There is more.

Revelation 1:10 *I came to be, in the Spirit, on the Day of the Lord; and I heard behind me a loud voice, like a trumpet ....*

So, there was this voice like a trumpet.

Revelation 1:12-13,17-18 *I turned around to see who was speaking to me; and when I had turned, I saw seven gold menorahs (candlesticks); and among the menorahs was someone like a Son of Man, ... He ... said, "... I am the First and the Last, the Living One. I was dead, but look!—I am alive forever and ever!"*

Whose voice was this that sounded like a trumpet? Yeshua! Yes. It was the risen and glorified Yeshua! So, Yeshua's voice was "like a trumpet!" Isn't that interesting?! Now you might be asking, "Was this a trumpet or a Shofar?" Well, it's hard to tell because the Greek word is not "Shofar" it's "sal-pinx" (G4536).

Hebrews 12:19 *... to the sound of a trumpet, and to a voice whose words made the hearers beg that no further message be given to them.*

The same Greek word, "sal-pinx" is used here referring to the event on Mt. Sinai. So, the conclusion is that Yeshua's voice sounds like a Shofar! Now, I want you to grasp this because this is going to be a leap of understanding. The Shofar sound is the closest thing there is to God's voice in this universe, in this physical world. That's why it is significant. That's why when we listen to it, it does something to us. It is like the voice of God. That's why the enemy had it hidden for 1700 years. And it's why we are capitalizing the word "Shofar" in this book.

Now I'm not saying God doesn't speak in other ways. The Scripture says that He speaks with a still, small voice, and that's not like a Shofar. And it says that He speaks with a voice of joy, and other ways. So, He speaks in many ways. But, one of the ways is with the voice of the Shofar.

Now, if we heard the fullness of His voice, I think there'd be a problem. I think the voice of the Shofar is a smaller manifestation of His voice. What would happen to us if we heard the fullness of His voice? It would probably blow us away, literally. We wouldn't be able to handle it. We'd be frightened like the Israelites were! So, when God wants to bring the power of His voice into the realm where we can hear it, it's the voice of the Shofar.

Now, what does the voice of the Lord do? Think about the story of Creation. How did the Lord create? He created with His voice! *"And God said, 'Let there be light and there was light"!* He *"said"*! When you *say* something you are using your voice, right? So, God's voice creates! Do you agree with me on that? So, that's part of the significance of this.

*   *   *

So, how important is it to God that we hear the voice of the Shofar? Well, Rosh Hashanah is a special holiday about it. What is the Hebrew name of this holiday? Yom Teruah, *the day of the sounding of the Shofar.* So, think about this. I never thought about this before. God appointed and set aside an entire day, a WHOLE DAY for us to hear the sound of the Shofar. That's how important it is to Him. That's why the blessing we say on this holiday is on listening and hearing the Shofar. In the traditional synagogues they sound the Shofar one hundred times during the day of Rosh Hashanah!

So, what do the Scriptures say the Shofar is to be used for by us? We're going to look through several passages from Scripture. As I studied this, I found there are six functions of the Shofar.

Psalm 150:3 *Praise Him with the sound of the shofar. Praise Him with the lute and the harp.*

There's a word that's understood in that verse, "you." It's the imperative, "You, praise Him!" It's a command. "Praise Him with the sound of the Shofar." And it's the first instrument mentioned in praise. Now, why is this to be used to praise God? It's supposed to be like His voice, but why praise Him with it? Well, it goes back to the definition of the word "Shofar." Remember it comes from the root word that means "to incise" or "to cut." When we blow on the Shofar, it cuts through the heavenlies. That's how I see this. It cuts through and the praises get through to the Lord. After all, who is the god of the air or the god of the atmosphere? The adversary, the devil is. So, there is interference. There is satanic interference between us and the Lord. And the sound of the Shofar cuts through that. It incises through that. So, God loves us to do this because then our worship comes up to Him clearly.

Now, it also cuts through something else—something in me and maybe in you. It cuts through the kind of fog that I'm sometimes in. It cuts through the fuzziness of my "flesh"—my carnal nature—to bring out my spirit, so that I can praise Him.

Now, also, when we praise the Lord with the Shofar in our worship, it cuts through to the heart of God. It cuts through and touches Him deeply. It's wonderful when we're worshipping and singing in the Spirit and we hear the sound of the Shofar also singing out and calling out to reach the heart of God.

So what we're saying is that the combined force of the Shofar blast and our shouts of praise incises and cuts through the powers of darkness clearing the way in our hearts and in the atmosphere for worship. This combined force clears out the spiritual garbage and the roadblocks satan puts in our way. It cuts through the enemy's realm, through his interference in our hearts and minds, making a love incision. It opens a corridor to heaven to the throne of God and keeps it open. It gets our praises through to God. It keeps us focused by blasting everything else away.

Now, in our congregation's purpose statement, our purpose in worship is "to connect with the God of Israel through His Messiah Yeshua, and to glorify Him and minister to Him through worship in Spirit and Truth, as led by His Ruakh (Spirit), and especially in His *Biblically appointed ways* and at His *Biblically Appointed Times* ...."

We think of those Biblical ways of worship as the Davidic dancing and the Messianic music. But this is a new revelation to me. What is blowing the Shofar? It's one of His Biblically appointed ways to praise and worship Him. And again, this is something that has been totally absent from the Body for 1700 years and only since the beginning of the Messianic Movement is now becoming a popular thing. So, through the Messianic Movement the Ruakh is restoring this Biblically appointed way of praise and worship.

So, the first Scriptural use or function of the Shofar is for clearing the way for praise and worship. The Shofar makes a nice noise for praise, but why a Shofar? Why not a trumpet?

Let me just take a minute now and explain the difference that maybe you have wondered about between the Shofar and the silver trumpets. If you've recently read the book of Numbers, you've seen the passage describing how to make the silver trumpets and what they are to be used for. (See Appendix III, p. 259) The Hebrew word that's used there is "kha-tso-ts'rah" which means a *trumpet (from its sundered or quavering note):—trumpet (-er)*. It's a totally different word than "Shofar." This is the silver trumpet that's made out of one piece of silver. It's beaten and formed into a trumpet, something like the brass trumpets we have today. It's very different from a Shofar.

The biggest difference is this. The Shofar can be played by anyone. But the silver trumpets can only be played by cohanim (priests). (See Numbers 10:8.) There were only two played together. They were signal trumpets for gathering the people, for moving the people, for heralding Appointed Times, etc.

The second difference is the silver trumpet is a musical instrument, while the Shofar is not. When we read about the time of David's Tabernacle, we find that the silver trumpets were among the instruments of worship. They were played with other instruments. So, I assume they could play tunes with them.

Another difference between the Shofar and the trumpets has to do with that Hebrew word "kol" or "voice." "Kol" is never used in conjunction with the silver trumpets, only with the Shofar. You never read "kol kha-tso-ts'rah." So, there's something special about the Shofar that is for worship but not for music. Do you see the difference? The Shofar is uniquely for the Lord. It is used in praise but not as a typical musical instrument. It's not used as part of an orchestra, for example. Its function is to make an incision in the heavenlies and keep that incision open.

Are the silver trumpets for today? Well, they are already in use as brass trumpets, but they are not to replace the Shofar. The Shofar is in a class of its own.

Second Function

Okay, I said there are six functions for the Shofar. We learned that the first one was for worship. What are the other five uses? In 2 Samuel we have the time when David was going to move the Ark of the Covenant from where it was to Jerusalem.

2 Samuel 6:15 *So David and all the house of Isra'el brought up the ark of ADONAI with shouting and the sound of the shofar.*

There's always shouting related to the Shofar. So, what was happening here? Who or what was on the move? The Ark. And what did the Ark represent? The presence of God! So, think in the Spirit now. You need to rise into the Spirit to understand these things. In the Spirit, the Shofar is used to herald the move of God. And what are we always praying for? A move of God! So, the Shofar heralds the moving of God.

So, sounding the Shofar can be a way of letting God know that we are ready to have Him move upon us. When we listen to the Shofar we are preparing ourselves for the move of His Ruakh among us.

I think we need a blast on the Shofar right now so that God would move right there where you are. Stand up and blow your Shofar. Then shout.

(Shofar blast.)

Hallelujah!! Hallelujah!! Praise Your Name!! Hallelujah!!

*   *   *

So the second use of the Shofar is for heralding a move of God and declaring our readiness and desire for it. Now, get ready to sound it again for the third use of the Shofar.

Third Function

1 Thessalonians 4:16-17 *For the Lord himself will come down from heaven with a rousing cry, with a call from one of the ruling angels, and with* <u>*God's Shofar*</u>*; those who died united with the Messiah will be the first to rise; then we who are left still alive will be caught up with them in the clouds to meet the Lord in the air; and thus we will always be with the Lord.*

Now, take notice. Who will blow on the Shofar when Yeshua returns? God Himself! God's Shofar will be blown. And I believe part of what God's doing in reviving the use of the Shofar is to get us used to that sound so we will recognize it when it comes because we don't want to miss that sound!

So Yeshua's return, the Rapture, will be heralded with the blowing of the Shofar. So, let's sound the Shofar again.

(Shofar blast.)

Hallelujah!!! Hallelujah! Come quickly, Lord, Yeshua. Come quickly!

Fourth Function

For the fourth function of the Shofar we go to the Old Testament. Nehemiah was organizing and supervising the rebuilding of the wall around Jerusalem. Workers were spread all around the city. This was a huge wall surrounding the entire city, and they had a problem! The problem was that they had some enemies who wanted to stop them from building this wall. These enemies were very, very interested in stopping them because, once the wall was built, they were going to be a lot stronger and not subject to attacks. So their enemies wanted to get them before they finished the wall!

Nehemiah 4:18-20 *Every one of the builders had his sword girded at his side as he built.* [So they were ready for battle.] *And the one who sounded the shofar was beside me. Then I said to the nobles, the rulers, and the rest of the people, "The work is great and extensive, and we are separated far from one another on the wall. Wherever you hear the sound of the shofar, rally to us there. Our God will fight for us."*

So, the Shofar was used to call the people together to fight where the enemy was attacking. Now, lest you think that this is something that is just for old time and long ago, it's not. It is desperately needed in the Body today. We have a city! A Kingdom city. And the leaders and pastors of this city are trying to build a spiritual wall around this city for spiritual protection. But we're scattered around. One is building here, one there. The enemy often comes to attack. We need the Shofar to be calling us to stand together.

Now, what does this mean? I think it means that the Messianic Movement has an important role in bringing unity to the Body of Messiah. Do you see that? The Shofar is a Jewish instrument! And, you know, we're seeing this happening! If you have been to some of the large events that have been held in the last few years, you've seen it, too. People always want a Shofar blown! Now we know why—it is Biblically appointed for this function!

I think of the Standing in the Gap rally held down in Washington D.C. in 1998. This was an event where people from all around the country, from all kinds of denominations came together, and you know how they started it out? With seven men blowing Shofars! That was a first. It was the first time many of them had even seen a Shofar. They sounded the Shofar to bring together all these men from all around the country, almost a million men.

This makes me believe we as Y'hudim Mishikhim (Messianic Jews) with our Shofars will have a part in bringing together the divided Body. So, the fourth use of the Shofar is to call the Body to stand together against the enemy, and we're beginning to see the fulfillment of this.

Fifth Function

Now we're going to look at the use of the Shofar in another area that is very important.

Ephesians 6:12 *For we are not struggling against human beings, but against the rulers, authorities and cosmic powers governing this darkness, against the spiritual forces of evil in the heavenly realm.*

This is the warfare against satan and his minions. We are called to fight in that warfare. We're not called to fight against each other. We are called to fight against the forces of darkness. But, what kind of weapons are we to use?

2 Corinthians 10:4 *The weapons we use to wage war are not carnal, but they are mighty through God to the pulling down of strongholds.*

"Not carnal" means they are not human weapons. They're not military weapons. They are spiritual weapons that we need to learn how to use. We must fight satan with God's weapons. You have to use spiritual weapons for this spiritual war. What are some of these weapons?

- Prayer
- Praise
- The Name of the Lord
- The Word
- Loving not our life to the death
- The word of our testimony
- The Blood

We're going to learn that the Shofar also belongs on that list, which was a new revelation to me. It might be to you, too.

Let's look at two stories of battles in the Tenakh (the Old Testament), and see if they tell us something about the weapons that have God's power, that are *"mighty through God."* And when we look at these, I want you to realize that these were natural battles, yet God gave the warriors spiritual weapons. So, lest you think, "Oh, that was just for then. That's not for today," I want you to grasp this. This is the most important thing to grasp here. These weapons that were given for these battles were spiritual weapons because the battles could not have been won with natural weapons.

So, first we're going to look at the story of Gideon. Gideon was a humble man who was called to deliver Israel from the attacks of two neighboring people, the Midianites and the Amalekites. And Gideon did a good job. He raised an army of 30,000 men. Then God pulled a fast one on him. He sent 29,700 of his warriors home. So, he only had 300 left. And with this tiny army of 300 men, he was called out to go against an army of hundreds of thousands, a huge army of two different people groups who were allied with each other. Their combined army was encamped against Israel.

Judges 7:16 *Dividing the three hundred men into three companies, he placed shofars and empty jars in the hands of all of them, with torches inside.*

Gideon's army was reduced by God from 30,000 to 300 men so that it would be clear it was God who did this. God had them use Shofars. Again, your Bible probably says "trumpets." But the Hebrew is "Shofar." It's actually "Shofarot." That's the plural. Hebrew doesn't use an "s" for plural.

You also need to understand the jars. They were not transparent like we think of jars. They were clay pitchers that were opaque. So, what happened was they covered the torches with the clay jars so you couldn't see the light.

Judges 7:17-19 *Then he said to them, "Watch me, and do what I do. When I get to the edge of the camp, whatever I do, you do the*

*same. 18 When I and everyone with me blow the shofar, then you blow
your shofars all around the whole camp, and shout, "For ADONAI and
for Gid'on (Gideon)!" 19 Gid'on and the hundred men with him arrived
at the edge of the camp a little before midnight, just after they had
changed the guard….*

I want you to grasp the faith and courage and bravery of these men.
They were literally unarmed! There were only 300 of them and they
were sneaking up on a huge army in the middle of the night with no
weapons! I mean this was a massive, mighty army!

*Judges 7:19-20 … They blew the shofars and broke in pieces the
pitchers that were in their hands. 20 All three companies blew the shofars, broke the pitchers and held the torches in their left hands, keeping their right hands free for the shofars they were blowing; and they
shouted, "The sword for ADONAI and for Gid'on!"*

But there was no sword! There were no physical swords there. The
sword was going to be the sword of God in the Spirit which was about
to come down and be unsheathed!

*Judges 7:20-22 … they shouted, "The sword for ADONAI and for
Gid'on (Gideon)!" 21 Then, as every man stood still in place around the
camp, the whole camp was thrown into panic, with everyone screaming and trying to escape. 22 Gid'on's men blew their 300 shofars, and
ADONAI caused everyone in the camp to attack his comrades; and the
enemy fled….*

Now there's a couple of interesting things about this. First of all,
when this came to Gideon that his soldiers were to carry Shofarot, he
didn't have to send out somewhere to find Shofarot. Did you notice
that? They seemed to have just appeared from nowhere. And I believe
it is because everybody carried a Shofar. They were kind of like our cell
phones! They really were because they were used for communication.
They were used to give signals to each other over long distances—from
one hilltop to another. In Israel, if you sound the Shofar from the top of a
hill, it can be heard throughout the whole valley. So, I believe that each
of the soldiers had their own Shofar with them already.

That is the first thing. The other thing to understand is the weapons.
What were all the weapons? The Shofar, yes, the torch which was light,
yes, the jar, yes. But we missed one. They had four weapons, actually.
Yes, their voices! The shout!

So, let's look at those weapons. First of all, the torch: We know what
that represents—the Light! And what is the Light? It's the Truth! The
torch was the Truth. And if you think about this, it's the Light penetrating

the darkness—the Truth penetrating the lies. And when we think about the ones whom the enemy has control over, they're blinded. They're in darkness. The Scripture says their eyes are blinded, so they can't see His Glorious Light or the Truth of the Gospel.

Now, the jar is an interesting weapon. But it was very important. I think the jars represent empty vessels. So, the symbolism here is this. The jars represented that the soldiers emptied themselves of their own ability and their own strength. They couldn't defeat this army! So, they were empty to allow God to fill them and do it His way. So, we have to be empty vessels.

So, what filled the jars? The Light! The Truth! So, we have to be empty vessels filled with the Light and the Truth to go out and do battle against the enemy. The Truth can be inside us only when we are empty vessels willing to be containers of God's Truth.

So, here's a list of Gideon's army's weapons.

- Shofar – Notice that the Shofar blowers were soldiers, not cohanim or leaders.
- Shout – Our voices, declaring God's authority.
- Torch – Truth and Light penetrating the darkness of the enemy and the blindness he has caused.
- Jar – The empty vessel we need to be for God to fill us with the Light and the Truth.

So, this is the battle plan for spiritual warfare. Be empty jars. Empty ourselves of natural power. Be filled with the Truth and Light. And blow the Shofar and shout.

Now, how was the enemy defeated? What happened to them? Confusion!! That's the word! They were defeated by confusion.

We had an incredible attack of confusion on Erev (the eve of) Rosh Hashanah, the night before I gave this message back in 2001. Someone ended up having to lead worship when she wasn't expecting to. That caused so many things in the service to be confused! I believe it was because the enemy was trying to prevent me from talking about this. Confusion is what the Shofar brings to the enemy.

Now, I want you to notice something. In this incident, notice the sequence. First, there was a shout, then there was the sounding of the kol haShofar, the voice of the Shofar. Let me say it again, first the shout, then the sounding. Now, remember "Shofar" means incision. What it did when the Shofar was blasted in the story of Gideon is it created a separation between the Midianites and the Amalekites. We just read that they began killing each other. And you know what, I don't believe Midianites were killing Midianites, nor Amalekites killing Amalekites because they knew each other. What I believe happened was the two sides began to attack each other. They were thrown into confusion by the blowing of the Shofar.

Now, I'm not saying that I understand this in the natural. I'm asking you to make a leap of faith here and a leap of understanding. I don't know how it happens, but somehow sounding the Shofar confuses the enemy! And we need to use it for that. It will enable us to confuse the camp of the enemy, to route the camp, to disperse the enemy, to cast out demons, to break down strongholds, to set captives free—from the things that keep them from hearing the Truth—and to recover what has been stolen.

The Shofar somehow makes the enemy vulnerable. It allows the Truth to enter. It penetrates the darkness and lets the Light shine in to illuminate people's minds, and allows God's power to be released. We are to use the Shofar when we engage in prayer and spiritual warfare.

Now, lest you think I'm making this all up, I want to quote you something. This is an amazing passage from the Talmud concerning Rosh Hashanah. The Talmud is the traditional Jewish commentary on the Scriptures.

In the Talmud, Rabbi Yitzakh says, "If the Shofar is not sounded at the beginning of the new year, at Rosh Hashanah, evil will befall the end of it. Why so? Because Ha satan (the adversary) has not been confused."

So the fifth use of the Shofar is in prayer and spiritual warfare to deal with an enemy attack.

Fifth Function In Action

[The following was what I said on Rosh Hashanah in 2001 when I originally gave this sermon. It was quite funny, yet very sobering. I continued this message with these next words.

"Now let's look at the story of Gideon. Gideon was appointed by Moses..."

(From the congregation: "Joshua!!!")

"Oh, I'm sorry. Joshua! You're right! Confusion! It's coming back! We're being attacked again!" (Laughter)

(From the congregation: "Blow the Shofar!")

"Yes, We need the sounding of the Shofar to clear the air!" (Chuckling)

(Shofar blowing.)

"Thank you, Lord! Hallelujah! Hallelujah!"

Why was there confusion? Well, this was obviously a message the enemy did not want us to understand right then! It was September 8, 2001, and what happened just three days later? 9/11 happened!!!]

Sixth Function

Let's move on. Gideon's battle dealt defensively with an enemy who was attacking Israel—an enemy dwelling in a camp. But, we, as a Body are supposed to be on the offensive. Right? We're supposed to be breaking down the "gates of Hell." We're supposed to be going against strongholds that are in place. So, what about an enemy in a stronghold, a walled city, entrenched and surrounded by the Gates of Hell? Well, we have the story of Joshua to help us deal with walled cities.

We already studied this story. So let me just quickly re-cap it here. Joshua was appointed by Moses (and God) to lead the Israelites into the Promised Land. He was given a battle plan by God to take the stronghold of Yericho (Jericho), a walled city. God didn't give him any battering rams or catapults. He gave him some very strange instructions. He said to carry the ark around the city once a day for six days while blowing Shofarot (plural of Shofar) with no "shouts or noise from their voices." Then they were to carry the ark around the city seven times on the seventh day, blowing Shofarot still with no "shouts or noise from their voices." The seventh time around when the Shofarot were sounded the people were to shout. Notice that it was the people who shouted, not just the leaders.

Joshua 6:20 *So the people shouted when the priests blew the shofarot. And it happened when the people heard the sound of shofarot, and the people shouted with a great shout, that the wall fell down flat....*

If you look at the Hebrew, it's very interesting the way it's phrased. It says "fell the wall under it." It's almost as if the wall fell under the sound of the shout.

...Then the people went up into the city, every man straight before him, and they took the city.

What were the spiritual weapons used here? What weapons did they use as they marched seven days once around and the seventh day seven times around silently? I see these four intangible weapons: Perseverance, obedience, courage, and unity.

One of the members of my congregation, Cathy, gave a testimony about two examples of people using these weapons, especially of obedience and perseverance in spiritual warfare. She told about a friend of hers who went with a mission team to Africa where several times the

Lord told them to go and pray for a certain person. The first time it was a blind person. They obeyed and prayed, but nothing happened. Later, it was a lame person. God told them to pray for this person that he will walk. Again, nothing happened. Later, they encountered the person again and the Lord told them to pray for him again. They said, "Okay," prayed again and still no change. This occurred several times. After they came back to America they heard that healing began to come, but they didn't get to see it with their own eyes.

Then Cathy told about this kind of thing happening with her and her husband in obeying the Lord concerning starting a new business: "The Lord tells us, 'I need you to do this, and now this and this,' and nothing changes at all once we do these great things. We struggle through and then we look around and we think, 'Oh, it all looks the same.' Or the second thing that happens is it gets worse. So those have been the two things. We either have nothing or it gets worse. Then the Lord tells us to do something else and we obey and have had more trouble.

"So the Lord has been taking me through Joshua 7, which is actually the next story. Right after Joshua had this great victory at Jericho, they went out and tried to defeat the next enemy and they lost. Joshua sought the Lord and found out why they were defeated. You can read the story. This place where they were defeated ended up being called Achor, which means 'trouble.' They called it the Valley of Achor or Valley of Trouble. The Lord showed me two promises in Scripture for when you are in the valley of trouble. I'm here to tell you that it is okay to be in the valley of trouble.

"Isaiah 65:10 *Sharon will become a pasture for flocks, and the Valley of Achor a resting place for herds, for my people who seek me.*

"He actually brings rest right in the middle of that. The other one is in Hosea.

"Hosea 2:15 (NIV) *There I will give her back her vineyards, and will make the Valley of Achor a door of hope.*

"In total amazement, I found out that this Valley of Trouble in Joshua became a border land, the borderland to Calev's (Caleb's) property. It was a borderland to the Promised Land! So, the Valley of Trouble bordered the Promised Land. It became the "door of hope" just like Isaiah said."

That was Cathy's testimony. Let me add that a few years after she gave that testimony, God began to really bless their business. They had a couple more devastating setbacks, but then the blessings began to break through! Their perseverance in obeying God won them the victory.

So, when we blow the Shofar, we shouldn't necessarily expect to see something happen right away. The battle is in the Spirit. God is telling us that the Shofar is a weapon. It's a powerful weapon. So, we need to be obedient in using it. But we might not see the results until later.

Cathy's examples talked about employing those intangible weapons of perseverance, obedience, courage, and unity.

Now, let's take a look at the tangible weapons for the Battle of Jericho. What were the weapons? Can you think of them? Of course, the Shofar. Their voices—shouting. What else was there? The ark! Yes, the ark, the presence of God, was there.

Here's a list of their weapons.

- Ark – His presence
- Shofar – Incising the walls or strongholds of the enemy and the gates of hell.
- Great shout – Hebrew: "teruah" – from the root word "ruah" (Strong's H7321) *to mar (especially by breaking); figuratively to split the ears with sound.* This is exactly the same word used for the "sounding of the Shofar and shouts of joy" for Rosh Hashanah! Isn't it amazing the depth of meaning there is in this little holiday, Yom Teruah?!

So, those were the weapons they used against Jericho. But there's an interesting difference here, if you noticed. In this case, they blew the Shofars first, and then they shouted. In Gideon's case, they did just the opposite. So, in the case of a walled city—a stronghold—the order is to blow the Shofar first because the Shofar is an "incisor." It cuts. And then the shout blasts things away.

Now, when you are incising something you are making an incision. The image here with the Jericho walls is splitting rock, like when part of a hill is blasted away to make a highway. Have you ever noticed the little straight lines along the cliff of this type of highway that look like a pattern? Those lines are from when they drill holes in the rock, and then push dynamite down into those holes. Drilling those holes is like making incisions in the rock. When the dynamite explodes, it splits the rock. This is the way rock is quarried and mountains are moved for highways. In ancient times water was used; when it froze, the rocks split.

For the walls of Jericho, it's much more amazing because they used spiritual weapons and yet had the same results!! Using only spiritual weapons, they actually physically broke those walls. The shout actually broke the physical walls down. If you think about it, they went around seven days, seven times blowing the Shofars. If you think about what they do in building roads, they drill lots of little holes. The Israelites were doing that, too. They were blowing the Shofars which were incising, or drilling holes in the walls, and then when the shout came, BOOM! There went the walls. It sounds wild, but that's the strategy God gave Joshua. It was a strategy to divide and demolish the walls of the enemies.

So, when we use the Shofar with "Teruah," shouts of joy, it divides the devil's kingdom and causes it to crumble and fall. The sixth use of the Shofar is for spiritual warfare against the enemy when he is entrenched in a stronghold.

*　　　　　*　　　　　*

We're going to stop there, but let me just explain something. We've just been talking, in these last two functions, about spiritual warfare. One of our purposes in our congregation's purpose statement is spiritual warfare. It says, "We are to be led by the Ruakh HaKodesh (the Holy Spirit) in spiritual warfare against the powers of darkness and in effective prayer."

Remember we learned that the Shofar sound is the closest thing there is to God's voice in this universe, in this physical world. And we also noted that God's voice creates.

Well, another thing God's voice does is it defeats satan. Adonai's voice terrifies and completely destroys the enemy. It's a powerful weapon we need to learn to use and use often.

Isaiah 30: 30-31 *ADONAI will make His glorious voice heard, and He will reveal His arm descending with furious anger in a flaming fire-storm, with cloudbursts, tempests and hailstones. 31 For ADONAI's voice will terrify Ashur, as with His scepter He strikes them down.*

May we learn to use the Shofar—our piece of God's voice here on earth—to crush the enemy and sweep him off the planet!

*　　　　　*　　　　　*

So let's review: Why has the Ruakh revived the use of the Shofar and the shout?

- To worship the Lord in His appointed way and hear His voice
- To cut through the enemy hindrances so our worship reaches the Lord
- To touch the Lord's heart
- To gather the people together to fight the forces of darkness.

- To give us victory in the spiritual warfare
- To defeat the enemy

This message about the Shofar was a new revelation to me. We are learning that it is a powerful, powerful weapon in the Spirit. And think about this. We're all looking for that End Time revival and the defeat of forces of darkness. Well, I believe the Shofar is going to be very instrumental in that. And that was not a pun! The Shofar and the Teruah shout are part of the arsenal we need to have before we can defeat the enemy and release the power of the Ruakh HaKodesh for revival. And now they *are* becoming part of the arsenal. Through the Messianic Movement the Ruakh is restoring these Biblically appointed spiritual weapons.

So, one more use of the Shofar is:

To release the power of the Ruakh for revival

Now that we see this wonderful revelation about the power of the Shofar, God is giving _us_ the authority to use this voice of the Shofar!

Joel 2:15 *Blow the shofar in Tziyon* (Zion)*!*

Just think. Shofar blowing occurs all day on Rosh Hashanah. It is to awaken sleepers. It is to bring remembrance. And it is also for another awesome function. Another Biblical purpose of Shofar blowing was to herald a king's arrival. That's the most exciting function of all! Some day in the future, our Yom Teruah Shofar blowing will help herald the coming of the King of Kings!!

*   *   *

Before I finish this chapter, I'd like to ask for your participation in an activity again. I'd like us to start using the spiritual arsenal we've been talking about right now. We're going to do some spiritual battling. So, get your Shofar ready and let's say the blessing over it.

Blessed are You, Lord our God, Ruler of the universe, who has sanctified us with Your commandments and commanded us to hear the sound of the Shofar.

Alright, now, let me ask you some questions. Does it seem like the enemy is attacking you in whatever you do? Do you feel like the enemy has you on the defensive? Okay. What we're going to do is follow the prescription that was for an attacking enemy. Remember that? It was to shout first and then blow the Shofar to confuse the enemy's camp, like Gideon's army did. So, we're going to shout first and then blow the Shofar over your situation. We're going to do this in faith that this weapon has power.

First, let's pray.

Father, we thank You for Your revelation about the power of this instrument to confuse the enemy. That is what we need here, Lord. The enemy has been attacking us. We need the enemy's power to be confused. We need him to start fighting against himself because Your Word says that a kingdom divided against itself shall not stand. So we need to see him confused. We see what You did through Gideon, Lord, so we are going to apply those principles now in Your Name.

So, Lord, we just want to apply first the other weapons and speak against this attack. In the Name of Yeshua, we command you enemy, satan, to stop attacking us. In the Name of Yeshua, we confound and confuse your forces. By the power of Yeshua's Blood, by the power of the Word of God, by the power of our testimony, by the power of faith, we break your power over us. We crush your power to attack us. We command you to retreat, in the Name of Yeshua. Amen.

Okay, we are going to shout now. You can shout whatever you want. You can shout, "Get out!" "Be confused!" "Leave!" "Hallelujah!" whatever you want on the count of three. One, two, three. BE CONFUSED! BE CONFOUNDED! BE TERRIFIED! BE DIVIDED. BE AGAINST YOURSELF. DESTROY YOUR OWN FORCES. GET OUT! FLEE! BE GONE! BE REMOVED AND CAST INTO THE SEA! HALLELUJAH!! HALLELUJAH!! HALLELUJAH!!

Now, blow your Shofar.

(Shofar blasts.)

Thank you, Lord. IT IS DONE! IT IS DONE!!

* * *

Now, let's do the Jericho kind of battling. This is for the kind of situation where you have been on the move with the Lord, but find that there's a stronghold in your life—meaning that there's something that you can't overcome. You're trying to move ahead, but you can't get by a certain obstacle. Maybe you've battled against it for years. You've prayed and prayed and nothing has happened. It's entrenched. It's strong. You can't break through it. Or maybe you've been praying for someone who just doesn't seem to get it. The Truth can't get through to them because there's a stronghold around them of unbelief or deception. To overcome this type of enemy, we're going to do the reverse. We're going to blow and then shout. Let's pray first and then blow the Shofar and then shout to break down the walls.

Father, we just thank You that the weapons of our warfare are not carnal, but they are mighty through You to the pulling down of strongholds—the crumbling down of strong walls!! We believe, Lord, that You have given us a new revelation of Your weapons, of using the Shofar and the Teruah as weapons.

And Father, we come to You now because somehow the enemy has gotten into our lives. There is something that we are supposed to move ahead with but the way is blocked because there's a fortified city of the enemy blocking us from doing what You are calling us to do.

So, we come against that stronghold now in the Name of Yeshua. By the power of the Word of God, by the Blood of Yeshua, with faith, with the word of our testimony, we command the strongholds to come tumbling down. We pray this in the power of the holy Name of Yeshua. Amen.

Now we're going to come against it first with the cutting power of the Shofar to penetrate it, to make holes in it. Then we're going to shout and demolish it. So, blow your Shofar! Let's drill some holes!

(Shofar blasts.)

Now shout!

COME DOWN!! BE BROKEN!! COME CRASHING DOWN! BE CRUMBLED TO THE GROUND! BE CRUSHED! BE DEMOLISHED! BE ANNIHILATED! BE GONE! BE REMOVED!

HALLELUJAH!! HALLELUJAH!! HALLELUJAH!!

CHAPTER 7

The Source Of Our Hope

Did you realize that the terrorist attack on 9-11-2001 happened just one week before Rosh Hashanah? Can you imagine how we felt? We were shaken! We were sure the end was very near!

Let me take you back to that week and give you a peek at what we did. The Twin Towers were attacked on Tuesday. On Wednesday evening we held the first prayer vigil for it. On the Friday after that infamous Tuesday we held another prayer vigil. After we prayed for a couple hours, I spoke the words starting in the next paragraph. Today the world continues to face terrorist threats and attacks. Perhaps right now while you're reading this, there is a new, frightening threat or event. If so, I hope this message that I gave that week will help give you direction and hope. As you read this sermon, keep in mind the fear and awe we were experiencing at the time. Read the words with reverence because that's how they were spoken—softly, gently, and very reverently.

*　　　　*　　　　*

*　　　　*　　　　*

It's 9:30 pm now. We've spent two hours in prayer and it's getting late, but I think there's something here that will really encourage you in these times, if you can stay. So, let's just pray and ask the Lord to open up our understanding.

Father, we need Your Word to speak to us here tonight, Lord God. We need instruction from You as to how to live our lives in these troubled times. So, we just pray that You would open our hearts to receive now. Speak to us as You will. In Yeshua's Name. Amen.

Matthew 24 is a long chapter where Yeshua is speaking of the future. Keep in mind that He was saying these things almost 2000 years ago. The disciples asked Him a question about the End Times.

Matthew 24:3, 6-7 *"... what will be the sign that you are coming, and that the olam hazeh* (this age) *is ending?" 4 Yeshua replied: "... 6 You will hear the noise of wars nearby and the news of wars far off; see to it that you don't become frightened. Such things must happen, but the end is yet to come. 7 For peoples will fight each other, nations will fight each other, and there will be famines and earthquakes in various parts of the world; ...."*

Now unless you've been totally isolated from television and your newspaper for the past ten years, this sounds very familiar to you. In Luke's version of this it adds in "pestilences" which would be AIDS (and SARS and H1N1, etc). So we are right in the middle of this.

Matthew 24:21 *"For there will be trouble then worse than there has ever been from the beginning of the world until now and there will be nothing like it again."*

So how are we to deal with what we experienced earlier this week and what we may experience in the future? Well, we've been doing some of it tonight. We've been praying. Obviously that's where to start. And I think all of us are somewhat frustrated that the other thing we'd like to do, which is to help, is difficult to do right now because not many of us are emergency medical technicians and not many of us can get down there. However, we can help. There are many places where you can give to the Red Cross. You can give money and you can give blood. They even had a station set up at the bank this afternoon. So, there are ways we can help.

And, of course, the Lord tells us we are to mourn with those who mourn. So this is a time to feel grief and to mourn in sorrow. But also in the book of Luke where He talks about this time Yeshua says, *"Now when these things begin to happen, look up. Lift up your head because your redemption draws near"* (Luke 21:28 NKJV).

So, how are we to deal with those whom the Lord brings us in contact with during this time—people who are afraid—people who are hurting? How many have had some interactions with people like that this week? I know I have. People are very open. They want to talk.

Well, first of all, we need to be able to encourage the people who believe that this is what the Lord predicted would come. And for those who don't believe, we need to draw their attention to the predictions that the Bible makes about current events—amazing predictions. Here's one of them.

Zechariah 12:2 *"I will make Yerushalayim* (Jerusalem) *a cup that will stagger the surrounding peoples."*

How much more clear could it be with what has been going on in Israel that this is being fulfilled in our day? So, one powerful way of sharing with people who are confused and searching is to say, "Look, this Book predicts all this. That's why this is a supernatural Book. That's why it is God's signature that is on this Book. He is the author! He knew all this was going to happen! He is in control. That's why the answers for what to do now are also in His Book!"

So, we can begin to give people hope in the midst of this tribulation. But we can't give them hope unless we have hope. And He is the only source of our Hope. And we have to be walking in that Hope. So, what is our Hope? Well, skip down to verse 29.

Matthew 24:29-31 *"Immediately following the trouble of those times, the sun will grow dark, the moon will stop shining, the stars will fall from the sky. And the powers of heaven will be shaken. Then the sign of the Son of Man will appear in the sky. And all the tribes of the Land* (all the nations) *will mourn when they see the Son of Man coming on the clouds of heaven with tremendous power and glory. And He will send out His angels with a great shofar and they will gather together His chosen people from the four winds, from one end of heaven to the other."*

Now, note that the gathering of His chosen will be with a great Shofar. Folks, that's our Hope—His return and our being gathered to be with Him. There is no other Hope! According to this Book, things are going to get a lot worse.

I'm sure there is one question on everyone's mind: "How close are we to this event?" Skip down to verse 32.

Matthew 24:32-33 *"Now, let the fig tree teach you its lesson. When its branches begin to sprout and leaves appear, you know that summer is approaching. In the same way, when you see all these things, you are to know that the time is near, right at the door."*

So, where are we in God's End Time plan? Well, the fig tree is always representative of Israel. And when did the fig tree blossom? In 1948. So, we can conclude that the Second Coming and the Rapture are near, right at the door.

I came across an interesting verse. It gives me some hope for what we're seeing right now. It speaks of the woman with the sun and moon under her feet. And on her head a crown of twelve stars. It's obviously Israel. And it speaks of her giving birth to a son. Toward the end of the chapter, there's this interesting thing when the devil comes against her and seeks to swallow her up.

Revelation 12:14 *But the woman was given the two wings of the great eagle, so that she could fly to her place in the desert, where she is taken care of for a season and two seasons and half a season, away from the serpent's presence.*

That three seasons and a half a season is obviously three and a half years, the bad part of the seven year tribulation after the anti-Messiah reveals himself. Who is this eagle? I have a hope that it's the United States because our symbol is the eagle. Now, I don't know that—whether the United States will stand by Israel during this time or not. It's just my hope. I have no proof.

So, we are in the midst of this time. The rapture might be very near.

Matthew 24:34 *"I tell you that this generation will certainly not pass away until all these things happen."*

What generation is He speaking of? The generation that sees what? The fig tree blossom and all these things take place. And what generation is that? That's us! That's our generation.

I Thessalonians 4:16 *The Lord Himself will come down from heaven with a rousing cry, with the call of one of the ruling angels and with God's Shofar. Those who died united with the Messiah will be the first to rise. Then we who are left still alive will be caught up with them in the clouds to meet Him in the air.*

We might soon rise to meet Him in the air. There will be chaos all over the world when millions of people everywhere disappear. Those left behind will go through a period of terrible tribulation as described in the Book of Revelation when God's judgment will be poured out onto the whole earth. Some of the people will turn to the Lord through that trial.

Matthew 24:36 *But when that day and hour will come, no one knows—not the angels in heaven, not the Son, only the Father.*

I don't know for sure when the Rapture is in relation to the tribulation. I'm not going to argue about that. But we're going to have to deal with some hard times. That's for sure. I'm not a pre-tribulation Rapture person because I don't think we're going to get off scot-free from all this. The warnings are that we're going to have to deal with some things. We're dealing with them now. I know there are many who might disagree with me, but that's where I stand. I guess I'm a mid-tribulation person. But I wouldn't argue about it.

So, how are we to make it through to that day when we'll be gathered? Let's say we have to get through half of the tribulation, the first three and a half years. How will we make it?

Matthew 24:42,44 *Stay alert, because you don't know on what day your Lord will come. ... 44 Therefore you, too, must always be ready; for the Son of Man will come when you are no longer expecting Him.*

We kind of take this lightly—this exhortation by Yeshua to be ready. Right? We say, "Oh, yea, yea, we're going to be ready." But I think many of us fall short in being ready and looking forward to that Hope, and living as if He could come back today. I want you to look in your Bible and notice something. Starting in chapter 24 verse 45 and going on to the end of chapter 25 are four parables, each one with the same theme: Be ready! You don't know when He's coming back, but He IS coming back! Be ready!

The first one is the parable of the faithful servant who is told to keep doing His Master's will until He returns. It applies to us. We are to keep seeking to establish His Kingdom—doing the work of the Kingdom until He comes. We are not to run off and hide out somewhere. We are to continue to be a light. There are many who have missed this and have gone off and waited on a mountaintop, saying the Lord's return is going to be this and this day. And they've all been proven to be wrong. We are to continue to work.

Then starting in the beginning of chapter 25 is the parable of the ten bridesmaids who have their lamps. Five of them have enough oil and five don't. Only five of them are able to stay awake until the groom comes. And the message for us is, "Watch out for yourself! Make sure you're staying awake. There will be others who won't be, but don't let them drag you down." Five of the bridesmaids come and say, "Can we have some of your oil so that we can stay awake?" And they tell them, "No! No! Go get some of your own." It sounds a little selfish. But it's saying that you've got to watch out for yourself to not let anyone influence you to not be ready.

And then there's the parable of the ten talents where three men are given different amounts of money. And they're told to invest it. Then the master who gave them the money comes back and says, "What did you do with my money?" The one who invested it wisely is richly rewarded. The one who just hid it in the ground is punished and he loses it. The obvious message is that God has given each of us talents, abilities, resources, skills, strengths. And we are to invest them into the work of the Kingdom and we will be rewarded. We're not to hide our talents. We're not to sit on them. We're not to say, "Oh, I'm too busy taking care of my own house. I'm too busy doing my own things." I think that was the crux of some of our prayers tonight. So many are just wrapped up in their own lives and not seeking to serve the Lord.

So, that's the third parable. The fourth parable is the one of separating the sheep and the goats. And what are the criteria for separation? What we do!!! Not what we believe! It's what we do!! Did you notice that? Visiting the sick. Visiting the prisoners, Feeding the hungry. Giving water to the thirsty. That's what separates. And it's to be done because we know He's coming back and going to judge!

So, all of a sudden as I read this, I said, "My goodness!! It is incredible how He is emphasizing this!" He's not just sort of saying, "Hey! You know, be ready! I'm coming back!" He gives four parables! I don't think there's any place else in the Bible where He gives four parables emphasizing the same point—over and over and over again!! And I said to myself, "You know, this is really important!" And it **is** really important! And I realize how short I fall from doing this—walking every day in the expectation that He's coming back, living my life in that expectation and that Hope.

Why should we do that? Well, the secret is that if we don't live in that kind of a Hope of His return and of our going to be with Him, we won't make it through these days! That's how tough they're going to be! That's the thing that's going to sustain us through these days. We must have this attitude through the time of tribulation.

We need to be people of Hope in His return so we can have the strength to go on. We need it so we can offer Hope to other believers, and so we can offer Hope to those who have none. As things get worse, those who don't know the Lord are going to have less and less hope. I mean they have hope now in our military might. We're going to go out there and we're going to knock out all those forces of terrorism. Well, I don't want to be a skeptic, but it's going to be hard to get all the forces of terrorism in the world wiped out. It's going to be hard.

And you know, when you have that Hope, some of the struggles that we go through, they don't seem so important. Some of the things that we're striving after just don't matter that much anymore.

Well, I want to confess to you that I talk a good game here, saying that's what we're supposed to do, but I struggle in living like that. And I think probably you do, too. Do you get caught up in the worry and the fear and the striving and the busy-ness? Yea?!

Well, God knew we would struggle in persevering in that state. And so, I want to tell you what He gave us. You never would've guessed what He gave us in order to help us through this. He gave us Rosh Hashanah and Teruah—Shofar blowing and shouts of joy!

Let's have a Shofar blast and give a shout!

(Shofar blasts.)

HALLELUJAH! WHEW!! Thank you, Lord!!

*   *   *

You know, I don't know if you experience what I do when I hear the Shofar. That sound resonates with the human body somehow. I actually feel the vibrations of it and it energizes me.

So, what does that have to do with this Hope? As believers we have something great to commemorate and remember on this day. We're supposed to remember something in the future. Kind of like the movie *Back to the Future*. We're supposed to remember the promise of His return and the gathering of His elect that will be announced with the sounding of the Great Shofar. I believe that, as Messianic believers, God planned for us that we would have a day once a year to remember that He's coming back so it doesn't fade from our memory. That we would hear the Shofar blasts once every year on Rosh Hashanah and in the weeks leading up to it to renew our Hope! And we can infer, prophetically, that not only is Rosh Hashanah a day to remember the Rapture, but on some future Rosh Hashanah that Great Shofar will sound and He will appear!

So, believers in the New Covenant, we have a Zih-kh'ron Teruah when we remember the promise of the sounding of the Shofar, and we renew our commitment to walk in that Hope and our commitment to sharing that Hope with the hopeless.

Now, I want to just take a minute to ask you a question. When that Great Shofar blows, will you be one of His chosen whom His angels will gather from the four winds? Will you be caught up together to meet Him in the air to be with the Lord forever? I've had the assurance supernaturally for twenty-four years now that I am one of His chosen. But believe me, I didn't talk myself into being sure! In fact, I resisted it. When I first began to study the Bible, I thought, "Awe this can't be! People have been talking about His return all through the ages!" And then the Lord brought me to one of those prophecies about Israel. I was shocked! "Whoa! We are near the end of time!" But I didn't figure it out on my own. God gave it to me as a gift. I want to just pray for you right now and ask the Lord to give you that assurance because you're going to need it. As we go through these next years, you're going to need it. You're going to need that Hope—Hope that He's coming and Hope that you will go with Him.

So, I'm going to pray now and if you don't have that assurance I want to give you a chance to make sure that you have it. So, let's just look to the Lord in prayer.

Lord, I just lift up to You now all of us. And I know according to Your Word that it is Your strong desire that when that Shofar blows, we will all rise to be with You. Lord, we know that You cry out for each of us, created by You, to be amongst Your elect. And we cry out for those we love to be among Your chosen. So, I just pray for each person that they would be honest with themselves right now and if they don't have that assurance, they would say, "Now is the time. Tonight is the night. Today is the day to receive that gift."

And Father, we thank you for Rosh Hashanah. We thank you that You appointed a time—a Moad—to remind us every year that there's going to be that Great Shofar call; that You're going to return and that we're going to rise to be with You forever. We thank You for that reminder. And we pray that it will last with us the whole year.

And we pray, Father, that we would know how to walk through this time of tribulation. Lord, we just ask that You would supernaturally place that Hope within us, that it would be strong; that we would live as that faithful servant, as the wise bridesmaids, as a sheep and not a goat, and as the one who invested his talents wisely. I pray, Lord God, that we would live in the knowledge of Your soon return. And Lord, especially during this time of great anguish as a nation, that we would be able to communicate that Hope to those who are without it—those whom we meet, those close to us, those who are strangers—that we would be able to give them that Hope. We pray for that Hope for all those who are in mourning right now. We pray for that Hope that they will see their loved ones again. In Yeshua's Name. Amen

CHAPTER 8

WHAT IS T'SHUVAH?

T'shuvah means repentance. We've been talking about Yeshua's Second Coming a lot, so I want to move on now to talk about something else that Rosh Hashanah or Yom Teruah should mean. We get some direction from the traditional way of keeping this Moad (Appointed Time).

As I explained before, traditionally, this is the New Year. But the greeting is not just, "Happy New Year." It's "L'shanah Tovah Tikkah Tevu." "L'shanah Tovah" means "to a good year." "Tikkah Tevu" means "May your name be inscribed." So, the greeting is "May your name be inscribed (in God's Book of Life) for a good year." This is drawn from Rabbinic tradition which says that God decides our fate for the next year between Rosh Hashanah and Yom Kippur. And those days are called, as I told you before, "Yomim Norim" ("Days of Awe"). But they are also called the "Aseret Yemai T'shuvah"—"Ten Days of Repentance." Rosh Hashanah is the beginning of those Ten Days.

Actually Rosh Hashanah is not a day of repentance, it's a day of joy, but it's the *start* of the Ten Days of Repentance. And they lead up to Yom Kippur the Day of Atonement. The Saturday in the midst of the Days of Repentance, is called "Shabbat Shuvah"—the Sabbath of Repentance. So it all fits together as you follow through God's calendar. We have these Ten Days of repenting before the time comes for the Day of Atonement, which is Yom Kippur—that awesome day when everybody needs to be right with God. So we need to get our attitude right—to be in a repentant attitude.

In Jewish tradition, what are these Ten Days all about? Well, they are days of t'shuvah (repentance), for examining our deeds, turning from evil, devoting more time to the Word, to worship, to prayer, devoting ourselves to good works, making amends for things we've done that we realize are wrong—in other words making reconciliation with others whom we might have injured.

But we, as believers in the Messiah, sometimes wonder if we should do the soul searching that traditional Jews do since, in Yeshua, we are forgiven. We ask ourselves, "Does God want us to make this a time of t'shuvah as they do?" And the answer, in my mind at least, is a resounding yes! There are several places in the New Covenant where we are instructed to examine ourselves, to search our hearts, and to ask the Spirit of God to search us. Here's one of them.

1 Corinthians 11:31 *If we would examine ourselves, we would not come under judgment. But when we are judged by the Lord, we are being disciplined so that we will not be condemned along with the world.*

So, Rabbi Sha'ul (Paul) is telling us here that God expects us to constantly be searching our souls and to be looking for ways in which we are falling short. Our walk with the Lord is not a static thing. It's not standing still. It's walking and following Him. And in following Him, the Scriptures say we are being changed into His image. So, we need to participate in that by taking time when we can say, "Lord, show me what things I need to change."

As human beings, I think we all periodically need a reminder to seek God in this way—to seek Him to change us—to change us from where we are into what He wants to make us. And that's why we need a Moad. That's why we need this Appointed Time to focus on our growing and maturing.

So what does the Shofar have to do with all this? Well, the Shofar is to be a wake-up call for our need to change. It's kind of God's alarm clock. Wake up! Because we can fall into a spiritual snooze—a spiritual lethargy—when we're not moving ahead with God. And you know, even as a nation we can fall asleep. That was what we prayed for after 9-11, and I think it was very appropriate. The World Trade Center terrorist attack was the biggest wake-up call that I think this nation has ever had. But America still hasn't awakened! It still needs to wake up!

So, what exactly is t'shuvah? It comes from the Hebrew word, "shuv" which means *to turn back, to reconsider, to repent, or to return.* I'd like to dig into that—to give us an understanding of what it means and how it applies to us.

I think the essence of t'shuvah is wrapped up in the English word, "contrite"—"having a contrite heart."

Psalm 34:18 (NKJV) *The LORD is near to those who have a broken heart, And saves such as have a contrite spirit.*

Isaiah 66:2 (NKJV) (This is an incredible verse.) ..."*But on this one will I look: on him who is poor and of a contrite spirit, And who trembles at My word.*

There is something very precious to God about having a contrite spirit. Now this word "contrite" is not very commonly used in our English language today. When I taught on this to some Russian speaking people, they said in Russian it's "tremble." So, what is a "contrite spirit"? Well, I've prayed about this and I'm sure I don't have the full definition, but I believe it means a heart that's open to change, a heart that's open to being taught, a person who does not have an attitude of "I've arrived," "I'm there," "I've got it made" or "I know better than everybody else." It's a heart that is humble; a heart that is correctable. That kind of heart is greatly pleasing to God because He knows we all have a long way to go. We're all being conformed to His image.

Now, there are really three groups of people that I'm going to talk about here that need t'shuvah. The first one is those who have already committed themselves to follow the Lord, and have given all they are able to Him. We (of this group) would think that we are not necessarily supposed to go through all that again, but we are going to see in a few minutes how the Shofar blasts are calling even us to t'shuvah, to turn—to return.

The second group I'm going to talk about consists of the people who have not given the control of their lives to the Lord yet. They're not sure He is the Messiah. They're not sure what relevance He has in their lives. I believe the Shofar is calling them to t'shuvah, to this contrite heart attitude—the attitude of being one who is open and saying, "God show me. God teach me."

The third group is all of America. Our nation is a nation that needs to have a contrite heart. Was the terrorist attack a judgment? I don't know. Could be. But I have no doubt that we are a nation that deserves judgment. There's no question in my mind. We have tolerated abortion. Sexual decadence is permeating our culture. Greed and materialism abound. Godlessness does, too. We allowed the removal of prayer from our schools and our government. We have been a nation of prejudice. We are a nation that is greatly in need of t'shuvah and waking up to God's call.

And, of course, we need to look at America's need for t'shuvah in the first person, in ourselves. Remember that Daniel the prophet, when he was praying for the nation of Israel, didn't say, "O Lord, they're such sinners. Change them!" We need to see that there's more we could've done. And there's more we *can* do. There are things we should have done that we haven't. And there are things that we need to do better. I'm talking about myself on that, too. We need to do t'shuvah and say, "What more can we do?" as we pray.

So, that's what t'shuvah means for the nation, but what about these other two groups? In Matthew the Lord says:

Matthew 7:13-14 *"Go in through the narrow gate; for the gate that leads to destruction is wide and the road broad, and many travel it; but it is a narrow gate and a hard road that leads to life, and only a few find it.*

The life that He's talking about here is eternal life—life in the presence of God. So, we can think of life as a journey—as a road. How about this first group that I'm talking about? Are these Ten Days of T'shuvah relevant to us? We've already made t'shuvah. I made the biggest t'shuvah I ever made twenty-four years ago when I turned to the Lord. But this analogy that the Lord gives us here is that our life is like a road, and we're walking that road and we're supposed to be following someone. Who is that? Yea, we're supposed to be following the Lord Himself down that road. And He describes that road as narrow and straight. The gates on it are narrow. It's a hard road to follow, not a hard road because its surface is hard. I used to wonder about this road. "How can you have a straight road that's hard to follow?" Well, it goes up hill! And it goes down hill. And we're supposed to follow Him up and down that road.

But, you know, our tendency is to wander off. It's like Isaiah said, *"All we like sheep have gone astray. We've wandered everyone of us our own way"* (Isaiah 53:6, my paraphrase). Even as believers, we go astray! I hope I'm not the only one here who will admit that there are times that I wander off that road! When I do get off, going this way, and the Lord's going that way down the straight road, I need to turn. The longer I walk off the path, the farther away from Him I get. I need to turn and get back on the road. And how do I do that? I need to have that contrite heart to be willing to admit I got off track. We need the Feast of Shofars—Yom Teruah to hear the Shofar to remind us that we have a Hope, like we talked about in the last chapter. I believe we also need to hear the Shofar on Yom Teruah to remind us that we need to wake up—that God is calling us to follow Him and have Him change us; that we're never done with changing; that we're never done with giving up all for Him.

And that's what I want to look at right now. I want to look at someone that all of us who are believers in the Messiah, and who are students of the New Covenant, look up to as one of the greatest examples of a follower of Yeshua who definitely had a contrite heart. And that is Rabbi Sha'ul (Paul), the man who wrote two-thirds of the New Covenant. I want to look at his attitudes in some of the passages he wrote and see some things that maybe you've missed about him. First of all, in I Timothy, he starts out with two statements about how what he's going to say is absolutely true.

1 Timothy 1:15 *So here is a statement you can trust, one that fully deserves to be accepted: the Messiah came into the world to save sinners,* [sounds like something that we all should accept and have no problem with, but then he says] *and I'm the number one sinner!* (Other translations say: "the worst sinner" or "the chief sinner.")

Now, I looked this up in several translations, but I couldn't find any that said it in the past tense, "I *was* the worst sinner." Every translation says, "I *am*." "I *am* the number one sinner."

Now why would he say that about himself? Well, we know something about this man's past. In the Book of Acts there are several places where it says things like this.

Acts 8:3 *But Sha'ul set out to destroy the Messianic community— entering house after house, he dragged off both men and women and handed them over to be put in prison.*

There are three other places where it talks about him doing this. This is before he met the Lord on the road and the Lord knocked him off his horse and blinded him and he had a t'shuvah experience.

But you know, there's a reason I brought this up. Now please don't take this out and disparage Rabbi Sha'ul, but he had an attitude and a zeal that could've made him like a terrorist! Do you see that? He was throwing people in jail because of what they believed! And in one of the passages it even says he was speaking *murderous* threats. So this man knows how low he could go. That's why he says I am the chief of sinners, because he *knows!* He knows that he constantly needed God's help to save him from his sinful nature. And his sinful nature in particular was being a religious fanatic.

He saw himself as a sinner because he knew himself better than anyone else. He looked at himself and said, "I know me. I don't know how bad anyone else is, but I know how bad I am. I know my iniquities." Remember, we talked about iniquity. It's the inclination to evil. So he knew how inclined he was to evil if he let himself go—how easily he could slip down the slope without God's grace. He saw that he still had the potential to be a terrible sinner. That's a man with a contrite heart! He was guarding himself. He was saying, "God change me. I know what's in my old man."

Now I want to look at another passage. It's kind of a long passage, but I hope you'll bear with me. It gives us some more insight into this contriteness of Rabbi Sha'ul's heart, as an example to us. Remember contriteness is in people who are open to change—open to God changing them—open to growing.

Philippians 3:7 *But the things that used to be advantages for me* (in other translations: "gain to me" or "to my profit"), *I have, because of the Messiah, come to consider a disadvantage* (or "a loss").

What things did Paul have? Well, he was born into a very prominent family. He was a Benjaminite and a Pharisee. He had position. He had a great reputation of being very brilliant. He had great knowledge and obviously great writing ability. He was probably relatively wealthy. But he counted that all as a loss.

Philippians 3:8 *Not only that, but I consider everything a disadvantage* (loss) *in comparison with the supreme value of knowing the Messiah Yeshua as my Lord. It was because of him that I gave up everything and regard it all as garbage, in order to gain the Messiah.*

Now, I think what he's talking about here is not just the things he had before he became a believer, I think he is even talking about the things that may have come to him as he was a believer, because he was a brilliant man and he was a great preacher and a great writer, and people would've looked up to him. So he would have had a reputation amongst the believers. And he had, as we know, incredible times in God's presence. He speaks about those times when he saw things that no one can see and God spoke to him and gave him revelations. So what he's saying is, "I count that all as loss. I count it as garbage. I count it as nothing compared to knowing the Messiah." Isn't that amazing?

Philippians 3:9 ... *and be found in union with Him* [your translation probably says, *in* Him], *not having any righteousness of my own based on legalism, but having that righteousness which comes through the Messiah's faithfulness, the righteousness from God based on trust* (faith).

This may remind you of the wedding garments. Remember the parable of the wedding? Remember those who came into the wedding feast without the wedding garments? What did the wedding garments represent? His righteousness! We're clothed in God's righteousness. So, he's talking about that here. He's saying he comes in Yeshua's righteousness, not in his own righteousness. Righteousness is right standing with God, not based on what we can do, but on the righteousness of what Messiah did.

Philippians 3:10 *Yes, I gave it all up in order to know Him ....*

Now let's start making this personal. We're to give up all our advantages—all the things that profit us—in order to know Him, Yeshua, personally.

Philippians 3:10 *I gave it all up in order to know Him that is, to know the power of His resurrection ....*

Why do we have to give it up? He says, "in order to" here. In other words, to know the power of His resurrection, you have to give it all up. Okay? What is the power of His resurrection in us? It's resurrecting us to a new life! So we can't experience the new life unless we give up what? The old life! That's what we have to give up. That's what he's talking about giving up here. Unless we give up our old nature—dependence on our carnal nature, our flesh, we can't experience the new life. The more of the old life we give up the more we experience His resurrection power and new life.

Philippians 3:10 *Yes, I gave it all up in order to know Him, ... and the fellowship of His sufferings, as I am being conformed to His death.*

Now that doesn't sound like fun. And it's not. It's not! But, you know, there is a fellowship, an intimacy we experience with Yeshua when we suffer as He did. That's what he's talking about here. Now what does that mean? It's similar to the intimacy we experience with another human being when we both go through the same trial together. For instance, if you have recently lost a loved one and you meet somebody else who lost a loved one, there's an instant bonding that happens there. You can comfort that person. There's an intimacy there.

Another example is if you're somebody who was rejected by your family when you came to the Lord. When you get to talk to other people who've experienced that, there's an intimacy in that suffering. And here's one for all of us. I think all of America experienced an intimacy after 9-11. I mean I did. I experienced a closeness with people. It was just like we were all in it together. There was an intimacy of suffering together.

So, what causes this suffering that is similar to Yeshua's? Well, it's the killing of the old self! It's not easy. He suffered terribly when He did it—literally! He killed His old self—His body—literally—when He died on that cross. Now, that was not His sinful self, because He had no sin. He was perfect. But we are called to kill the old nature—to kill our old, sinful person. And we're called to do that daily and that is a painful process.

When I preached this message to my congregation, I asked, "Anybody here enjoy crucifying the flesh?" And to my surprise, someone said yes. "You enjoy it?" I asked. The person answered, "The fruit that comes after it!" That's what Rabbi Sha'ul is talking about, the fruit that comes afterwards. We're called to kill—to crucify—the old nature for the fruit that comes afterwards.

Now, when does crucifying the old nature begin? When is that point where we're supposed to look back and say, "That's when I crucified the old man"? Immersion in water! Right! Immersion is to be that time. When we go down under the water, we die to the old man and come up in the resurrection. But that's just the start because, as you know, we have to walk that out every day; because the old man tries to resurrect himself all the time. It's a continuing process, and it's painful and causes suffering. Therefore we have a little of that fellowship in suffering with Him.

We experience more of that fellowship of suffering with Yeshua when we speak out for Him and we are rejected and persecuted for Him. All those things are the fellowship of His suffering. So Paul is looking forward. He's saying, "I *want* to experience the fellowship of His suffering."

Philippians 3:11-12 *... so that somehow I might arrive at being res-urrected from the dead* [that he might be totally the new man]. *It is not that I have already obtained it or already reached the goal—no, I keep pursuing it* (pressing on) *in the hope of taking hold of that for which the Messiah Yeshua took hold of me.*

Now here's the thing, Rabbi Sha'ul, the author of two-thirds of the New Covenant, is saying, "I haven't reached the goal"! You see that? Why? Because it's a moving goal! Every time you get near it, it moves! Yes! It moves! We'll explain that a little bit later.

Philippians 3:13 *Brothers, I, for my part, do not think of myself as having yet gotten hold of it; but one thing I do: forgetting what is behind me and <u>straining</u> forward toward what lies ahead,*

Now, this is not the picture of somebody just sitting back and saying, "Lord, just do this. I'm just going to trust you to do this." Is it? No! "Straining forward, pressing ahead …."

Philippians 3:14 *… I keep pursuing the goal in order to win the prize offered by God's upward calling in the Messiah Yeshua.*

Now, I had a revelation about this verse as I was studying this. What is Sha'ul's goal? What is he striving towards? The prize is the upward call. It's not a place, or a state of spirituality, or some sort of level of holiness that we achieve, that we arrive at! The prize is the getting there. Let me say that again. It's the process of getting there that is the prize! "The *upward* calling." See it's the "upward" part not the arriving that he is emphasizing here.

Are you wrinkling your brow at me? Let me explain this again. It's the work of getting there that is the prize. That's what Paul is striving after. He wants to continue getting there, because we never get there in this life! There's always more for us to grow in. There's always more for us to learn. There's always more of God transforming us—conforming us into the image of His Son. We're not going to get there until after we die. Then we will be complete. So it's a continuous thing.

Let me give you a little story that John Maxwell tells in his leadership training class. Now, John is an author. He's written about 15 or 20 books. I never knew this, but what he shared was that authors don't get to choose the titles of their books. They write a book. They suggest the title, but it's up to the publisher and their marketing people what the title will actually be. Because you know those marketing people, they don't think anybody else knows how to sell anything so they have to pick a title that will grab people. So, John had written many books. And he had always submitted the title for the book that he wanted and when it came back from the publisher it was always a different name. And he had always just kind of said, "Oh well, I'll let it go. They know better," and agreed to it.

But, one time he was writing a book that, in his mind, was titled *Success is a Journey.* He sent it to the publisher with that title. And he got back the title, *The Journey to Success.* Now, I didn't catch right away what he was talking about. But when he got that title back, he said, "I can't accept this." He made a special trip to another city to visit the publisher to insist that they could not change the title to *The Journey to Success.* The reason was this. The whole point of the book is that success is not a place that you get to. John's teaching, by the way, is not just spiritual; it's for every area of life. Success is the process of getting there. In other words, to be a successful person doesn't mean in business, for instance, that you establish a company and make a million dollars. That's not, in his mind, a successful person. A successful person is one who develops the skill and ability to do something like that and after that's over can do something else that's bigger, and then something else that's yet bigger than that. The successful person has the mindset that says, "I'm going to keep growing." "I'm going to continue to improve." That's success in John Maxwell's mind.

So he went down there and he made them change the title, because, you see, *The Journey to Success* was exactly what he was trying *not* to say, because you don't journey *to* success. Success is not a goal. It's the process, the ongoing pursuit. Now, there's a spiritual parallel to this. It's the same way with our spirit. The prize is not at the end of the journey. The prize *is* the journey. We don't achieve some level of spirituality—a closeness with God—where we can then sit back and say, "Whoa, I'm there!" or "You know, I've had these revelations and everybody can just applaud me all the time, and I can just sit back and relax." No!

Success in the spiritual sense is to be on a journey with Him—to be walking with Him. That's success. The prize is being in contact with the One we're walking with on the journey! That's the prize! Now, this is really important because most of us have a different concept of life. We think that it's to get to the end, but it's not. It's just like that old saying: it's not who wins or loses; it's how you play the game. It's not that you're going to win or lose; it's how you walk your life. If you walk your whole life with the Lord, that's success! No matter where He leads you. Okay? So, here's the motto:

Success is not a goal. It's a process, an ongoing pursuit.

The journey goes on for our entire life. And here's the thing. It requires us to keep moving because He's moving. If we sit down and say, "You know, I think I've gotten as far as I'm going to go. I don't need to get any closer to the Lord. I don't need to do anything more that God is calling me to do. I'm just going to hang out at this level." Well, He just keeps walking. And we get further away from Him. You see, we can't stop. You have to keep moving. Standing still means we've stopped succeeding.

And it's an upward calling. In other words, it takes effort. It takes effort to climb hills. He's taking us places we have never been before— to new heights, to new altitudes. And I hope that's what He's doing in your life, because that's success when He's taking you to new things.

And we should not be surprised that there are new things, saying things like, "Oh no, I have this new challenge. What am I going to do about it?" Well, part of that walking with God is accepting new challenges, because that's one of the biggest growth things that He calls us to. And when God puts His finger on something and says, "You know, you need to stop doing that," don't be surprised because cleaning up our act is part of that challenge, too.

So, let me just read the rest of what he says here about these things, because it's really interesting.

Philippians 3:15 *Therefore, as many of us as are mature, let us keep paying attention to this; and if you are differently minded about anything, God will also reveal this to you.*

So, what he's saying here is that the evidence of maturity is that you are on the journey. Do you see that? The evidence is that you are on a journey, asking God to move you, to change you, to grow you. That's the evidence of maturity. It's the opposite of what you might think! You might think maturity is having arrived. But if you think you've arrived, you see, you've stopped moving. Once you get to that place where you think you've arrived, you're not a success anymore, because you've stopped going upward.

Philippians 3:16 *Only let our conduct fit the level we have already reached.*

Now, this is really important. We have to live a life demonstrating how far God has brought us. Are you with me? Revelations, doctrinal soundness, and gifts of the Spirit are *not* proofs that God is changing us. Conduct is proof. Holy living is proof. What kind of conduct? Well, it means being a person:

- Of Prayer
- Of Intercession
- Of good works
- Of evangelism
- Of compassion
- Of worship
- Who studies the Word
- Who reaches out

Those are the kinds of conducts. I'm not talking about not doing this or not doing that. I'm talking about being a person who is doing things that demonstrate that there is good fruit in their lives. (By the way, those things on the above list are the seven purposes of our congregation.) We're to do those things that demonstrate that God is doing something in us.

Philippians 3:17 *Brothers, join in imitating me, and pay attention to those who live according to the pattern we have set for you.*

He's saying, "You don't have to do this alone. Look to others for your example."

This is something we learned in our leadership training class. Be open to being discipled. Seek out people who are more mature than you who can mentor you. John Maxwell talks about always being in an environment where there's somebody whom you look up to, and say, "I'd like to be like him or her." Always put yourself in an environment like that because it inspires you. Be mentored. Search for people who can mentor you.

Philippians 3:18-19 *For many—I have told you about them often before, and even now I say it with tears—live as enemies of the Messiah's execution-stake* (cross). *They are headed for destruction! Their god is the belly; they are proud of what they ought to be ashamed of, since they are concerned about the things of the world.*

This is what we are to turn from, making the things of this world higher priority than the things of God's Kingdom.

Philippians 3:20-21 *But we are citizens of heaven, and it is from there that we expect a Deliverer, the Lord Yeshua the Messiah. He will change the bodies we have in this humble state and make them like His glorious body, using the power which enables Him to bring everything under His control.*

I wasn't thinking of this when I looked up this passage, but that gets right back to the future theme of Rosh Hashanah. Did you hear it in there? A deliverer will change our bodies into glorious bodies, talking about His return, and transform us into immortal bodies! It's amazing!

So that's the challenge for those who have already made t'shuvah and are following the Lord. But what about that other group, those who have not committed their lives to following the Lord? I want to tell you that you need to obey the call of the Shofar to make that initial turn and go through the Narrow Gate. Not to change everything in your life, because that's not your job, but simply to start following Him down that straight and narrow path, that "*road that leads to life.*"

Why should you heed that Shofar call and do t'shuvah, to turn to follow Him? Well, here's one of my favorite things that the Lord said:

Matthew 11:28 "*Come to me, all of you who are struggling and burdened, and I will give you rest* (shalom).

What a wonderful promise—no more struggle, no more burdens—rest. And I can tell you personally that I was struggling and burdened.

And since I made that turn to follow Him when I heard Him say, "Come to Me," He has given me rest in the midst of great trials, and I've taken on great responsibilities that I never thought I would or could take on. And yet, He has given me rest. So many others could tell you this personally, too.

I had an interesting thing happen a week ago. I was over at the retirement home with a ninety-three year old woman. I was sharing with her, and she asked me how old I was. I said, "Fifty-five." She said, "You don't look fifty-five! Why do you look so young?!" I don't know if my congregation thinks I look young, but she did. And I was able to say to her, "The reason I look young is because God has given me rest for the past twenty-four years." I haven't struggled and striven and carried a heavy burden. That doesn't mean I haven't gone through trials. If you want to hear a whole evening's worth, I can tell you about all my trials! They are numerous. But I had *Him* through those trials, and that's the secret that is in the next verse.

Matthew 11:29 *Take my yoke upon you and learn from me, because I am gentle and humble in heart, and you will find rest for your souls.*

I have walked through many difficult trials, but He has been with me. He has continued to call me on that upward call, and I have found rest for my soul.

But what is this yoke thing? Well, His yoke has been upon me, meaning I have been His servant. I have committed myself to serve Him because that's what it takes, because He is God! We can't come to Him and say, "I'm going to go my way." We have to come His way—put His yoke upon us. There are those who hesitate. But what I think they don't understand is that He is a gentle master. He is the perfect master. There are lots of masters who have heavy yokes. The enemy, satan, is a heavy yoke master. We ourselves can be heavy yoke masters. If it was up to me, I'd probably drive myself harder, and work harder than what the Lord wants me to work. Maybe some of you are like that—workaholics. We can be heavy on ourselves.

Matthew 11:30 *For my yoke is easy, and my burden is light."*

His yoke is easy and His burden is light. So, I challenge you to listen to Him calling out to you, "Come to Me." Heed His call. Go to Him. Accept His easy yoke and light burden. Give the weariness and stress of your life to Him and enter into His rest.

Go ahead and bow your head right now and talk to Him.

CHAPTER 9

JERUSALEM, A PRAISE IN THE EARTH

So, as we learned in the last chapter, it's good for us to once a year begin to say, "Lord, show me. Show me the things that are displeasing to You. I want to change. Help me to know what those things are." However, I also believe that we as Y'hudim Mishikhim (Messianic Jews) and as Gerim Mishikhim (Messianic Gentiles) have more to do in these Ten Days than personal repentance. God has another assignment for us.

1 Peter 2:9 *But you are a chosen people, the King's cohanim* (the King's priests or a royal priesthood) ....

Back in the time of Moses, God established that one clan of the tribe of Levi, the descendants of Aaron, would be the cohanim. (Remember, "cohane" is singular; "cohanim" is plural.) They would serve in the

113

Temple. They would make the sacrifices. They would do the things that needed to be done. And even to this day, there are many, many Jewish people who have the name, Cohen. You probably know someone named Cohen. Well, they are descendants of that priestly clan. And someday those priestly clans are going to be gathered back together to begin serving in the Temple in Israel. It's a very Jewish thing to be a cohane—to be a priest.

So, if we're supposed to be cohanim, we need to understand what it is that cohanim do. What are we called to do? What is our role? Well, I thought of three things that the cohanim did in the times of the Temple.

First of all, they repented and made sacrifices for their own sins. They couldn't serve as cohanim unless they acknowledged that they were human, and that they fell short and needed to make sacrifices for themselves.

Then they made sacrifices and repented for the sins of the people of the community of Israel, even though they themselves had not committed those sins with the rest of the community. And, third, they were called to make intercession for the nation of Israel, their community.

Intercession is more than just spending a lot of time in prayer. It's certainly praying for others rather than yourself, but it's also offering up to God a sacrifice. And I'm not saying we are called to physically lay down our lives as Yeshua did for other people; although, during times of danger, many have been called to do that. There are many who have been martyred for the Kingdom in the past and it is still happening today in many areas in the world. (To learn more about that go to *The Voice of the Martyrs* at persecution.com.)

I'd like to ask you to do something right now. Would you please take a minute to review all that is involved in intercession? Turn back to the chapter called *Intercession* (Chapter 3, p. 33) and re-familiarize yourself with what we learned about it.

Now that you have refreshed your understanding of what intercession is, I'd like to turn your attention to a song about intercession, "*On Your Walls O Jerusalem*" from Barry and Batya Segal's CD, "<u>Go through the Gates</u>". The song is on You Tube. Take a minute to find it, so you can listen to it while you read on. At first you will hear the sounds at the Western Wall. If you listen closely you can hear them chanting this verse in Hebrew.

Isaiah 62:6-7 (NKJV) *I have set watchmen on your walls, O Jerusalem; They shall never hold their peace day or night. You who make mention of the LORD, do not keep silent, And give Him no rest till He establishes and till He makes Jerusalem a praise in the earth.*

We're going to study through this Scripture. I have been singing this song for a long time now. After I first heard the song, I bought the CD and I just couldn't stop listening to it. I've been praying about what these verses really mean. Barry and Batya, who wrote this song, live right in Jerusalem. So, you can understand why they would be asking for watchmen. So, let's go through these verses and try to understand what it means to be a watchman for Jerusalem.

Isaiah 62:6 (NKJV) *I have set watchmen on your walls, O Jerusalem; ....*

So, first of all, who put these watchmen on the walls? Yes, God has set these watchmen on the walls. And where are the walls? Jerusalem. And the walls are there to do what for Jerusalem? Protect Jerusalem! Yes! Walls are what protected Jerusalem in the past.

Jerusalem has always been and is now in danger. It has been under attack all through history. There have been incredibly numerous attacks *on* Jerusalem, battles *over* Jerusalem, and slaughters *in* Jerusalem. Why is that? It is because it is the spiritual center of the earth. It is the place where the Kingdom of Light and the kingdom of darkness collide. The kingdom of darkness wants to eliminate it. We're seeing that right now in our own time.

Isaiah 62:6 (NKJV) *I have set watchmen on your walls, O Jerusalem; They shall never hold their peace day or night. You who make mention of the LORD, do not keep silent,*

So, what do these watchmen do? They pray. They are not watchmen like watching out for danger and warning people. They are prayer people. It's to the Lord they are speaking. *"Do not keep silent ... day or night."* So the watchmen pray day and night. And by the way, it's watchwomen, too, among those who are called to pray to protect Jerusalem.

Let's read on because verse 7 is just fascinating. It goes back to that thing about Moses changing God's mind. Listen to what it says.

Isaiah 62:7 *And give Him no rest till He establishes and till He makes Jerusalem a praise in the earth.*

That verse has been going through my mind. What is it saying? Let's start with the first part. *Give Him no rest.* So God is telling these watchmen basically to harass Him, hound Him, bug Him, keep bothering Him. Give Him no rest. Right? Sometimes I have this thing that will happen. (I don't figure you've had this experience, but maybe as parents or if you're leading some organization, you have.) Somebody will say to me, "We should do such and such" and I'll say, "Yea, that's a great idea, but I know I'm going to forget it. I'm too busy. So I'm telling you to bug me. You come to me. You call me. You get it ready. You come and you do it." I think that's what God is saying here. "If you think this is important, you bug Me about it. You stay on My case about it. You keep telling Me about it if you really want to see it happen." This is a form of true intercession.

And you know it's an incredible mystery, but God needs intercession like that. Why does He need this from us? I mean, He has a plan. He can carry out His plan. Why does He need us interceding this way? I don't know the answer to that. But somehow that is what He has appointed us to do on this earth.

Sometimes I will actually test people this way. I'll tell them, "If you really want to see this happen, you call me." And if it is really important to them, I get a call from them. But if it isn't really that high up on their list of important things, they forget about it, and I never get the call. If they believe it is really vital, they bug me until it is taken care of. Perhaps that's sort of what God is doing here.

Isaiah 62:7...*till He establishes and till He <u>makes Jerusalem a praise in the earth</u>*.

What will it mean for Jerusalem to be "*a praise in the earth*"? As I thought about this, I could see three different levels of this. On the first level, the narrowest meaning is Jerusalem will be a beautiful, peaceful city that people will love to come visit. Many tourists will come and will give praise when they see it. The key word there is "peaceful." That would be the miracle right there. That has been the issue all through history. So, watchmen on the wall will pray that Jerusalem will be a city of peace and beauty where everybody will want to go.

That's the narrowest interpretation of it, but there's a broader meaning. I don't think the prophet Isaiah is talking about buildings, streets, parks, memorials and museums. He's not talking about walls of stone. What is he talking about? Why is he saying that they should intercede for Jerusalem? Well, I think the answer to that is in a verse that probably every single one of you knows.

Psalm 122:6 (NKJV) *Pray for the peace of Jerusalem:* (In Hebrew it's: *Shalu Shalom Yerushalayim.*) *"May those who love you prosper."*

I'd like you to read what follows that verse. I don't think many people do. It explains why you should pray for the peace of Jerusalem. Yes, you should pray for them so you prosper, but there's a bigger reason.

Psalm 122:7-8 *May shalom be within your ramparts, prosperity in your palaces. 8 For the sake of my family and friends, I say, "Shalom be within you!"*

And then verse nine.

Psalm 122:9 *For the sake of the house of ADONAI our God, I will seek your well-being.*

Why pray for the peace of Jerusalem according to Psalm 122? *Because the house of ADONAI* is in Jerusalem. It was in Jerusalem in the past, and it will be in Jerusalem in the future. That's the reason. It's not because it's special for some other reason, but it's because the presence of God is in that place. That's why I said it's the center of spiritual conflict on this planet.

So the broader meaning of God making Jerusalem *"a praise in the earth"* is linked to the fact that God's presence is in Jerusalem. Now what does this mean? I believe it means that everywhere on the earth it will be acknowledged that the manifest presence of the Living God— who is the Creator God, who is the God of all nations, *who is the God of Israel*—dwells in Jerusalem. Not the New Jerusalem that will someday come down from heaven, but the earthly Jerusalem made out of the stones of Israel.

What is going to happen in Jerusalem according to the prophetic Scriptures? The Temple is going to be rebuilt there (Matthew 24:15). The Lord is going to return there (Acts 1:4-12). He's going to set His foot on the Mount of Olives (Zechariah 14:4). The millennial Kingdom of God is going to be established there (Isaiah 65:18-25). And according to the prophet Zechariah, the nations of the world will go up to Jerusalem to celebrate Sukkot (the Feast of Tabernacles). And if they don't they won't get any rain (Zechariah 14:16-17). All of these things are very tangible. They're not like heaven. They are very earthly things.

Jerusalem will have the presence of God in it in a way that has never been seen before in human history. So, it will be a praise in all the earth. Do you see that? That's what this passage is talking about. And that's why we're to intercede for Jerusalem.

Then we need to ask the question, "Who will be the citizens of Jerusalem?" The Muslims think they're supposed to be the citizens of Jerusalem. That's why the Dome of the Rock was built there. And that's why violence started in 2001 when Ariel Sharon set foot on the Temple Mount.

And there was a time back in the tenth or eleventh centuries, when the Pope decided that the Christians should own Jerusalem, right? And something happened after that called the Crusades, which were the battles of Christians trying to conquer Jerusalem. So, who do you think are supposed to be the citizens of Jerusalem and be in control of Jerusalem when it becomes *a praise in the earth*?

I believe it's the Jews! Israel will have control of it. Do you know the reason why that is? It's because there are so many promises in the Bible about the Jewish people having Jerusalem and being in the presence of God there, that if it didn't happen—if Jerusalem came into the hands of some other peoples in the end—the Scriptures would not be true. It would mean that the God of the Bible is not capable of keeping His promises!! God has chosen the Temple Mount as His dwelling place on this earth. In the End Times, according to His promises, He is going to re-take His property, which will be the re-establishment of His authority on Earth. And all the nations and peoples will acknowledge that the God of Israel is the Creator God, the one true God.

Now, let's take that one step further. We see that Jewish people are scattered all over the world. Someday they're all going to be back in Israel, but right now they're scattered. So, if Jerusalem gets to be a praise in the earth, that would mean that Jewish people all around the world would be loved, not hated.

We have to ask this question. "Can Jerusalem be *a praise in the earth* while the citizens of Jerusalem are despised?" Do you think that's possible? Can you imagine all the nations of the world recognizing that Jerusalem has the presence of God—the God of *Israel*—in it, and yet hating God's chosen people—the Jewish people—the *people* of *Israel*? I can't imagine that. I believe Jerusalem being *a praise in the earth* means that there would also be this love and respect for the Jewish people.

That would be a miracle in Rochester, NY where I live! Actually, it's not bad here, but in Paris where it's getting pretty bad? In Berlin where it's getting worse and worse? Yes! That's what is going to happen when Jerusalem becomes *a praise in the earth*. The Jewish people will be loved! In Baghdad! In the Gaza Strip! And even in Tehran! What an amazing miracle it will be!

And it's not because we are a better people, or a smarter people, or a more spiritual people. That's not the reason at all! It's simply because God chose us to be part of His plan. We have a role to fill, and that role involves being the landlords of Jerusalem where the presence of God will be. And the peoples of the world will come to love the God of the Jewish people.

So, in this broader interpretation of the walls of Jerusalem, I think the walls extend. They're not just around that city. They extend to all the places in the world where Jewish people live, which is a large part of the world. And the watchmen on the walls are to pray for the protection of the Jewish people—whom the adversary has tried to destroy all throughout history. So wherever there are Jewish people living, if we are watchmen on the walls, we're to be praying for their protection.

Now we're also to pray that the House of the Lord be established in those communities all around the world. Like in the city of Rochester where I live and the city or town where you live—that in the Jewish community, the House of the Lord would be established; that His presence would be there.

Genesis 12:3 *I will bless those who bless you, but I will curse anyone who curses you; ....*

Now I want to conclude here with the broadest interpretation of this. According to the New Covenant, the followers of Yeshua are said to be Temples of the Spirit of God. So wherever we go, when we gather in families and communities, we establish the Kingdom of God in that part of the world. We bring the presence of God to those places. And remember Gentiles are grafted into that olive tree which is Israel, and Jewish people are grafted *back* in. We're all part of the Commonwealth of Israel. So, the walls of Jerusalem extend really to everywhere we go to bring the Kingdom of God—to Haiti, or Ecuador; to China, or to Irondequoit (a suburb of the city of Rochester). The Kingdom of God is there because you're there. And the walls of Jerusalem, in that sense, protecting the House of God are in that place.

So, that's you're commission. We are all called to be on the walls of Jerusalem in Israel, in the Spirit, interceding for the city and the Land of Israel, but also interceding for the Kingdom to be established in the Jewish community near you; for the presence of God to be known. And I think it's happening right now. I think actually my congregation is experiencing a wave of the Spirit of God in the area of prayer. Our leadership team had a prayer meeting recently that was just incredible. There was such strength that was there. We as the leadership had decided that we've had such attacks from the enemy that we need to periodically get together and pray for each other and for our congregation.

The Hebrew word for watchmen is "shomrim." The singular is "shomar." I want to end by encouraging you to be willing to stand on the wall—to be willing to be a shomar—a watchman on the wall—to bug God! To not give Him any rest, until He makes this place a praise on the earth—until He makes your city a praise on the earth—until He makes *Jerusalem a praise on the earth.*

Are you called to be a shomar a shomrot—a watchman or a watchwoman? If so, I'd like to challenge you right now to make a commitment to intercede and ask God to make Jerusalem a praise in the earth. This doesn't mean you have to pray continuously all day, but it means that you will frequently take some time to go before God and intercede.

If you're willing to do that would you stand up? Go ahead, take your book and stand up while you read as a sign to God of your commitment. I'm going to pray for a shomar or shomrot anointing upon you right now.

Father, thank You for those who are standing. We don't understand it, Lord. Why would You want us to be bugging You? Why would You want us to be giving You no rest day and night? Yet somehow it's in Your plan that we have to do this for Your plan to be fulfilled! We don't understand it, Lord, but we are willing to be obedient and to do what you ask.

(Lift up your hands to the Lord right now.)

Father, I ask that You would put a shomar anointing upon this person who is standing right now, who is committing to spend time to pray for the peace of Jerusalem, to pray that You establish it, and make it a praise on the earth, and to understand that the walls of Jerusalem are spiritual walls that even extend to their own family, to their own community, and to their own congregation. Father, I don't know what You're going to do through this. But I believe You told me to do this. I pray that this anointing would come down upon the people right now. I don't know if they're going to feel anything, but Lord, I know that when they go to prayer, something is going to happen. There's going to be a new zeal—a new connection with You in this time of these Ten Days of Awe. I pray that there will be many reports of a new connection with You, of an ability to pray that wasn't there before, of a persistence, of a zeal, of an ability to intercede—whatever that means in their lives. We pray and agree with this in the Name of Yeshua.

And all God's people said, "Amen!" That means you believe it will happen.

CHAPTER 10

Upside Down Kingdom Part I

I want to get back to the subject of doing t'shuvah during the Yomim Norim (Days of Awe) and to the Shofar waking us up to repentance. As I said before, those of us who have already committed ourselves to follow the Lord and are trying with all our hearts to follow Him, the wakening call of the Shofar is for us, too. When we give our hearts to the Lord, we give all that we are aware of and all that we are capable of at that time. But I found in my own walk that sometimes circumstances will bring about a situation and I will realize there's something that I'm holding back. I realize, "O, I haven't given that to Him yet. I'm still trying to control that. I'm still worried about that." And God is saying, "I want you to give that to Me now."

Yom Teruah (Rosh Hashanah) is the day to start. But you may be thinking, "How do I start? If I don't know what to change, how can I change?" Well, in Romans it tells us why we all need to change.

Romans 8:29 (NASB) *For those whom He foreknew, He also predestined to become conformed to the image of His Son, so that He would be the firstborn among many brethren ....*

One time I asked my congregation, "Is there anybody here who would be willing to stand up and say that they are fully conformed to the image of Yeshua?" And you know what? No one stood up. How about you? Could you truthfully say that? No? I didn't think so. Why can't any of us say that? It's because we're all on the way to that. And it involves continuing change. What is this image of His Son? Well, Isaiah 55:8-9 is a real foundational passage that speaks of this. The Lord speaks to us here about the difference between Him and us. The Lord calls us to be like Him in this way.

Isaiah 55:8-9 *(NASB) "For My thoughts are not your thoughts, nor are your ways My ways," declares the LORD. "For as the heavens are higher than the earth, so are My ways higher than your ways And My thoughts than your thoughts."*

God's way of thinking and doing things is different from the world. God's thoughts are different from our thoughts. His ways are different from our ways. The word that He uses here is "higher." In other words, we are to grasp, to understand, that they are above us. They are more than we are.

The God that we worship is the Creator of the universe. And that universe, we can't even comprehend. We can't grasp how big it is. We still haven't measured it. We've got great telescopes and we can see tremendous distances out there in the universe, but the astronomers tell us we can't see to the end of it. And our God is bigger than that.

And then, if you look at the opposite, we can't grasp how small the universe is either. We have great microscopes, and we can see down to the tiniest particles, and yet we're always discovering new, tinier ones. We don't even know what those tiniest particles are. And our God put all that together. He is much, much greater than we are. We have some concept of what He is, but we don't really grasp all that He is.

He is different from us, but He calls us to be like Him. He calls us to think like Him. He calls us to learn to walk with Him and to understand His ways. It's His desire to conform our thinking to His way of thinking—to get us to do things and to think about things, as it says in this verse, the way that He would do things and think about things.

So, the way I like to think about this is that God's Kingdom, which we have entered in and want to be citizens of, is an upside down Kingdom. I got this concept from a class that I took in 2003 where it talked about how God's Kingdom is upside down from the world. The concepts of the world are what people would consider right side up, but in God's concept, or way of thinking, they are actually upside down. His ways are so different from the world's that it's almost like the Kingdom of God is an upside down Kingdom.

We're going to look at a bunch of verses that show these upside down ways. They are the opposite of the way the world thinks. As you look at them, I don't want you to just say, "Oh, that's interesting." I'd like them to challenge you. They challenge me because in many of these upside down ways of thinking I haven't arrived. I'm still thinking the wrong way. I'm not thinking "upside down" yet.

So, I'd like you to look at them and say to the Lord, "Am I thinking the way You think about this subject, Lord? Am I acting the way You act about this subject?"

You may be thinking, "I don't know if I'm capable of changing. How can I change myself? There are some things that I do that I know are not Godly things. I know I'm acting the way the world does. How can I change that?" I want to encourage you to believe that if God calls you to change, He will enable you to change. He never calls us to do anything that He doesn't equip us to do. That equipping may come through circumstances. It may come through revelation. It may be difficult! It may be easy. But once we begin to cooperate with Him and say, "Lord, change me," God will begin to work those things in our lives. That's the essence of t'shuvah—of being contrite.

So, let's look at some of these upside down concepts.

First Upside Down Concept

How do we deal with people who hurt us? How do we deal with someone who is out to get us? The world would say you need to take revenge. You need to get back at them. But here's God's upside down way.

Romans 12:19 *Never seek revenge, my friends; instead, leave that to God's anger; for in the Tanakh* (Old Testament) *it is written, "ADONAI says, 'Vengeance is my responsibility; I will repay.'"*

So, do you see? That's upside down! The world teaches revenge, get even. God says, "Never do that!" Why? Because that brings us down to the level of the person who did something wrong to us. A lot of the problem, I believe, that we're seeing in the Middle East right now is because that is a way of life in that culture. "If you killed somebody in my family, I'm going to kill somebody in your family. We have to even the score." In much lesser ways that's how our society works here. So, how can we obey this upside down way? Well, there's an unseen factor that's spoken of in this verse. The unseen factor is that God says, "It's my responsibility." So, we can have faith that God will repay. Now, it may not be in this life. It may be in the next life. But God says He will judge and give to everyone according to what they have done. So, He will repay. So, once we can get hold of that, we can say, "Okay, I won't take revenge. I will leave it to you, O God."

Second Upside Down Concept

To get your enemies to stop hurting you, the world would say to put up walls, to put up a fence. Move out of range. Get away. Or take something that you can beat them down with so they are afraid to hurt you anymore. But the Word of God says something very different.

Matthew 5:44 *But I tell you, love your enemies! Pray for those who persecute you!*

Romans 12:20 *On the contrary, "If your enemy is hungry, feed him; if he is thirsty, give him something to drink. For by doing this, you will heap fiery coals [of shame] on his head."*

So, in the verse from Matthew, we're called to pray for our enemies. In the verse in Romans, we're called to do something—actually go out and help them. That's radical! It's actually upside down from what the world would say. Again, there's an unseen factor here. What are these fiery coals? What is that about? The fiery coals were placed on the altar in the Temple when they made sacrifice. The fiery coals represent cleansing fire. So, what the Spirit of God is saying here is that as you pray for your enemies, that will cause the Spirit of God to move in their lives and this cleansing fire will come into their lives and they will be changed! So, you will have something better than having your enemies just stay away from you. You'll have your enemies transformed! What an awesome promise! But it's totally upside down: Pray for and feed your enemies.

Third Upside Down Concept

When confronted with evil, the world would say fight back with a stronger force. When we're confronted with evil people in our society, we want to bring judgment upon those people. Right? That's the way of the world, but here's what Romans says.

Romans 12:21 *Do not be conquered by evil,* [That sounds good! But then the rest of the verse is a little hard.] *but conquer evil with good.* So, what does this mean? This means if somebody is doing evil to you, do good to them. And again there is the unseen factor that God will use your doing good to convict and change that person. (Now I don't necessarily mean evil that physically harms you. You may need to get away from that person.)

There's also another application of this verse—a personal application. What happens when evil is ruling you? When evil is causing you to sin—tempting you to do things that are wrong; when you are being controlled by evil. This verse is saying, *"Do not be conquered by evil. Don't let it rule over you. But conquer evil with good."* This is very practical advice here. What it's saying is, if you're being tempted to do evil, don't just sit at home and say, "I'm not going to do evil. I'm not going to do that." Go out and do some good. Occupy yourself with doing good and that will help you to resist the temptation to do evil. So, don't be conquered by evil, but overcome evil with good.

Fourth Upside Down Concept

How about this one? To be free, we must fight against oppression. We must stand up for our rights. We must make sure that nobody takes advantage of us. That's what the world teaches about freedom, right? But listen to what the upside down advice from the Lord is.

John 8:32 *You will know the truth, and the truth will set you free.*

So, to be free, you must learn and understand what the truth is. You must get through the deceptions of this world which are placed there by our adversary. You must get through those to the truth. And what we see here is that true freedom is on the inside. You can be a prisoner in jail. I've known people who have been in jail and have been totally free because they have freedom on the inside. They understood the truth. And what is that truth? They understand that the purpose of our lives is to serve God. Even if they landed in jail because they weren't serving God, if they turn and start serving God while they are in jail, they're free. They're totally free. Someday they might also get out, but they're free on the inside. You shall know the truth and the truth will set you free.

Fifth Upside Down Concept

To have direction for your life, to know where you're going, to know what you're supposed to do, the world would say do research. Consult wise people. And here's the one that gets me because I'm a lot like our father, Jacob. Think through all the possibilities. Think of life as if it was a chess game. You know, some of these chess masters, they can anticipate 20 to 30 moves in advance. Many people think that's the way to be successful in life. Just figure out, if I do this, this will happen, and if I do that, that will happen. Those are people who are like Jacob, like I am—schemers. Do you ever have that problem? You're mind is running full speed, I'll do this and then this and this will happen. I think I see you nodding your head. Well, listen to what the Lord says the upside down Kingdom is like.

Proverbs 3:5-6 (NKJV) *Trust in the Lord with all your heart, And lean not on your own understanding; In all your ways acknowledge Him, And He shall direct your path.*

This is totally upside down from what the world says because it's saying here, "Don't try to do things based on your own understanding." Why is that? It's because our understanding as human beings is finite. We can't see the future. We can't see around the next corner. But there is someone who can see around the corner. Who is that? God can see around the corner.

Here's an example I've used before. Let's say I'm walking down the road and I come to a fork. I look down this way. It looks like a nice, smooth road. It goes on for awhile and I see a curve, but I can't see around the curve. I look down the other way. Oh, it's a broken, bumpy road. And I look down a ways and there's a curve and I can't see around the curve. Well, what would I choose? I would choose the smooth road because it's smooth as far as I can see, right? But what's around those curves? There could be an abyss around that curve. There could be a volcano! And there could be a pleasant, beautiful lake around the rough curve. I don't know. But somebody is up above looking down. That's the Lord. He can see around those curves. That's the essence of this verse. If we trust in Him to direct our paths, He'll show us even the paths we can't see.

Now, the problem I think all of us have with this verse, at least I have, is that it uses the word "all" twice. Do you see that? In verse 5 it says, *"Trust in the Lord with ALL your heart."* And then in verse 6 it says, *"In ALL your ways acknowledge Him."* I think that's the thing most of us struggle with because we don't know our own heart. We think we're trusting in Him with all our heart, but we're not really.

"In all your ways...." So often we come up against something— at least I do (I won't project my sins onto you.)—I come up against something and I think, "Oh, I can handle this. I don't need to pray about this. I can just go ahead and do this. I know how to do it!" But

that's not seeking Him and acknowledging Him in ALL of our ways. This "*acknowledge*" is an interesting word, too, because it's really "knowledge" —knowing Him. In other words, in all the ways that we go, know Him in those ways. Know what He wants. Know how He is leading us in those ways.

Sixth Upside Down Concept

To be wise—we all want to be wise. Do you know anyone who doesn't want to be wise? To be wise, get a lot of education. Study hard. And, of course, be old. Wisdom comes with age, right?

Well, the Kingdom of God is upside down.

Proverbs 9:10 (NKJV) *The fear of the Lord is the beginning of wisdom; and the knowledge of the Holy One is understanding.*

The fear of the Lord is the BEGINNING of wisdom! You don't even have any wisdom, according to God, unless you have the fear of the Lord. Now what IS the fear of the Lord? People get confused by this. The fear of the Lord is not something that makes you afraid of being in God's presence. That kind of fear drives you away from God. The fear of the Lord is reverence, respect, and obedience to God. That kind of fear draws you TO God. So, the fear of the Lord is the beginning of wisdom.

Seventh Upside Down Concept

Okay, two more here and then we will wrap up.

To deal with the pressures of life…. Oh, our society has lots of ways to deal with the pressures of life. You can take pills. Right? You can drink. You can use other kinds of drugs. You can go talk to a psychiatrist. You can share with friends and some of the pressure will go away.

Listen to what the Word of God says.

Philippians 4:6-7 *Don't worry about anything. On the contrary, make your request known to God by prayer and petition with thanksgiving. 7 Then God's shalom, passing all understanding will keep your heart and your mind safe in union with the Messiah Yeshua.*

So, yes, you are supposed to tell somebody, but not the psychiatrist. Nothing against psychiatrists, but what it's saying here is when you have problems, tell God! Pray about your troubles. Give them to God. Make your requests known to Him. And notice that it says, "with thanksgiving." Well, the reason it says "thanksgiving" is because when you make your request known to God and you feel like He's going to answer, then you can be thankful. If you have the faith to believe He will answer, you will be thankful. Then it says, *"God's shalom,"* or *"the peace of God."* I remember when I was a brand new believer, receiving this shalom, this peace just by praying. It did pass all understanding. You can't figure out where it comes from. It's just all of a sudden you have peace. I've experienced that so many times, I can't tell you. When I've taken some things that troubled me and I've prayed about them and I've committed them to God, saying, "Thank You, Lord. I'm putting them in Your hands and leaving them there," then the peace of God just comes upon me

Final Upside Down Concept

This one is a really important one.

The world says, if you want to save your life, if you want to preserve your life, what do you do? You take good care of yourself. You have the best doctors. You make sure that nobody is in control of you, that you are the one in control of your circumstances. You make and save enough money so you can live well. This is what the world says is how you save or prolong your life, right?

Listen to what the Lord says about this.

Luke 9:24 (NKJV) *Whoever desires to save his life will lose it, but whoever loses His life for My sake will save it.*

"Whoever loses His life for My sake…." What is He talking about here? Well, the whole point of the teachings of Yeshua is to say that we are to give our lives to Him. We are to be obedient to Him and follow Him. We are to let Him lead us. And He has wonderful blessings for us if we'll do that. So, when we lose our lives for His sake, that's exactly what it means. It doesn't mean that we commit suicide or that we go out and purposely martyr ourselves. It means that we lay down what we want. It means we lay down our will and we say, "Lord, I want to do Your will. I want to follow Your way." And as we do that, the Lord has this incredible promise. You will save your life. So, it is simply a matter of obeying Him and serving Him and seeking Him, and we will save our life.

Well, I'm going to end there. Here are all eight of the upside down things listed for you. Read them over and then we will pray.

1. To deal with people who've harmed you, don't take revenge.
2. To deal with your enemies, care for them and love them.
3. To deal with evil, respond with good.
4. To be free, seek the truth.
5. To have direction, trust in God and don't lean on your own understanding.
6. To be wise, fear the Lord.

7. To deal with pressure, make your requests known to God with thanksgiving.
8. To save your life, lose it for Yeshua's sake.

So, let's pray.

Father, we thank You that You have revealed to us Your Kingdom and that it is an upside down Kingdom. It is totally contrary to the ways of this world. And we just come before you, Lord—I come before you and I pray for everyone reading this that you would reveal to us ways in which our thinking is not like Your thinking; ways in which we still do things in the world's way. I pray, Father, as we enter into these Ten Days of Awe, that each of us would be thinking about these upside down principles and where we've missed them—where we are still in the world's ways. We want to begin to bring these things before you, Lord, and we ask you to change those things in our lives, so that we might begin to think Your thoughts and do Your ways. So, I just ask right now, Father, for Your Spirit to begin revealing things to us.

[Do you want to have those things revealed? Just lift up your hands.]

Reveal to us, God, the ways in which we are not thinking like You or doing like You. We will be open, Lord. We will be contrite. And we ask, Father, that as You reveal those things to us, and as we repent, that You will change us into Your wonderful image.

We ask these things in the mighty Name of Yeshua our Messiah. Amen.

CHAPTER 11

UPSIDE DOWN KINGDOM
PART II

Celebrating the Torah

On Rosh Hashanah morning in 2003, we did what we do every holiday and what Jewish synagogues everywhere do every Shabbat morning. We celebrated the Torah. I'll let you peek in on how that went.

"We're going to do something this morning that is a whole lot of fun. And I hope all of you will participate with us. I have in my hand here my palm pilot! [Remember, this was 2003!] You might say, 'It looks like a phone.' That's because it is. It's both. But it's a palm. And in here all I have to do is click on the correct icon and I can bring up the Bible! Isn't that amazing?! The whole Bible exists in here in electronic form. I don't even know what kind of storage they are using, but it's in here. Palm pilots have been around for about ten years or so already.

"Now I also have here my Bible. And we think about this as having been around for thousands of years, don't we? But, you know, this form of the Bible—with pages where you can easily go from one place to another, with chapters and headings to guide you—it's only been around for about 400 years. But the Bible has been around for 3500 years! So, for 3100 years or so, the Scripture was kept for us in the form of a scroll.

"Well, we have a Torah scroll here that we're about to bring out and rejoice in because this is a time for remembering. The thing that we want to remember today, as we do this, is that God gave us His Word.

"These old Torah scrolls, like ours, are parchment scrolls that are rolled up. They are hand-lettered and they contain all five books of Moses in Hebrew. Now, we don't have a 3000-year-old Torah scroll. We have maybe a 150-year-old scroll. Yes, it is an antique.

"We are going to bring out our scroll and do what we call, Celebrating the Torah. The thing that's fun about this is that when we bring it out we rejoice that God has given us His Word. What an appropriate thing to do on this day of sounding the Shofar with shouts of joy.

"So, we're going to bring the Torah scroll out and parade it around the room as we sing the traditional Hebrew song, "*From out of Zion Comes Forth the Law.*" I would like to ask all of you to get in line behind the Torah Scroll and dance and sing and shout and give thanks to the Lord.

"Some of you might have seen the dancing over here in the corner during worship, and you might have thought, "I'd like to do that but I don't know the steps." Well, there are no steps to this dance. Okay? (Chuckles) So feel free to join in.

"Now when we do this, there's a Jewish custom to take the corner of your Tallit, your prayer shawl, kiss it and touch the scroll as it comes around. Or if you don't have a prayer shawl, you can use your Bible. This is in fulfillment of "*kissing the Son*" (Psalms 2:12). The Scroll is the Word of God, and Yeshua is what? The Living Word! So "kiss the Son!" So, let's rejoice together that God has given us both His written Word and His Living Word!"

*   *   *

At the end of the service after my message and prayer, we closed with the Post Torah Blessing. Here is how we always do that. First everyone rises and our cantor chants the blessing in Hebrew. Then we all recite it together in English.

"Blessed are You, O Lord our God, King of the universe who has given us a Torah of Truth and has planted eternal Life in our midst. Blessed are You, O Lord our God, giver of the Torah. Amen."

The Torah is then carefully covered with its special cloth covering and placed in its special place called the "Torah ark." The cantor says, "Now as they close the Torah ark, please join with me in the "*Etz Khaiyim Hee*" (The Tree of Life). We sing it in Hebrew, then we recite it together in the English.

"It is a tree of Life to those who take hold of it. And those who support it are praiseworthy. Its ways are ways of pleasantness and all its paths are peace. Bring us back, Lord, to You and we shall come. Renew our days of old. Amen. Amen."

So, that was your peek into our congregation's Torah celebration. Why not come to a Messianic synagogue and participate? I give you my personal invitation to come to ours in Rochester, NY! Visit our website at shemayisrael.org.

*   *   *

Now to continue our soul searching that we started in the last chapter, we are going to look at some more of the ways that God's thinking is so far beyond our ways of thinking and the world's ways of thinking that His ways actually seem totally opposite, or "up side down" from ours. We're going to look at a few more passages in the Scriptures today where it speaks about these upside down ways of thinking. And, again, I'd like you to receive them as a challenge, not to just say, "This is interesting" or "What does this mean?" Instead, I'd like you to ask yourself, "Am I thinking upside down like that," or "Am I still thinking world side up?" or "Is my thinking being transformed into the way God thinks?"

Now, again if you feel a little apprehensive about that, you might be thinking, "How can I change my way of thinking?" I want you to know that the grace of God is very much in that process because it is very much His desire to change all of us. And I think of the time when God was dealing with Paul about his flesh and his pride. And when Paul complains about this God says, *"My grace is sufficient for you. My power is brought to perfection in your weakness"* (2 Corinthians 12:9 NKJV and CJB).

So, if there's a way in which you're convicted and you say, "Well, I'm not thinking like that" "I'm not walking like that." Don't get discouraged. Don't get depressed about it. First believe that if God has revealed this to you, He's going to give you the way to change. It might not happen overnight, but He's going to get you to the way to be transformed.

So, let's look at some more of these upside down things with the hope that over these next ten days God will start to change us. I'm going to just tell you how the world thinks and operates, and then show you the Scripture about how God says, "No, no, that's upside down! I think differently."

Eighth Upside Down Concept
In difficult circumstances, keep a stiff upper lip. Be tough. Get through those things however you can. Isn't that the way the world teaches us? Well, here's what God says.

I Thessalonians 5:18 *In everything give thanks. For this is what God wants from you who are united with Messiah Yeshua.*

Is that a stiff upper lip? No, it's faith. It's faith saying that if I give these things to God, if I pray about them, if I tell my request to the Lord, He is going to move in these areas. So I can be thankful in every circumstance. It's also faith in the understanding that whatever circumstance comes into your life, and this is so important to grasp, *God works all things together for good to them that love Him* (Rom. 8:28). So whatever the circumstances are of your life, no matter how tough they seem, you can have faith that God is going to use them for good to transform you into the image of His Son. And that's what you can be thankful for.

Ninth Upside Down Concept
The world teaches that to be rich, to have a lot of resources, to have a lot of things and money, you have to look out for number one. You have to guard your investments. You have to be competitive—weed out all your competitors. You have to outsmart others. You have to invest well and you have to save! Right? You have to gather it all and find a good place to put it.

Isn't that the way the world teaches? Well, listen to what God's economic system is. It's not capitalism. It's not socialism. It's not communism. But it's upside down because God says, "Give!"

Luke 6:38 (NKJV) *Give, and it will be given to you: good measure, pressed down, shaken together, and running over will be put into your bosom. For with the same measure that you use, it will be measured back to you.*

Isn't that totally upside down? If you want to be rich, if you want to be prosperous, give! Now this shouldn't be our motivation for giving. The motivation for giving should be out of love to help, to see God's Kingdom extended. But! God gives us this promise as an encouragement. He gives us this promise so that we can have faith to step out and give. And God will take care of us. Why does God have to encourage us with a promise? Because it's hard to give! It's hard to give up time, money or energy if you think that you're the only one that's taking care of you. But God is taking care of you. He will supply. The promise here is awesome. *"Pressed down, shaken together."* That's like if you were to take a container, let's say a bucket for flour, and you pour the flour in there and it fills it up. Now if you were to shake it and then to take something and press on it, you know what would happen? You could put a lot more flour in there because it would compress down. That's how He says He's going to do it, *"pressed down and shaken together."*

Now how can this be? It is because there is another unseen factor here. And the unseen factor is that God is the one who arranges for the giving back to us. We have no control over that. We get the excitement of waiting to see what God will do!

I tell you we have seen this so wonderfully since we started giving away food a few years ago. We had never done anything like this in our congregation before. We started to do this as an act of faith. And it has been absolutely amazing! The first remarkable thing is where we get the food to give away! And then second is how so many people come and volunteer to help us. We've got people from several different congregations helping. And then people have started giving us money to fix things up so we can do this better. We've even had an anonymous donation to remodel our kitchen because we're doing this. It's really not for any other reason. We've also been given a van. It isn't working yet, but we're going to get it working. When people see you giving, they want to get on board. They want to get along side of that. So *"give and it shall be given to you."*

Tenth Upside Down Concept

However, when you do give, the world says if you want to get some benefit from it, from giving, you have to let everyone know you're doing it! You have to get credit for it! If you start a grant or a foundation or something like that, you should put your name on it.

Well, the Kingdom of God has totally different rules.

Matthew 6:2-4 (CJB) *So, when you do tzedakah,* [That's Hebrew for "good deeds."] *don't announce it with trumpets to win people's praise, like the hypocrites in the synagogues and on the streets. Yes! I tell you, they have their reward already! But you, when you do tzedakah, don't even let your left hand know what your right hand is doing. Then your tzedakah will be in secret; and your Father, who sees what you do in secret, will reward you.*

That is just the most amazing passage. What it's basically saying is if you do it in a way that people reward you for it, God won't bother! But if you do it in a way that keeps it secret, God will reward you for it.

Now, I don't personally apply this to not getting a tax break for donations. Some of you may think of it that way. But I do list my giving on my income tax return. I think our government put that in place to encourage contributions to non-profit organizations. So I don't want anybody to say that I told you to stop doing that—to stop getting a tax receipt and getting it off your income taxes. Remember it's not like you're getting more because you do that. It's that the government isn't taking away more. Okay? So, I encourage you to keep doing that.

I believe God put this rule in place to encourage and enable giving. Keeping my giving a secret enables me to give more because God rewards me with more to give!

Eleventh Upside Down Concept

Well, how about this next one?

To have lasting riches, you have to know how to guard your things from thieves. You have to find good investments. You have to find a safe bank to put it in. You have to keep others from even knowing you have it! Or they might steal it away! You have to hide all the things that you have. Listen to what the Lord says that is upside down from that.

Matthew 6:19-20 *"Do not store up for yourselves wealth here on earth, where moths and rust destroy, and burglars break in and steal. Instead, store up for yourselves wealth in heaven, where neither moth nor rust destroys, and burglars do not break in or steal.*

So to have lasting riches, don't even think about the things here on earth. Store up treasure in heaven. Now, let's think about this a minute. What is the lasting fruit of our lives? Will it be that we built a beautiful home or that we had a great car or that we left a lot of money to our off-spring? On the Day of Judgment when the works that we do that are of value to God are preserved and the other works are burned up with fire, do you think that house is going to last? Of course not! What is going to last? The things that we do out of love and out of obedience to the Lord. The things that we do in bringing other people into the Kingdom. The things that we do to cause others to bear fruit. That's the lasting fruit that we will have. Just think about how worthless all the accomplishments of this world will seem when our fruit is judged on that day! So it's upside down.

Twelfth Upside Down Concept

To be promoted, you have to perform the best and advertise it. Make sure you're given credit for your accomplishments. And convince others you are the best. But the Kingdom of God is totally upside down on this, too.

Matthew 23:12 ... for whoever promotes himself will be humbled, and whoever humbles himself will be promoted.

So, how do you humble yourself when you do something good? Well, you don't take credit for it. Give credit to the others who worked with you! Give credit to the Lord who inspired it! And notice what it says. This is very important to see here. It says if you do promote yourself, you WILL BE humbled. You know what that means? That means God will humble you! We don't want God humbling us! The better alternative is to humble ourselves. It's always easier to humble yourself than to have God humble you. Actually, recently I've been very frequently humbled by the Lord. And it's not pleasant! But you know, I've come to value it. Because it shows me those places that really need to change.

Thirteenth Upside Down Concept

Alright, we're down to the last two.

The world teaches that to be a leader, you have to dominate everyone else. You have to be able to boss people around. You have to be able to maybe intimidate people—and have the goods on them. That's how some leaders operate. They're able to blackmail other people. They know the things that would embarrass them.

Or you have to be so charismatic that people will like you and follow you. Those are the three marks of a leader in this world: 1. having charisma—being a great orator so people follow you, 2. having the goods on people and 3. using intimidation. Those are how some of the great dictators—I shouldn't say "great"—some of the *terrible* dictators of this world have functioned. But listen to what Yeshua says.

Matthew 20:25-26 *But Yeshua called them and said, "You know that among the Goyim (or among the Gentiles, among the non believers), those who are supposed to rule them become tyrants, and their superiors become dictators (dominators). Among you, it must not be like that. On the contrary, whoever among you wants to be a leader must become your servant.*

Isn't that upside down? Do you see how upside down that is? If you want to lead, serve! If you want to go up, go down!

Sounds crazy, but if you think about this for awhile, it actually makes right side up sense. Because if there's a group of people that are milling around trying to figure out what to do, you know what they need? They need a leader! A group of people doesn't get anywhere without a leader. So, a leader really does <u>serve</u> the people. But he has to have an attitude of service, not an attitude that the people are doing things for his benefit. He needs the attitude that he is doing things for the people whom he is serving. And I've found that you don't get to lead in the Kingdom of God, in God's organization, until you demonstrate that you're a good servant. Because if you're going to rule over the people and dominate and be a tyrant, God isn't going to put you in leadership. It has to be by being that best servant.

Fourteenth Upside Down Concept
Okay, the last one.

To save your life you have to have really good medical care. You have to have good insurance. You have to be careful that you don't get infected somewhere. You have to be careful of all the diseases that are going around. And in a lot of ways, you have to have control of your life.

You know, many people when they get to be very old, are very afraid of going into a care place where they don't have control. That's the big issue. I remember my father when he was up into his eighties, the big thing with him was he wanted to keep driving because as long as he could keep driving that car, he had control of his life. He could go where he wanted and do what he wanted.

So, that control of our lives, that's the thing—not letting anybody take advantage of us—those are the things that help us keep our lives, that save our lives. But look at what the Lord said.

Mark 8:35 (NKJV) *For whoever desires to save his life will lose it, but whoever loses his life for My sake and the Gospel's will save it.*

Okay, yes, I tricked you. I did this one in the last chapter. But it is so important that I wanted to go over it again. Don't you agree it is important and very, very upside down? What's God saying to us here? Well, we're called to be part of the Kingdom of God, and one of the benefits of being part of the Kingdom of God is something called eternal life. We're told that we're going to live forever, not necessarily in this mortal body, but we are going to live forever. And how do we come into that eternal life? Well, we come into that eternal life by giving our lives to Him. So, He's saying that as you lay down your life for Him, as you give your life to Him, you receive Life. You save your life. But if you refuse to do that, if you say, "No, I'm going to run my own life. I'm never going to submit to You as Lord," well, the Scriptures tell us that we don't get life.

We get eternal death. And that's eternal separation from God which is a frightful prospect. So, in order to save your life, you must lose it. What does it mean to lose it? To lose it means I'm not going to keep control of it. I'm going to give the control over to the Lord. And I'm going to let Him be the One who shows me what to do.

I think the greatest example is what is traditionally taught in the synagogues on this holiday, the story of Abraham and Isaac. So, here Abraham was promised a son. For years and years he waited. Finally he had this son that he was promised—Isaac, and then the Lord says, "Go and sacrifice your son." And what did he do? He said he would do it. And then he went and did it. And the Lord stopped him just at the last instant before he actually did it. He said, "I was just testing you, Abraham." But what was he testing about Abraham? He was testing Abraham as to whether he would give everything to the Lord. Would he be obedient even of the thing he treasured the most? And that's what this is talking about. If you want to save your life, you lose it. But if you lose your life for His sake and for the Gospel—for the spreading of the Kingdom of God—you will save it.

So, that's the upside down Kingdom.

Here's a list of all fourteen of them.
1. To deal with people who've harmed you, don't take revenge.
2. To deal with your enemies, care for them and love them.
3. To deal with evil, respond with good.
4. To be free, you must know the truth.
5. To have direction, trust in God and don't lean on your own understanding.
6. To be wise, fear the Lord.
7. To deal with pressure, make your requests known to God with thanksgiving.
8. In difficult circumstances, give thanks.
9. Give and it shall be given unto you.
10. To be rewarded for your good deeds, don't brag about them.
11. To have lasting riches, store up your treasures in heaven.
12. To be promoted, humble yourself.
13. To be a leader, become a servant.
14. To save your life, lose it for Yeshua's sake and the Gospel's.

Let's pray.

Father we thank You for these Ten Days that are coming up. I thank You right now for this list of all these upside down ways in which You think and do things. And I pray Father that we would consider these passages over these next ten days. And we ask You right now, Lord, in the Name of Yeshua, that Your Spirit, Your Ruakh, would reveal to us the ways in which we are not thinking according to Your ways and doing according to Your deeds. Reveal to us, Lord, that we might change, that we might operate according to the Laws of Your Kingdom and not the laws of this world; that we would function in a different way—Your way, O God. And as You promised us in Your Word, Lord, we ask You to change these things. We trust You that You will accomplish these changes in our lives. And we will be conformed more and more into Your wonderful image. And we thank You in the mighty Name of Yeshua. Amen.

CHAPTER 12

THE JOY OF THE LORD IS OUR STRENGTH

We know now that even we Y'hudim Mishikhim and Gerim Mishikhim are to have an attitude of t'shuvah, of turning around, of repenting during these coming Yomim Norim, the Ten Days of Awe. We also have learned in previous chapters that the essence of t'shuvah is having a contrite heart.

Well, there is a wonderful story in Scripture about some people who had contrite hearts. The Israelites had returned years before from Babylonian captivity with the amazing favor of the Persian king, Cyrus. Persia conquered Babylon and then allowed the captive Jews to return to their homeland. They had rebuilt the Temple, their own houses, and the city wall, while at the same time overcoming lots of opposition. They had also re-started the regular sacrifices.

Nehemiah 8:1 ... *all the people gathered with one accord in the open space in front of the Water Gate and asked Ezra the Torah-teacher to bring the scroll of the Torah of Moshe, which ADONAI had commanded Isra'el.*

With one accord—in unity! They told Ezra to read to them. Ezra did not initiate this reading. What did he read? The Torah—Law of Moses, which is Genesis through Deuteronomy.

Nehemiah 8:2 *Ezra the cohen brought the Torah before the assembly, which consisted of men, women and all children old enough to understand ....*

Notice, it even included children.

(Cont.) *It was the first day of the seventh month.*

So, Rosh Hashanah!

Nehemiah 8:3 *Facing the open space in front of the Water Gate, he read from it to the men, the women and the children who could understand from early morning until noon; and all the people listened attentively to the scroll of the Torah.*

He read from early morning until noon. That's at least four hours! And all the people listened attentively. Have you ever attended a four hour preaching service? Would you want to? Would you be able to pay attention the whole time?

Nehemiah 8:4-7 *Ezra the Torah-teacher stood on a wood platform which they had made for the purpose; beside him on his right stood* (six men) *...; while on his left were* (seven men) *.... 5 Ezra opened the scroll where all the people could see him, because he was higher than all the people; when he opened it, all the people rose to their feet.*

6 Ezra blessed ADONAI, the great God; and all the people answered, "Amen! Amen!" as they lifted up their hands, bowed their heads and fell prostrate before ADONAI with their faces to the ground. 7 The L'vi'im (Levites) *... explained the Torah to the people, while the people remained in their places.*

It appears to me that they stood while listening to the reading. Do you see where it says they stood up? If you want to stand while you read, you can. We've only got a few more verses.

Nehemiah 8:8 *They read clearly from the scroll, in the Torah of God, translated it, and enabled them to understand the sense of what was being read.*

Much like what I am doing now. Commenting. Clarifying.

Nehemiah 8:9 *Nechemyah (Nehemiah) the Tirshata (Governor), Ezra the cohen and Torah-teacher and the L'vi'im (Levites) who taught the people said to all the people, "Today is consecrated to ADONAI your God; don't be mournful, don't weep." For all the people had been weeping when they heard the words of the Torah.*

What would they have heard that would have made them weep? It was the Laws they had not been keeping. The Temple had been rebuilt. They were making offerings, yet they hadn't been keeping the Laws concerning Temple worship, concerning the Moadim; Laws concerning how they should treat servants and Laws concerning agriculture—Laws about everything in life.

Why did they weep? I believe it was in repentance, but I believe they also wept in fear. They knew there were curses for those who didn't obey. Ezra had read those curses to them.

Deuteronomy 27:26 *"'A curse on anyone who does not confirm the words of this Torah by putting them into practice.' All the people are to say, 'Amen!'"*

They knew they deserved punishment for neglecting His law.

Nehemiah 8:10 *Then he said to them, "Go, eat rich food, drink sweet drinks, and send portions to those who can't provide for themselves; for today is consecrated* (holy) *to our Lord. Don't be sad, because the joy of the ADONAI is your strength."*

The Hebrew here is "Ki khed-vat ADONAI he mah-ooz-khem." *"For the joy of the LORD is your strength"* (NKJV) is a very familiar phrase. We sing it. You probably know it by heart. But what does it mean exactly? I don't know how you understand the phrase, but here's what I've always understood it to be saying. "Have the joy of the Lord in you and it will strengthen you." This is true. But, let's look at what it really says in context.

Ezra told them, "This day is consecrated to the Lord" —meaning He considers it holy. Why does God consider Rosh Hashanah holy? Well, I believe there are four reasons.

1. It was His Moad, Yom Teruah. A Moad by definition is a holy day.

2. The people were in unity: "*... all the people gathered with one accord in the open space in front of the Water Gate and asked Ezra the Torah-teacher to bring the scroll of the Torah of Moshe*" God considers it holy when His children are in unity, especially when they are in unity wanting to hear from Him, and His word.

3. They listened: "*and all the people listened attentively to the scroll of the Torah.*" Not only did they ask to have the Word read, but they really listened—all of them, including the children!

4. They were touched: "*all the people wept, when they heard the words of the Law*" (NKJV). They didn't just hear the words of the Law, they were so touched in their hearts that they wept openly. Something holy was happening in their hearts.

Ezra and Nehemiah said, "*The day is holy to the Lord. Do not sorrow*" (NKJV).

Why shouldn't the people sorrow? They were convicted of their great sin. But they were told, don't sorrow because "*the joy of ADONAI is your strength*" This doesn't quite make sense, at least how I've always understood it: "have the joy of the Lord in you and it will strengthen you." I wouldn't have said that to a people who were repenting. The people didn't need strength; they needed to be comforted in their great sorrow and fear.

So I began to study the Hebrew and have concluded that the words "*the joy of ADONAI is your strength*" is a poor translation.

"Ki khed-vat ADONAI he" means "for the joy of ADONAI it is." So far it is good.

"Mah-ooz-khem" is translated "your strength," but this is a poor translation. "Mah-ooz-khem" actually means "*fortified place; defense, fortress, stronghold.*" So, a more correct translation would be "*the joy of ADONAI is your defense, stronghold, fortress*"

So, in other words what this passage is really saying is, "You have made the Lord have joy. You have caused His heart to rejoice by your repentance. And His joy is your stronghold. His joy is your defense against the punishment and curses you should have received for violating His laws.

Now, let's go back over it. How did they make Adonai have joy? Much the same way my congregation makes me, as their rabbi, have joy:

- By being in unity about wanting to hear God's Word
- By listening intently when God's Word is read and explained
  By openly weeping in repentance, in fear of the Lord, and fear of the consequences of sin
- By having contrite hearts

Now, the question is, "Does our repentance really bring joy to God?" Let's read and see.

Luke 15:10 *In the same way, I tell you, there is joy among God's angels when one sinner repents.*

It brings joy to the angels!

2 Corinthians 7:9 *Now I rejoice, not that you were made sorry, but that your sorrow led to repentance ....*

The Corinthians' repentance brought joy to Paul!

Isaiah 66:2 *...on this one will I look: on him who is poor and of a contrite spirit, and who trembles at My Word.*

Part of being contrite is trembling and fearing His Word. God looks with favor on the contrite. And do you remember what else it means?

Contrite means being:
- Open to correction from the Lord. (This correction may come through others.)
- Willing to see our shortcomings
- Willing to see things about ourselves through other's eyes
- Wiling to repent, to do t'shuvah, make changes in our lives

So, having a contrite spirit causes joy to the Lord. His joy over our repentance is our stronghold or defense against the consequences of our sin; against the punishment we deserve; and against the curses we have incurred by our disobedience.

Nehemiah 8:11-12 *In this way the L'vi'im* (Levites) *quieted the people, as they said, "Be quiet, for today is holy; don't be sad." 12 Then the people went off to eat, drink, send portions and celebrate; because they had understood the words that had been proclaimed to them.*

Because they understood the words proclaimed to them, they could celebrate rather than weep. Do you understand the words just declared to you?

We are beginning the Ten Days of Awe which are God's especially Appointed Time for having contrite hearts. By having a contrite attitude, you will make these days holy to the Lord. You will bring joy to His heart. If your repentance is from your heart, you can celebrate because God sees your heart. It is so precious to Him that it will be a stronghold to protect you from the consequences of your sin.

Perhaps you're thinking I haven't sinned recently, so why do I need to be contrite? That attitude is evidence of an un-contrite heart. Do you still have a human nature? Do you still struggle against your carnal nature or are you so spiritually mature you don't have a carnal nature any more? How about your iniquity, your inclination to evil, your flesh? Do you still struggle with pride, envy, exaltation of self, doubt, bitterness, anger, gossip, evil thoughts, lust, greed, covetousness? Any of those? We're supposed to be contrite about those things.

Even if we don't give in to our carnal natures—our inclination to evil—we still need to be contrite about that being our nature. That's what Paul meant when he said he was the chief of sinners.

1 Timothy 1:15 *So here is a statement you can trust, one that fully deserves to be accepted: the Messiah came into the world to save sinners, and I'm the number one sinner!*

As I pointed out before, he says "I am the number one sinner", not I was the number one sinner. Do you think Paul was still going around breaking God's laws? In the Greek, "hamartia" is used for sin and iniquity. Here it means iniquity. He meant he was still struggling with iniquity—with his carnal nature. Since he knew himself better than anyone else knew him, he could say he was the number one.

We need to be thankful the Lord has made a way for our sins to be atoned for and our iniquity to be borne.

Isaiah 53:5-6 (NKJV) *But He was wounded for our transgressions, He was bruised for our iniquities; the chastisement for our peace was upon Him, and by His stripes we are healed. 6 All we like sheep have gone astray; we have turned, every one, to his own way; and the LORD has laid on Him the iniquity of us all.*

I can think of another meaning of "the joy of the Lord is our stronghold" or as the literal Hebrew would put it, "the joy of the Lord, He is our stronghold." Who is the "he" who is the joy of the Lord? It's Yeshua! He is our stronghold. He is the reason we don't have to experience the consequences of our sin and iniquity because He paid the price by being wounded for our transgressions, and bruised for our iniquities.

So, during the Yomim Norim, the Ten Days of Awe:
- Pray for contrite hearts during the whole time.
- Pray for Ruakh HaKodesh to reveal our iniquity to us.
- Pray for a heart of repentance.
- Pray for our repentance to be so genuine that God would have joy over it.
- Pray that His joy would be our stronghold against the consequences of our iniquity.
- Give thanks that Yeshua is the Joy of the Lord.
- Give thanks that He is our stronghold against the consequences of our sin and iniquity.
- Give thanks that He was wounded for our transgressions and bruised for our iniquity.

- Pray for those who have never received Him as that stronghold to receive Him now.
- Pray for us to know when our repentance is complete.
- Pray for the Ruakh HaKodesh to bring us to times of celebration.

<u>CHAPTER 13</u>

A TIME TO HEAL
PART I

Rosh Hashanah begins a season known in the Jewish community as "The High Holidays." In today's Jewish culture these holidays are, I think, most primarily marked by having family gatherings and attending meetings—long meetings.

The Biblical meaning of this time of the year is very significant. In the book of Leviticus there are three Moadim that are commanded for this part of the year. They are Appointed Times that God has appointed for something to happen. These Appointed Times have a theme to them that runs through them. It starts with Rosh Hashanah which is Yom Teruah a "Day of Remembrance with the Sounding of the Shofar and Shouts of Joy." And what are we to remember? Well, as I've said, I believe we are to remember God Himself. Remember that He is the awesome Creator. Remember His Word—the Laws—the instructions that He gave us. And remember our past year—the good things that God did, the struggles we've had. And perhaps also remember the ways in which we have fallen short in the last year.

In the afternoon of this day there's a traditional ceremony we mentioned before, called Tashlikh. It's a very important ceremony where we go out to a stream and cast bread crumbs into the water in fulfillment of Micah 7:19 (NKJV) that says, "*You will cast all our sins into the depths of the sea.*" It's important because the Tashlikh reminds us that at the end of the Yomim Norim there is forgiveness—that these Ten Days are not to be entered into with a very sad attitude of, "Oh, I have to try to find out the things that I'm struggling with. How terrible that I'll find some of these things out," but a hopeful attitude of "I'm going to find these things out and this is going to help me because I'm going to deal with those things and God's going to help me deal with them."

Dealing with those things happens on Yom Kippur—the Day of Atonement—the day in the Bible when atonement was made for the whole nation of Israel. All who were repentant were covered by that atonement—the covering over of sin. Because of that atonement, four days later there is a holiday of great joy where the atonement is celebrated. It's called Sukkot—The Feast of Tabernacles. The joy is there because the people know that the things that have come up during the Ten Days have been dealt with and have been forgiven. It's also a time of thanksgiving for the provision of food for the year and praying for rain for the next year.

In the year 2005, as these holidays were drawing near, I began to pray about what the theme should be and where we should go, and God gave me something new: a series of messages with a title based on the phrase in Ecclesiastes 3:3—a very familiar passage in the Bible—where it talks about there being "a time for this and a time for that." That's why the title is "A Time for Healing."

The direction I got from the Spirit of God about this is that there is healing power in these three Appointed Times. There's healing power for physical ailments and emotional ailments, and there's power to keep us in health. So, I'm very excited about this. I hope you are, too, because I believe that when we get to the end of this, we're not just going to be rejoicing that we've been forgiven of things, but that we've been healed of things. Are you excited about that?! Good!

Over the course of the series I'll be addressing some questions that I'm going to throw out to you now. You might want to underline them. I think that they are very interesting questions. First, "Why is our healing prayer so ineffective?" I've talked to many Messianic rabbis and pastors and they all feel like they should have a higher batting average. Yes, when we pray, people do get healed, but it's not the percentage we'd like to see. Everybody struggles with this. The second question I'm going to look at is, "What does the Bible say about the source of sickness and disease?" Where do they come from? The third question is, "Does God want to heal us?" The fourth one is, "Is there a block to our healing prayers?" The fifth is, "How can I learn what that block is in my life?" The sixth is, "Beyond healing, how can I walk in health?"

Answering these questions will lead us through a process that will involve some humbling because we are going to have to be willing to let the Spirit of God show us if there's something in us that needs to change. It will involve some revelation—some repentance—some faith. And I believe it's going to come to some healing in your life. I was with eleven Messianic rabbis a while back down at Ground Zero. We got to spend some time to pray together and this question came up immediately. I thought about it later. There were hundreds of years of ministry represented amongst those eleven men and their wives—hundreds of years, yet all of us agreed that our batting average was too low—that we need to be more affective in this area of praying for the sick.

So, we're going to look now into what the Bible says about sickness and disease. Where does sickness come from? What is its source? So let me take you all the way back to the time of creation and the Garden of Eden. Understand with me that the Bible describes that God created human beings and He put them in a place called "Gan Eden," in Hebrew, or the "Garden of Eden" in English. It was a wonderful, perfect place and He gave them all that they needed to live in that place in perfect happiness and harmony and joy, and to live in connection with Him. And He set one condition before them. And I believe it was a test. Let's read the condition.

Genesis 2:16-17 (NKJV)   *And the Lord commanded man saying, "Of every tree of the garden you may freely eat, but of the Tree of Knowledge of Good and Evil, you shall not eat; for in that day that you eat of it, you will surely die."*

Well, the penalty of the disobedience of this was death. And as we read on in the book of Genesis, our fore-parents Adam and Eve were tempted by the adversary, ha-satan.

Genesis 3:6   *When the woman saw that the tree was good for food, that it had a pleasing appearance and that the tree was desirable for making one wise, she took some of its fruit and ate. She also gave some to her husband, who was with her; and he ate.*

And so these two gave into temptation and they disobeyed God. The consequences of that rebellion came upon them and upon all their offspring. The Bible speaks of a loss of innocence and a loss of immortality. We understand from this that death did not exist before this rebellion—not even in the animals. In fact, the way I understand it, there were no meat-eating animals. Every animal was a vegetarian. So, there was no death. But this all changed because of Adam and Eve's disobedience—which we call, "the fall of man."

So, here's the question. If there was no death, do you think there was sickness? I don't believe there was any sickness or disease before that. Death, disease, and physical decay of our bodies due to old age became part of life on earth because of sin! Now, I'm not the only one who has thought this. In the New Covenant, this is what we read.

Romans 5:12 *It was through one individual that sin entered the world, and through sin, death; and in this way death passed through to the whole human race, inasmuch as everyone sinned.*

So because Adam's offspring (us and all our relatives) have inherited the fallen nature, we sin also. And death, decay, and disease have ever since been a part of life on this earth. Now the Tanakh, the Old Testament, goes on to describe God's plan to deal with this mess that was caused by the fall of man. God began by forming relationships with individual people. He formed a relationship with a man named Enoch, then with a man named Noah, then Abraham and Isaac and Jacob. With each of these people, after Enoch, He established a covenant, an agreement, a contract. Each of these people taught their children the ways of God.

Then God established a covenant through a man named Moses. Moses received from God instructions on how to deal with sin. The instructions were that Moses was to put into place a system of sacrifices. Innocent animals were to be sacrificed to pay the price for the sin of the people. So the innocent animal would die instead of the guilty person. And, of course, the guilty person had to be repentant. They had to want to be forgiven. If you were a person who didn't care, it didn't work.

But after He established this covenant with Israel, God spoke further to us through Moses connecting sickness with sin and health with obedience. I'd like you to look at this verse. This was just as our forefathers were coming out of Egypt. God gave them instructions. In fact, He was about to give them the Ten Commandments and the written Law.

Exodus 15:26 *He said, "If you will listen intently to the voice of ADONAI your God, do what he considers right, pay attention to his mitzvot* (commandments) *and observe his laws, I will not afflict you with any of the diseases I brought on the Egyptians; because I am ADONAI your healer."* The Hebrew is *"... Ani ADONAI roph-eh-khah." "I am ADONAI who heals you."* What God was doing in that phrase is He was naming Himself. He was saying, "This is one of My names, 'ADONAI your healer.' " So, this promise to Israel is really a promise of a disease-free society if the people are obedient. And, of course, the sicknesses that God was talking about include the ten plagues that He brought upon Egypt.

I'd like to point out that scientists are aware today that there are sicknesses that are directly connected to or are the result of sin. Are you aware of that? We have a plague in this world of huge dimensions called AIDS! And what is it a result of? It's the result of sin! It's the sin of sexual immorality that causes this plague. So, I want you to see here that God's instruction was that health is dependent on obedience, and disease is connected with disobedience. Now, of course, this connects diseases with many kinds of disobedience because God gave us many commandments. God gave us commandments concerning adultery, stealing, lying—all of these and many more. When we disobey these commandments, this gives the potential for disease in our midst.

Now the promise was to Israel as a nation, but I personally believe, and I think you will agree with me as we go through this, that this promise also applies to individuals, and that this promise still applies under the New Covenant—perhaps even more so.

And here's the point that I hope you get excited about. If it's true that there's a connection between sickness and sin, then, to me, that is a great source of hope because there are lots of sicknesses that doctors don't know how to deal with, but we do know how to deal with sin! And if we can identify those connections and deal with those sins, we have some hope for healing some of those things that doctors are not able to cure.

So, what have the Jewish Holidays got to do with this whole thing—this connection between health and obedience, and sickness and sin? Well, as I mentioned before, the holidays are days on which God has made an appointment with us. Why is that significant? Well, when people make appointments with me, they say, "Jim, can I have an appointment? I want to come in and talk to you about something." So I make an appointment with them. And when they come in and sit down with me, because they've made the appointment, I say to them, "Well, what did you want to talk about?" The agenda is theirs, not mine.

Now, we can call upon God at any time. It's like us making an appointment with God. We set the agenda. We go to God and we say, "Oh, God, help me with this!" "Oh, God, speak to me about that!" "Oh, God, give me direction for this!" It's our agenda. But when God sets an appointment with us, He has the agenda! That's one of the great powers of what is being revived through the Messianic Movement: That we are looking at these Moadim and we're saying, "Okay, what does God want to do during these Appointed Times? What does He want to say?"

Now, I believe the period of the Ten Days of Awe is also an Appointed Time. So, it's very clear to me that these Ten Days have a very clear agenda for us from God. The agenda is introspection. They are days of asking God to reveal things to us, to answer the question, "Are there things that we are doing that are not pleasing to You, Lord?" I believe that we are going to have a very fruitful time because it's God's time to do this! You may have gone to Him in June or in April and said, "Lord, show me if there's anything that I need to change in my life" and didn't hear anything. But this time, because it's God's Appointed Time to reveal those things, I believe we are going to hear from Him.

Now, the other part of the tradition of Rosh Hashanah or Yom Teruah that connects with this is the Shofar because in Jewish tradition, the reason for the Shofar sounding is to wake us up. It's a holy alarm clock. What is it supposed to wake us up to? It's supposed to wake us up to consider the spiritual side of our life, to consider the things of God, to open our ears to what God is speaking to us. The Shofar wakes us up to look at our past year. "Where have I fallen short? Where have I gotten into trouble? Where have I fallen into temptation? Where are the things that I'm not even aware of that have been a problem to me?"

Now, there are two kinds of people, well, it's really three kinds. There's the kind of people that are in total agreement with this. They're like, "Yes, this is wonderful! Let's go for it!" But there are two other kinds of people and I just want to clarify some things with you. The first group is the "no connection" group. (You don't have to tell anybody if you are in this group. You'll know it when I explain it.) This group doesn't really believe that there's a connection between sin and sickness. If you're this kind, your reaction might have been, "How can he say that sickness is the result of sin? Isn't that terribly judgmental? Here you've got someone who is suffering from a terrible sickness and now you're condemning them by saying, 'It's your fault!' You're going to blame them!" Did you have that thought? It's very common to think that. You might also be saying, "And besides, I know some very Godly people who have suffered from some serious sicknesses and I can't believe that it's because of something they did!" If you are saying or thinking things like that, you are in the "no connection" group of people. The second group is what I call the "no problem" group. Nobody's going to admit that they are in this group. Let me tell you! These are people who don't believe that they personally have a problem with sin. Their reaction is, "Oh, this is interesting, but it doesn't apply to me because since I came to the Lord and I repented of my sin, it's not a problem for me anymore! I may be suffering from some illness right now, but it has no connection to anything I do. It's an attack from the enemy!" So, maybe you think that way. You're not going to admit to it, though. Right?

So, let me just give a couple clarifications. First of all, I want to speak to the "no connection" group. The Bible does teach that not all sickness is a result of sin, but it also teaches that some of it is. Here's a Scripture where both of these concepts come out clearly.

John 9:1-2 *As Yeshua passed along, He saw a man blind from birth. His talmidim (disciples) said to Him, "Rabbi, who sinned—this man or his parents—to cause him to be born blind?"*

Now what His disciples were expressing there was the already well understood Jewish belief that there was a connection between sin and sickness.

John 9:3 *Yeshua answered, "His blindness is due neither to his sin nor that of his parents. It happened so that God's power might be seen at work in him."*

So, Yeshua said that there are times when it's not due to sin. This case was one of those. He told the disciples, "This man was born blind so that when I heal him it's going to bring great glory to God."

Here's a similar case.

John 9:4-7 *"As long as it is day, we must keep doing the work of the One who sent Me; the night is coming when no one can work. While I am in the world, I am the light of the world." Having said this, he spit on the ground, made some mud with the saliva, put the mud on the man's eyes, and said to him, "Go, wash off in the Pool of Shiloach (Siloam)!" (The name means "sent.") So he went and washed and came away seeing.*

If you read on, you'll see this caused a great stir in Jerusalem. So, this man, in God's plan for his life, we don't know how old he was, had to suffer through years of blindness and be gloriously healed as a testimony to God. So, the Bible does teach that not all sickness is the result of sin. That's one clarification.

Now, another clarification is for both groups, the "no connection" group and the "no problem" group. The Bible also teaches that sickness can be the result of someone else's sin. In fact, that was what was expressed here by the disciples. Did you hear it? "This man was born blind. Was it because of his parents' sin?" I am an example of that. When I was a child I had terrible problems with allergies. But all of those problems went away when I moved out of my parents' home. It wasn't because my parents didn't keep a clean house or because they had something that I was allergic to in their home. God rest my mother's soul. I'm not criticizing her for this, but I believe it was because of my mother's anxiety. She was always nervous about everything that I came in contact with. I believe that it became a pattern in my life. I constantly had these struggles with allergies. It was terrible. I took shots for years. Then I went away to college and I never had another problem with it. So, I believe that was what was happening in my life! I was sick because of someone else's sin.

Now, we mentioned before that AIDS seems to be a terrible illness that is connected with sin, but right away you think, "What about people who get AIDS through a transfusion?" Well, that's not that person's sin. It's somebody else's sin. Somebody got that virus into that blood—gave blood that way, but it wasn't their sin. And what about an AIDS baby? It's the same type of thing. And here's another example. How about an abused child who grows up in constant fear? Doctor's have made connections between living in the state of fear and lots of diseases. For instance, ulcers are a connection there. So, is it the person's sin or is it because of the way they were treated as a child? There are many other traumatic experiences that people go through that cause them to have fears and phobias—all kinds of things—emotional problems and mental problems and inabilities to cope. So, sometimes it can be someone else's sin, but it's still sin that caused it. But dealing with the sin of somebody else is also possible! We can be healed of the things that we struggle with due to someone else's sin.

Now, here's another clarification for the "no problem" group. Remember the "no problem" group. "I don't have this problem because I don't sin. It's an attack of the enemy!" Well, it *can* be an attack of the enemy. It happens sometimes when we are going ahead and doing the will of God. We're right there in the center of His will. We're doing exactly what He's wants us to do to advance His Kingdom. Because of that, the enemy is so opposing to us that a sickness comes on us. I've had that happen personally. Yet I believe that somewhere there's a chink in my armor when that happens—that there's something that I'm doing, that I'm not aware of, that has allowed the enemy to get in there and slow me down with that.

Now, if you're part of the "no problem" group, maybe it's also because you're personally not struggling with any kind of sickness or emotional problem, which is great. But if you have loved ones who are struggling with an incurable condition or with emotional problems that nobody knows how to deal with, I hope you will grasp the understanding of this teaching so you can help them.

I want to make a clarification for both groups. It is very important that we all understand just what sin is. I think when we use that little word, people often think of the big things: murder, stealing, adultery, etc. And we're not guilty of those things. We struggle with what the Bible talks about as secret sins. What are secret sins? They're things we're doing that other people can't see. Sometimes they're things that even we don't realize we're doing that are not in line with God's will or God's ways.

Let me give you some examples. In counseling, I've met numerous people who hate themselves. Maybe you are like them. They really hate themselves. They hate the way they look. They hate the way they act. They hate everything about themselves. Now, this is maybe a harsh thing to say, but I believe, in God's eyes, that is sin. It's sin because God says we're created in His image. If we're created in His image and we hate that image, then what are we saying? We're saying we hate God!

How about fear?! Many of us suffer from different kinds of fears. We don't often think of that as sin, but, you know, in several places, the Bible speaks in the imperative and says, "Fear not!" The opposite of fear is faith—trusting in God! And conversely, the opposite of faith is fear. Many of us fear lots of things which means we're not trusting God in them. And doctors know very well that having anxiety and fear does things to our bodies!

Another secret sin is Envy. In Proverbs there is a very interesting verse.

Proverbs 14:30 ... *envy rots the bones.*

How many people struggle with bone diseases, such as arthritis or joint problems? It could be from envy or jealousy! Bitterness is also a secret sin! Bitterness in the Bible is described as a root that defiles many. There's also the sin of judging other people. Many of us are not even aware when we do this.

I'm just going to list some of the others here: covetousness, greed, gossip, disrespect of parents, elders, and those in authority. Pride is a huge one. Unbelief is also a sin in God's eyes. Unbelief in God's promises! How many of us don't struggle with that at one time or another? Unforgiveness! That's a big one! And then there's just the simple area that's not even a moral issue. It's when God's wants us to go do something and we decide we want to do something else. It's disobedience.

So, with those clarifications, I hope that you can agree that there's a connection between our behavior—our level of being able to obey God—and the possibility of physical ailments or emotional ailments—all those kinds of things—coming upon us. And I hope you can also see that we are all vulnerable to them. Even if you're in that "no problem" group, you're still vulnerable to them.

Now, through His prophets, God began to reveal that He had a plan. He had a way to deal with the mess that was made by the fall. Someone was coming who would change everything. The whole rule of the game would change. Let's read where Isaiah predicts that this person is coming. He describes the person this way.

Isaiah 53:4 (NKJV) *Surely He has borne our griefs and carried our sorrows, yet we esteemed Him smitten, stricken by God and afflicted.*

So, this person that the prophet is predicting came to be known as HaMashiach—the Messiah—the Anointed One. It says here, He would carry away our grief and our sorrow. Yet, it would seem like God was afflicting Him! So, it's kind of a mystery there why God would be afflicting Him, yet He would be carrying away our grief and sorrow.

Isaiah 53:5 (KJV) *He was wounded for our transgressions. He was bruised for our iniquities. The chastisement of our peace was upon Him, and by His stripes we are healed.*

So, this is saying that this Messiah would suffer for our transgressions and iniquities, be chastised to bring us shalom or peace, but notice it says this strange thing: He would be striped to bring us healing. This striping—what this means is being beaten with a whip. When you're struck with a whip, it creates a stripe on your body. So, in these prophecies there were predictions that the Messiah would come and God would deal with sickness and disease, using Him and what He went through.

So, six hundred years later, after this prediction was made, a man came. He claimed to be the Son of God. He claimed to be the Messiah—the Anointed One. His name, Yeshua, actually means in Hebrew, God saves. He began to teach people about God and His ways. He was a powerful teacher. He used parables and He taught from the Scriptures. As you read about His life, you discover that the most visible thing about His anointing—that revealed His anointing—was that power flowed through Him to heal. That was the way people could tell that He was anointed. I want to read just one passage here in Matthew which ties this all together.

Matthew 8:16 *When evening came many people held in the power of demons were brought to Him* [to Yeshua]. *He expelled the spirits with a word and He healed all that were ill.*

And that word "all" is "all," as in everyone.

Matthew 8:17 *This was done to fulfill what had been spoken through the prophet Yesha'yahu* (Isaiah), *"He Himself took our weaknesses and bore our diseases."*

So, the author of the book of Matthew specifically makes this connection that Yeshua would take upon Himself the punishment to pay for not just our forgiveness, but also for our healing. His ultimate purpose was to be a sacrifice for sin—pour out His blood and give His body to make atonement for sin. But He spent most of His time while He was here amongst the people, healing people—dealing with their sicknesses!

Well, that's as far as I'm going to go with this right now. I'm going to continue with this teaching in the next chapter. We are going to talk about the connection that Yeshua made between sickness and sin. And then we're going to talk about whether God wants to heal us.

I hope that this has been an encouragement to you to again seriously seek the Lord. We need to ask Him to show us because we are blind to many of these things. Jeremiah said our hearts are desperately wicked, who can know them? The heart being described here is our inner self. Who can know all the things that go on inside of us—what our real motivations are? I'm having faith that God is going to bring new revelation. People are suddenly going to have the thought, "Oh, it might be a problem in my life, that I'm doing that!" Then there's going to be repentance. And there's going to be faith that God's going to touch us. I believe there's going to be healing and joy. You're going to say, "It worked. It worked! It really did work!"

Let's close in prayer.

Father, I thank You for the clear direction that I've had in this, even the e-mail that I got from someone who was teaching on this same thing. So, Father, I just want to pray first for the "no connection" group, those who struggle with the idea that there is a connection here. I pray that You would use the words of this message and the Scriptures that we've read and just show the truth because it's Your Spirit that reveals truth.

I pray also, Father, for the person who is struggling with a physical or an emotional problem, that You give a revelation to them of the meaning of this connection that they would be able to grasp this. And I pray especially for the "no problem" group—the group that thinks they don't have any problem with sin, that they don't do anything wrong. Lord, I pray that Your Spirit would just bring conviction to them, that their conscience would come alive and would be speaking in their ear.

And I pray, Lord, that You would prepare our hearts for these Ten Days, that You would give us revelations on the things that we need to deal with. Perhaps some things will be connected with the problems we have, but perhaps some will just be, "You need to deal with this." I pray, Father, that You would increase our faith that You desire to see us overcome these things. And give us that faith and that hope that we are going to see healing in our lives, and even in the lives of our loved ones. And we just commit these things to You in this season. In the mighty name of Yeshua, we pray. Amen. Amen.

CHAPTER 14

A TIME TO HEAL
PART II

So, again, what had happened to me is I felt like the Lord directed me to have a series of teachings called, "A Time to Heal" out of the passage in Ecclesiastes that says, "there's a time for this and a time for that." One of them says, "There's a time to heal." The Ruakh Ha-Kodesh seems to be giving the direction that "there is healing Power in the Moadim (Appointed Times) of Rosh Hashanah and the Ten Days—physical healing, emotional healing, and the power to keep us in health. We need healing Power for that, too. Good health doesn't just happen. It is because of the healing Power of Yeshua.

Could you use some healing Power right about now? Yea! Me, too! Well, before we ask for God to heal us there are some questions that need to be addressed. Are you ready to answer some hard questions before asking for healing? Oh, you didn't want to have to answer to anything first, did you? You just wanted to be healed without needing to be responsible for anything on your part, right? We all would like that, wouldn't we?

Well, the questions are the ones I mentioned in the last chapter. The first important thing to be asked is, "Why is our healing prayer batting average so low? Why are so few of our prayers for healing being answered?" Now I pray for a lot of people to get healed and people DO get healed, but not all of them—a lot fewer of them than I'd like to see. We're going to answer that question later. Another question is, "What does the Bible say about the source of sickness and disease?" We talked about that in the last chapter. We're going to talk about it a little more in this chapter. And then we're going to ask the question, "Does God want to heal us?" And finally, we're going to ask the question, "Is there a block to healing prayers being answered, and if there is, how can I learn what that block is so that I can be healed and I can walk in health?"

Now, in the last chapter, we asked the question about what the source of sickness and disease is and we learned that the Bible says there's a connection between sin and sickness. So, if it's true that there's a connection between them, we need to be very excited about that because there are sicknesses that nobody knows how to cure, but we all know how to deal with sin! It's very clear from the Scriptures how we are to deal with it. The hope here is that by discovering these connections and dealing with the sin, we will see healing. We will see the power of God move in healing.

Now before we go any further, let me explain that in the Hebrew Scriptures there are three different words that are translated as sin. Probably everybody has a different concept of sin. The first word that is translated as "sin" is "avone." It really should be translated "iniquity." Iniquity, as I explained before, is not things that we do or say, or laws that we break. The rabbis define "avone" as our "inclination to evil." It's the fact that we, as human beings, have to struggle against evil. It's easy for us to do evil. It's easy to fall into sin, but it's hard to do good. It's like we're leaning over toward evil and we have to push ourselves back toward good. I doubt that I'm the only one who experiences that. For example, it's easy to be lazy, right? It's hard to be diligent.

The second word for "sin" in the Hebrew language is "khatahah." This is the one that is most often translated as "sin." But it actually means "missing the mark." So, this word is not really speaking about intentional things that we do that are against God's will. It's more like when we don't live up to His standards, when we fall short. When we try but it doesn't work.

And then the third Hebrew word for "sin" is "pesha." Often it is translated as "transgression." And this is intentional sin. One time we had a visitor who was a scholar from Israel, and he called "pesha" "organized crime." It is things that you planned to do that you know are wrong. You didn't just happen to do them. Our legal system deals with this third level of wrong doing. The punishment for premeditated murder is much stricter or worse than the punishment for murder that happens as the result of a fit of rage. So we can understand these definitions.

Well, the Yomim Norim is the Appointed Time for the express purpose of uncovering and dealing with sin in our lives—all of these different kinds of sin. And I believe it's a special time of anointing for going through this process because God has appointed it! And since God has ordained it, it's going to be very fruitful! One of the fruits will be in receiving healing. Do you believe this, too?

So we're going to start looking in the Scriptures now. We're going to start out with Matthew 8. We're going to just review a little bit. In the last chapter we looked at the connection between sin and disease in the Tanakh (Old Testament). And now we'd like to look at some of the things that were said in the B'rit Hadashah, the New Covenant, about the connection between sin and disease.

Matthew 8:16 *When evening came, many people held in the power of demons were brought to him. He expelled the spirits with a word and healed all who were ill.*

"All" as in every one that was ill. "All" doesn't leave anyone out, does it?

Verse 17 *This was done to fulfill what had been spoken through the prophet Yeshayahu (Isaiah), "He himself took our weaknesses and bore our diseases."*

So, as I pointed out in the last chapter, Matthew here connects Yeshua's healing power back to Isaiah's prophesy. God's ultimate purpose was for Yeshua to be the final sacrifice for sin, to pour out His blood and to give His body to make atonement for the transgressions and the iniquity of all people, Jew and Gentile. That was God's purpose for sending Yeshua to the cross. But Yeshua spent most of His time while He was here on this earth dealing with sickness. Why do you suppose that is?

Well, let's look at when He healed people. Let's see if He made a connection between sickness and sin. First we'll read just an amazing story in Mark 2. Yeshua had been teaching and praying for people for quite awhile. Word of His amazing power spread all throughout Israel. So the people were expectant.

Mark 2:1-4 *After a while, Yeshua returned to K'far-Nachum* (Capernaum). *The word spread that he was back, and so many people gathered around the house that there was no longer any room, not even in front of the door. While he was preaching the message to them, four men came to him carrying a paralyzed man. They could not get near Yeshua because of the crowd, so they stripped the roof over the place where he was, made an opening, and lowered the stretcher with the paralytic lying on it.*

Can you imagine this scene? These men climbed on someone's roof, lifted their friend up there on a stretcher, and tore a big hole through the roof, big enough to let that stretcher down through it! They were determined to get to Yeshua, weren't they? But what you have to understand is that they had straw roofs on their houses. So it wasn't that they had to go get out hammers and rip off asphalt shingles and plywood and things like that. They just pushed the roof away, maybe dug through some dried mud or clay, put a rope on each corner of the litter or stretcher and lowered this man down in front of Yeshua. As I was about to say here, I think Yeshua was amazed to see the faith, not of the man, but of his friends. Well, maybe of the man, too, to be willing as a paralytic to be taken up on a roof and then lowered down. That took a lot of faith, too, right? Let's read on.

Mark 2:5 *Seeing their trust, Yeshua said to the paralyzed man, "Son, your sins are forgiven."*

Now that's not what the people, or the paralytic, or his four determined friends who went through all that trouble had been expecting to hear! They didn't expect their friend to be put on the spot like that.

But, Yeshua could see that this man's sin was the cause of the paralysis. We don't know what his sin was, but Yeshua knew. And the interesting thing to note here is that the paralytic hadn't even asked to be forgiven! Did you notice that?! Why was that? Well, I believe that this paralyzed man probably wasn't just a passive participant in this whole ordeal. I believe that part of the reason his friends were willing to go to all that effort is that he must have asked them to bring him into Yeshua's presence. Perhaps he begged them. Perhaps he had a deep longing to see this One he believed to be the Messiah. Once he was there in His presence, Yeshua could see that this man had a contrite and repentant heart.

Again, "contrite" means to be humble; to be open to being shown your faults. This man was open to having Yeshua tell him he had sins that needed forgiving. The word "repentant" means to be willing to turn from your faults. This paralyzed man was willing to stop living in wrongdoing and to receive forgiveness for his past. So, Yeshua, seeing this in his heart, was able to declare the paralytic forgiven. However, this didn't set too well with some of the people.

Mark 2:6-7 *Some Torah-teachers sitting there thought to themselves, "How can this fellow say such a thing? He is blaspheming! Who can forgive sins except God?"*

Their theology was that only God could declare that a person's sins were forgiven. So what Yeshua did was blasphemy in their way of thinking. It was blasphemous against God.

Verse 8 *But immediately Yeshua, perceiving in his spirit what they were thinking, said to them, "Why are you thinking these things?"*

With this supernatural insight, Yeshua showed them He was more than human. He was showing them that just as He could read their thought, he could also read the inner secrets of the man on the stretcher. The same supernatural insight that told him what the Torah-teachers were thinking, also enabled Him to know the paralytic had a repentant heart.

Yeshua asked them "Why are you thinking these things?" What was it that He knew they were thinking? Well, I believe they were saying to themselves, "Who does this man, Yeshua, think He is? Only God has the authority to forgive sins! Does He think He has God's authority? What blasphemy!" So, knowing that this is what they were thinking, He says,

Mark 2:9 *"Which is easier to say to the paralyzed man? 'Your sins are forgiven'? or 'Get up, pick up your stretcher and walk'?"*

He was making a very strong connection between sin and sickness here. A very strong connection. One of the strongest connections in the whole Bible. It is like He is saying that having his sins forgiven would cure this man of paralysis! Do you see that there? He even makes the connection stronger in what he says and does next.

Mark 2:10-12 *"But look! I will prove to you that the Son of Man has authority on earth to forgive sins." He then said to the paralytic, "I say to you: get up, pick up your stretcher and go home!" In front of everyone the man got up, picked up his stretcher at once and left. They were all utterly amazed and praised God, saying, "We have never seen anything like this!"*

Now this is a very different story from what we'd expect. For instance, if you noticed, Yeshua did not lay hands on this man. He didn't anoint him with oil. He didn't pray for his healing. He just told him to get up! That's all Yeshua did. He just told the man to stand up, and the man was able to do it! But why was He able to do it? Why was that all it took? Well, I think it was because His sin had been forgiven. It was his sins that had him bound. It was his sins that hindered his healing.

And Yeshua was demonstrating here, I hope you all catch this, that He did have the authority to forgive sins because when He did it, this paralytic got up and walked! What greater demonstration of His authority could there be? But it's also a lesson to us, that sin was the cause of this man's paralysis. Now other authors in the New Covenant reinforce this. I'd just like to read some of these things to you.

James 5:14-16 *Is someone among you ill? He should call for the elders of the congregation. They will pray for him and rub olive oil on him in the name of the Lord. The prayer offered with trust will heal the one who is ill—the Lord will restore his health; and if he has committed sins, he will be forgiven. Therefore, openly acknowledge your sins to one another, and pray for each other, so that you may be healed. The prayer of a righteous person is powerful and effective.*

Notice again the connection between sin and sickness. Also here there is the understanding that confession of sin to each other is a way to help us deal with our sin. If we hide our sin, it will only fester and cause trouble and pain and sickness. But if we confess it, then it is brought out in the open. It is exposed and we can be free of it. We can be washed clean.

But also notice there's a little bit of a softening of it here. It doesn't just say, "his sins will be forgiven." It says, "**if** he has sinned!" In the last chapter we looked at whether all sickness is caused by sin, where we found it isn't. But we understand that some is.

Now Yeshua also taught that sickness can be the result of satanic bondage. Here in Luke 13 we have another incident where Yeshua heals someone, and once again, we find it very strange in how He does it.

Luke 13:10-13 *Yeshua was teaching in one of the synagogues on Shabbat. A woman came up who had a spirit* [She had a spirit!] *which had crippled her for eighteen years; she was bent double and unable to stand erect at all.*

Now a spirit is something ethereal, something we can't see or put our finger on, but the Scriptures tell us that this spirit crippled her! She was bent double and unable to stand erect! That's pretty crippled. In essence, she was a paralytic, too!

Luke 13:12-13 *On seeing her, Yeshua called her and said to her, "Lady, you have been set free from your weakness!" He put his hands on her,* [This time He put His hands on her.] *and at once she stood upright and began to glorify God.*

Now notice the difference here. This time we don't see Yeshua dealing with the woman's sin at all. He just put His hands on her and said, "You're free!" Now things again get a little testy. And we might as well look at how the testiness went because it's important to see.

Luke 13:14-17 *But the president of the synagogue, indignant that Yeshua had healed on Shabbat, spoke up and said to the congregation, "There are six days in the week for working; so come during those days to be healed, not on Shabbat!"* [The president of the synagogue was complaining here that He shouldn't have done this because in Jewish tradition, healing was not allowed on Shabbat. It was considered work.] *However, the Lord answered him, "You hypocrites! Each one of you on Shabbat—don't you unloose your ox or your donkey from the stall and lead him off to drink?* [Isn't that work?] *This woman is a daughter of Avraham, and the Adversary kept her tied up for eighteen years! Shouldn't she be freed from this bondage on Shabbat?" By these words, Yeshua put to shame the people who opposed him; but the rest of the crowd were happy about all the wonderful things that were taking place through him.*

So again we see opposition. But back to the point of this, what was the cause of this woman's physical ailment? A spirit! It was satanic bondage. Satan had bound her. Now, how does satan gain power over someone to bind them in this physical way? Or other ways? Well, we can find the answer in one of Sha'ul's writings. In this particular passage Sha'ul (Paul) is speaking to one of his disciples named Timothy and he's giving him instructions as a teacher, exhorting him to be gentle.

2 Timothy 2:25-26 *Also he should be gentle as he corrects his opponents. For God may perhaps grant them the opportunity to turn from their sins, acquire full knowledge of the truth, come to their senses and escape the trap of the Adversary, after having been captured alive by him to do his will.*

What is Rabbi Sha'ul saying here? What is it that will help a person be able to escape the trap of the Adversary? Do you see that there? Yes, by coming to a full knowledge of the Truth. So turn that around and we can see that it is through our lack of the full knowledge of the truth that the adversary can trap us into doing his will. This trap of the enemy can have physical manifestations. So we all had better start studying the Word and learning the Truth that is in there!

The phrase that Rabbi Sha'ul uses, "come to their senses" indicates that the person is not necessarily aware that they have been trapped. Their mind is in a fog. Sometimes we don't even know we are bound up. The Ruakh HaKodesh has to bring us to our senses. So that's the reason we see from Sha'ul's writing that a person can become trapped and shackled. But why was the "daughter of Abraham" bound? Well, we're not really told why.

I love the way the program we've been involved in called "Cleansing Stream" describes it. It talks about how satan can get a hook in you, almost like the image of a fish that a hook gets set in and then it can be dragged around by that hook.

So the adversary had set a hook in her. How that hook got set in, we don't know, but very often it can be through sin. A person can open the door to being put into bondage by satan through sin. For instance, if a person is extremely greedy, and they're always thinking about how much money they can make, etc., the enemy can get a hold of them through that; in a sense put a hook in them and draw them around and manipulate and control them by that. Sometimes he can use a phobia or fear caused by a traumatic experience to bind a person in anxiety and worry. It could be a spirit of fear that traps us so much that we can't go anywhere or do certain things. A spiritual force is manipulating us.

But it could also be through something that someone did to her. Perhaps it was the sin of her parents or others in her life that provided legal right for the devil to set a hook in her. For instance, we know that sometimes when people are mistreated or abused that puts a hook in them. A real simple example would be a mother who might reward her children with candy all the time. Well, what can that cause? It can cause the child later on in life to look to food for a sense of well being. This could turn into a life of gluttony and we all know where that leads.

Perhaps it had nothing to do with sin. Perhaps it was just the enemy's way of preventing her from fulfilling God's plan for her life. Sometimes when we're right on with God, trying to do His will, trying to accomplish the things of His Kingdom, the enemy can just bring us sickness to try to resist that. So we need discernment on all of this.

So let me just summarize. The Bible teaches there's a connection between sin and sickness. And we learned in the last chapter that the Scriptures tell us that sickness entered the world through sin. Death entered through sin. Medical science tells us that sickness is often spread through sin, for instance, the AIDS epidemic. But what we're learning now is that sickness could be due to a person's own sin: known or secret. Or it could be due to somebody else's sin. Or it could be due to some kind of traumatic experience, etc. The enemy can use any of these things to hook us and cause demonic bondage.

So we see this connection between sin and satan and sickness. Do you follow me so far? Okay.

So the next question we want to look at is, "Does God want us to be healed?" This is an important question. We have already read that Yeshua healed all who were brought to Him. In the previous chapter, we read an amazing passage which says that one of the names God gave Himself was Adonai Ropheh-khah, which means "the Lord who heals you." So He calls Himself our healer. Now I'd just like to read a few more Scriptures here, a couple of them from the Tanakh (Old Testament), which speak to us about this desire of God to heal us. The first one is in Psalm 103, a familiar passage.

Psalm 103:2-3 (NKJV) *Bless the LORD, O my soul, and forget not all His benefits: Who forgives all your iniquities, who heals all your diseases.*

And again, right in that verse we see that connection: iniquities and diseases in the same verse! Did you see that? And remember what iniquity is. It's really the most pervasive kind of sin. It's an inner attitude type of thing. Sin brings destruction and disease. Yeshua brings the opposite. In the New Covenant Yeshua says this.

John 10:10 *The thief comes only in order to steal, kill and destroy; I have come so that they may have life, life in its fullest measure* (or abundant life).

All of us have probably experienced this. It's hard to have a full, abundant life when we're sick, right? That's one of the main things that stops it. So Yeshua came to bring us abundant life—life in its fullest measure. Let's take a look at the atoning work of Yeshua, what He did, to see if it has a provision for healing. Isaiah 53 is this incredible passage written 600 years before the time of Yeshua, predicting what He would do, predicting that He would be the final sacrifice in God's plan.

Isaiah 53:5 (NKJV) *But He was wounded for our transgressions* [That's pesha], *He was bruised for our iniquities* [our avone]; *the chastisement for our peace was upon Him, and by His stripes we are healed.*

As noted before, the "stripes" in this passage refer to the whipping Isaiah predicted Messiah would endure. And his prediction came to pass. Yeshua received the 40 lashes minus one—the whipping that brings a person right to the brink of death. It was shown very realistically gruesome in the Passion movie.

Now we need to notice one thing here. Notice that it wasn't Yeshua's death that brought healing but His stripes. Do you see that? It doesn't say, "...by His death we are healed." It says, "...*by His stripes we are healed.*" So what can we learn from this? Well, I think we can learn something very special about God's desire to heal us. Just think about this for a minute. If Yeshua had not come to deal with our healing, He could have been spared the extra, terrible suffering of the whipping. But He wanted so much to heal us, too, that He was willing to suffer more excruciating pain for it. He endured those flesh-ripping lashes so that we could be healed from all our diseases.

So, we can see from the Word of God that Yeshua had to endure the stripes for our healing and He did it willingly. Now let's go over what we've learned so far about healing. We've learned that it is God's will to heal in most cases. We know that there can be exceptions like the man born blind for the glory of God.

Just an aside here about that man born blind. Let's not lose sight of the fact that he did receive a glorious healing. He was blind for a long time but not his whole life. He got to experience an awesome miracle that astonished the whole community, and gave him the opportunity to give testimony even to high up Jewish officials. So God received widespread glory from his healing. Who else was ill for the glory of God? Yes, Lazarus.

There's one other exception—when we won't be healed. When would that be? It would be when it's time for us to die! There is a time appointed for each one of us to die. When that time comes, we won't be healed, we will get to go and be with God in Glory!

So, does God want to heal us? What is the answer to that question? What does the Bible tell us? Does God want to heal you? Yes! A resounding yes!! So, if God wants to heal us, and we aren't getting healed, then there must be a problem somewhere. There must be something blocking God's will from happening. So we must ask the next question, "Is there a block to our healing prayers being answered?" Yes, there must be a block. If I'm praying for healing and no one is getting healed, then something is blocking the healing.

Well, I believe the block is this. Are you ready? This is important! The block is the belief that many Bible believers have that because we have repented, because we have given our hearts to the Lord, because we have turned to Him and are following Him, that the affect of sin in our life is gone! This is not what the New Covenant teaches. The New Covenant teaches that we are progressively being conformed to His image and we are being cleaned up of those things in a slow process. Let's look again at Romans 8:29, one of my favorite verses.

Romans 8:29 ... *because those whom he knew in advance, he also determined in advance would be conformed to the pattern of his Son, so that he might be the firstborn among many brothers.*

So what this is speaking of is we are all being made like the Messiah. How are we being made like the Messiah? Are we starting to look like Him physically? No. We are being made like Him in our character. We are having the fruit of the Spirit grow in our lives. In this way our act is being cleaned up. We are having more victory over sin. Our character is becoming more like the Messiah. But this is a life-long process that all of the followers of Yeshua go through. Take a look at Yeshua's disciples, for example. It was a process over their lifetime of being perfected. And the word that describes this process is an old-fashioned word that we need to use more often. It's the word, "sanctification." The word comes from the Hebrew word "kadosh" which means "to be separate from evil." So, sanctification is a separating of us from evil. It's an ongoing, maturing process whereby we are separated from evil, separated to the Lord.

As we are going through this process, we begin to produce the Fruits of the Spirit. What are the Fruits of the Spirit? Let's name them. Love, joy, peace, patience, gentleness, meekness, kindness, and self-control. These are what we will start to display in our lives. And the natural, rather the *super*natural way this should work is we will also have greater and greater victory over the things of this world and the things of the evil one as we mature in Yeshua. We will have more and more victory over sin. The sins that used to bother us so much and "so easily beset us" and made us fall, will eventually no longer tempt us.

We need to get one thing clear. We need to see that sanctification is different from justification. Justification happens the instant we place our trust in Yeshua's atoning sacrifice and make Him Lord of our lives. Justification is instantaneous when a person realizes who the Messiah is and turns their heart to Him. In that instant, they are justified in God's eyes, and they are covered by the sacrificial blood of Yeshua! Justification wipes our slate clean. We call this "being saved," or "being set free." But justification is just the beginning of this ongoing process of sanctification. How is sanctification accomplished? Well, Yeshua speaks about this in John 17. He says it very clearly here. In the Complete Jewish Bible here, He doesn't actually use the word "sanctification," but many of your Bibles will use it.

John 17:17 *Set them apart for holiness by means of the truth—your word is truth.*

That phrase, "set them apart" in Greek is "hagios." Other Bible versions translate it as, "sanctify them." Let's read on.

John 17:18-19 *Just as you sent Me into the world, I have sent them into the world. On their behalf I am setting Myself apart for holiness, so that they too may be set apart for holiness by means of the truth.*

So, how does it say we are sanctified? By His Word of Truth. It's His Word that sanctifies us. As His Word fills our hearts more and more, we become more and more holy; more and more set apart for Him; more and more sanctified. The way I understand this and what I have experienced and maybe you have experienced this, too, is that this is like peeling the layers of an onion. It just keeps on going. (But you don't necessarily have to cry during it.) You take off one layer and it's like, "Wow, I've been delivered of that." "I've been set free of this." "And I have victory over that." And then you find there's another layer. And this goes on all through our lives because we have a very high standard that we're being conformed to. Who is that standard? It's Yeshua Himself! So this is just part of the normal life of followers of Yeshua. Layers of sin, bondage, and wrong thinking are being taken off one by one. Things ingrained in our sinful nature, like pride, are removed layer by layer.

Many times there is a block to sanctification. What is that block? Well, one block is in the group of people that I mentioned before, the "no problem" group. These believers think sin is "no problem" because they don't do it any more. They no longer do the same sinful, ungodly, immoral things they did before they became believers. Their life has changed drastically, so they think all sin is gone from their life. They say, "I don't need to worry about sin anymore because now it doesn't bother me. I'm free of that." They haven't grasped the ongoing need to be sanctified. Perhaps it's partly because we don't teach on it enough.

The New Covenant teaches that followers of Yeshua are still susceptible to the temptation to sin. And I can testify to that! It teaches that our sin can affect our lives physically, emotionally, relationally, and financially. It's very clear to me from the New Covenant that past sin can continue to cause problems in my life, even after I've repented of it. Oftentimes, I still suffer the consequences of it, especially if the enemy has gained some kind of hook in me to manipulate me because of it.

Now I understood something very interesting in studying this. I had never seen it before. I have to credit a gentleman named Henry Wright whose book, *A More Excellent Way* (Whitiker House, 2009), I was reading. If you look at the structure of the New Covenant, it's actually got two very distinct parts to it. The four Gospels and the Book of Acts make up the first part which is full of miraculous healings, right? It's all in there! All throughout! But then if you start reading the letters—the letters of Rabbi Sha'ul (Paul), and Ya'akov (James) and John and Peter, you know, there's hardly any mention of healing going on. Have you noticed that? Hardly any mention! They say a couple things about it, but really not much. What we see there is this. The Gospels and the Book of Acts describe all the healing miracles and say that it's available, but the writings—the letters—deal very strongly with our sanctification. They deal with how we can live a holy life and how we can walk with the Lord! Do you see the pattern there? It's really amazing when you think about it. Our appetite is whetted by reading the Gospels and the Book of Acts. We want to see those kinds of things happening, but what we miss is, well, read the rest of the Book where it tells you how to see those things happening! Follow the instructions and seek God to get your life cleaned up and my life cleaned up, and we'll see those kinds of miracles. And this is where that verse in 2 Timothy comes in.

2 Timothy 2:26 *...come to their senses and escape the trap of the Adversary, after having been captured alive by him to do his will.*

We escape these snares of the adversary one by one. As we are sanctified, we are layer by layer set free from sickness and satanic bondage. In my life, I've seen one by one those traps being broken. I believe there are still some other traps that I'm in that I don't even know about. I think that's just the way life is. There may still be something the enemy's using in my life, but gradually we are set free.

Now this is interesting. I was reading in the newspaper about Rosh Hashanah. They had a couple articles in there. One of the articles was quoting from a local rabbi saying, "Rosh Hashanah is a time to turn to God so we can change the world." And somebody commented on that saying, "Well, you know, really the change begins in the home." And I thought, "You know, it really doesn't. Change really begins in our hearts. Each one of us must allow God to begin to change us, to sanctify us from within.

Now I, personally, have experienced this peeling of the onion many times in my life. One of the really interesting ones that I experienced was in the area of finances. Some of you may know my story. My parents were communists. They were against the whole capitalistic system. And they raised me that way, to be against it. My father actually taught me that to think about money, to think about saving, to think about investing, especially investing, was a terrible thing to do because nobody really should be investing. We all should be working for the good of everybody. That was what communists thought.

After I left my father's home and was on my own and began to work, I noticed I just didn't seem to have any ability to deal with saving any money, or investing any money. And I began to realize that as a father I had kids that were going to go to college. And old age—I had to deal with that someday. I needed to be dealing with these things, but I couldn't bring myself to do it.

Then one day I was praying about this and it came to my mind, "This is something that your father taught you. This is a way of thinking." It's not a Godly way of thinking because God speaks about investments in the Bible. But this was something that my father had taught me and I couldn't break free of that. So finally I went to the Lord and I repented of it because it's not a Godly way of thinking, and I asked Him to deliver me from it. And I WAS delivered from it. I never had that problem after that.

It was really interesting. As my father got older, he had actually managed to set aside some money for his older years. But he had his money in something that was earning very little. And when he was in his mid-seventies, I began to talk with him saying, "Can we put that in something else where you could earn a little more on it?" And, you know, he wouldn't deal with it. He was still like that. He just plain wouldn't deal with it. So I finally had to give up and just leave it there.

So that's just an example of how these things can work, not just in sickness but even in our finances. So if the enemy has kept us in the dark about the root causes of these problems in our lives: sickness, bondage, financial problems, relationship problems, then it is good that we are entering into the Ten Days when we'll be seeking God to reveal those roots! If we spend these Ten Days doing what God designed for us to do, then He will be able to reveal to us the things that are blocking our healing and our sanctification, right? That's what I believe God is calling us to do. Isn't that great?

The sad thing is that the need for these days has been denied by the church for 1700 years! Just think, the church could have been experiencing this special time all these centuries! There is awesome Power in what God is showing us today. The church denied people this Power in the past. But we can have that Power today.

What do we have to do to hear from God about this Power to be freed from all the things that block us? Well, it is wrapped up in that word, "contrite," being willing to be shown our faults, our shortcomings, the things that we struggle with. This is someone who trembles at God's Word because that's the standard by which we determine we do have faults.

Does anybody like to be told what all their faults are? No, no one! We don't like to be told what is wrong with us. But we need to be that way with God. We need to be a person who trembles when we see ourselves falling short of the standards of thinking and behavior He sets in His Word.

Now have you ever met any un-contrite people? I have. They don't want to hear about anything that they're not supposed to do. They just don't want to hear it. That's a big problem. It's hard to work with someone like that, isn't it?

Now, lest the days we are facing seem too fearful and depressing to us, we have the tradition of Tashlikh—casting our bread on the water—taken from Micah 7:19. *He will turn again, he will have compassion upon us; he will subdue our iniquities; and thou wilt cast all their sins into the depths of the sea.* We do this at a stream or a river and watch the bread representing our sins float away.

This ancient tradition gives us a nice visual reminder that God does forgive our sins; that He carries them away, never to hold them against us. This whole process of sanctification is a very good thing. Discovering our faults and the places where we fall short of God's standard is not a negative thing. It's not a bad thing. It's a wonderful thing because this is the thing that will set us free. And Yeshua said, *"You shall know the truth and the truth will set you free."* Now part of that is the truth about Him, but also it's good to know the truth about us to set us free. The end result is to be gloriously free in our lives; and to begin to see miracles and healings and answers to long-time prayers. Now who wouldn't want that?

So let's pray.

Father we come before You as we enter these Ten Days and we thank You for placing these Ten Days on Your calendar as an Appointed Time, Moad. And I thank You, Lord, for the revelation of the connection between sin and sickness and bondage.

Lord, I pray You will give each of us a new revelation of the connection between our own sicknesses and the sin in our own lives, between the bondages we are under and our sins. And give us faith that You do want to heal us.

Also, give us a revelation of our ongoing need to be sanctified. Help us to have contrite spirits willing to be corrected by the Ruakh HaKodesh. Help us to be willing and open to having our faults revealed. Shine the light of Your Ruakh HaKodesh on us. Give us a joyful attitude about what is about to happen because when those roots are revealed,

You are going to show us how to deal with them. Hallelujah. Thank You, Father. Thank You. Thank You. And we ask all this in the Name of Your Son, Yeshua. Amen. Amen.

CHAPTER 15

A TIME TO HEAL
PART III

The Shabbat (Sabbath) during the Ten Days of Awe is called the Shabbat T'shuvah. It means Sabbath of Repentance. There is always a Sabbath of Repentance between Rosh Hashanah and Yom Kippur.

Do you remember the greeting for Rosh Hashanah? It's "L'Shanah Tovah" (for a good year) "Tikkah Tevu" (May your name be inscribed—for a good year.) The greeting for Yom Kippur is the same, but you add on "v'Tikkah Temu" (Temu instead of Tevu) and that means "and sealed" ("v" is "and.") So, it's "May your name be inscribed and sealed unto a good year." In traditional Judaism the belief is that, during the Ten Days of Awe, God decides everybody's fate for the coming year. Then the fate is sealed on Yom Kippur. So, here's the whole Yom Kippur greeting: "L'Shanah Tovah, Tikkah Tevu v'Tikkah Temu."

*   *   *

I want to continue with this series called A Time to Heal. The Spirit's direction to me has been that there is healing power in this Appointed Time of these Ten Days—physical healing power, emotional healing power, and power to stay in health. We've looked at what the Bible says is the root cause of sickness and disease. And we've learned that there are spiritual causes. Then we spent some time looking through Scriptures that showed that God does want to heal us, that physical healing is part of God's plan for our lives. Then we asked, "Well, what's blocking His healing? Why do we not see it more frequently?" We looked at some of our attitudes in that. Now we are going to dig a little deeper to find some more blocks and how to hear from God about those blocks. And finally, we're going to look beyond healing to "How can we walk in health?"

Now, keep in mind that the success of our going to God to seek answers about our healing is all wrapped up in having that contrite heart that is willing to hear from God—is willing to be corrected—is willing to have the dirt dug up so that it can be washed away. I can't emphasize this point enough. If we're not willing to let the Spirit of God reveal to us our faults and the things that are causing these things, we're not going to get anywhere with this. So, how do we hear from God once we have this contrite heart?

This is a subject that is very dear to my heart. Before I came to the Lord, I was searching to find the meaning and purpose of life. As part of that search, I began to pursue Eastern religions. I took lessons and learned to be a yogi. There was a very, very strong and difficult discipline to practice to do that kind of exercise—that kind of Yoga meditation. You had to learn all these ways of dealing with your mind, and even with your body. You had to learn to sit in certain positions and stay in that position, dedicating long periods of time so you could hear. What I ended up hearing was definitely NOT the Lord. It was all deception. But my point is that there was all this work that had to be done to get to that place. I still remember an amusing situation that I got into once. I had finally learned to get into the lotus position where you get your legs crossed and all that. I was so pleased with myself. I sat there and sat there and did all the exercises that the leader had taught me. Then it was time to get up, but I couldn't move. I was stuck. Diane had to come and un-pry my legs. Then they wouldn't work. They were totally asleep.

I had to develop all kinds of special techniques in my yoga studies. It took extreme discipline and difficult, hard work. So, when I came to the Lord, I was totally amazed at this Book, the Bible. I thought it would have all these instructions on all these techniques and disciplines you had to do—first this and then that and that, but the Bible was nothing like that! It just said that God will speak to you. It was so amazing to me to learn that God would speak to me just because I had given my heart to Him. And I found it was true! It happened! When I had turned to Him, God began to speak to me.

How did I hear from Him? I heard from Him by reading the Word. I heard from Him by singing praises and worshiping Him. I heard from Him by being in prayer. And I heard from Him through other people speaking into my life—being in fellowship.

But the thing I want to touch on goes back to the Yoga-type thing. I have found that to really get in touch with God and hear from Him, I personally need to do something. Something that I don't hear taught about very much as I listen to different speakers. A lot of them talk about reading the Word and all these great things which are all very important. But there's one thing that I don't hear which is so simple. It is this. To hear from God, I simply need to learn to be quiet. Right? Because I can't hear anything when I'm talking! We need to learn to take time to be silent before the Lord. I don't know if you do this regularly or not, but I do it everyday. I take some time, apart from praying for people, apart from interceding, apart from confessing or declaring and even apart from worshiping to just plain being quiet, focusing on Him, and listening for His voice.

His voice is inside. It comes into my thoughts. But I need the discipline to hear it. I don't know about you, but I suspect you're probably like me. It seems like that's the last thing I do. I do all these other things, worshiping, praying, interceding, etc., and then I remember, "Oh, yea! I need to just be quiet for awhile and let God speak to me." So, I want to encourage you today that it needs to be the number one thing because when it comes down to it, those are really the best times when I hear from God—when I stop all my thinking and just get quiet.

What I've learned in myself, and I think it applies to everyone else, too, is that when I come to the Lord and I want to hear from Him, I need to come with a certain attitude. To me, that attitude has been captured in Paul Wilbur's cover song on his CD, *"Let the Weight of Your Glory Cover Us."* Do you know that song? There's that wonderful line in there that says, "We do not seek Your hand, we only seek Your face." What that means to me is that I often go to God seeking His hand. "Lord, do this. Lord, show me how to do this. Lord, I need this. I need that." It's all me talking to Him about my agenda. "This is what I need. This is what You have to do, Lord, please." It's all about His hands. The symbolism is His hands moving. I want to see His hands move. I want Him to do this or do that.

And what I find is I have to get beyond that. I have to get to the place where I'm seeking His face. What I mean by that is I'm just being open to whatever He wants to say to me. Maybe He wants to say something to me that totally has nothing to do with what I'm asking Him about. But as long as I'm focusing on "Lord, you've got to do this" or "You've got to do that, Lord," I don't get to hear that. Having the correct inner attitude—I find that hard to do. It usually takes me awhile. I'll go to Him and say, "Lord, I need this and I need this and this" and then all of a sudden it will come into my mind, "Wait a minute, why don't you just shut up and let Him say what He wants to you because it might have nothing to do with all the things you're listing there." That's what seeking His face is—just coming and looking to Him without an agenda and letting Him speak to us.

The Lord says,

John 10:27 *My sheep hear My voice. I know them and they follow Me.*

This is our inheritance. It is part of the Covenant that we would hear His voice. Now I don't often hear His voice audibly. But I'll tell you what I do hear. I do receive thoughts in my mind that I know are not my thoughts because I know my thoughts. Sometimes something comes in there that I know is beyond anything I could've thought of. Often times it's a breakthrough. I would never think that way. It is God giving revelation.

Sometimes the Lord speaks a reference to people, "Isaiah 42 verse 7" and you can open up and He'll speak that way. But other times it might just be a thought that comes into your mind. "I never thought of that before. Why didn't I ever think of it?" It solves your problem often times. It solves many of my problems. Or it gives me new insight to show me that it really wasn't my problem. It was someone else's problem and I should just get away from it. It's with the discipline of quietness that we can hear such things from the Lord.

There's another thing that the Bible tells us about this in Jeremiah 29:13—a foundational verse to me—*You will seek Me and find Me when you search for Me with all your heart.* So, what does this mean to search for Him with all our heart? Well, if we can't set aside five minutes to just be quiet, are we searching for Him with all our heart? I mean, how could we say we are? It would be complete hypocrisy. This is the verse right after the verse about His plans for us being good. No one ever quotes verse 13. They just quote verses 11 and 12. But this is such a wonderful promise that if our heart really wants to find Him, He's saying, "You'll find Me!" But you've got to take the time. You've got to get alone and be quiet! Then you will find Him.

So, I need to quiet my thoughts and not have an agenda. Now you see, when I go to prayer, a lot of times I'll be thinking about my plans, how I'm going to do this, and how this has got to work out, and I need an idea for this. Then I get into this line of thinking, "Well, what if this happens? Oh, that would be terrible! Oh." You know all these things going through my mind. It's like I'm meditating on all of these plans and I just have to quiet them down and listen for His voice.

Now there are a couple of other ways of hearing. In Joshua 1:8, the Lord instructs Joshua, "*Yes, keep this book of the Torah on your lips, and meditate on it day and night, so that you will take care to act according to everything written in it. Then your undertakings will prosper, and you will succeed.*"

So, this is another way of hearing from the Lord—meditating on the Word. Actually, for me, this is the greatest benefit of being in ministry and having a teaching ministry. Every week, sometimes a couple of times a week, I have to go and get into the Word and bring forth a teaching. And this is how I do that. I get some direction as to what it should be about. I then read it very carefully making sure I take notice of every word. Then I just think about that passage over and over again. I let it roll around in my mind. I imagine the event. I read it over and over, thinking about what's really happening. And pretty soon insight starts coming—new revelation. That's meditating on the Word.

The other thing I want to encourage you to do, and I don't really know how to explain this, but I do something that I call having my spiritual senses attuned. What that means is that if I'm seeking the Lord for some kind of direction, I sort of am on the lookout for Him to speak to me in various ways. So, someone might just say a casual word to me and I will wonder, "Is that what God is saying to me?" Or I'll drive by a billboard that says something that will catch my eye, and I'll ask, "Is that God's message?" Or I'll hear a song. It's being in that listening type of place. So, I hope that helps you.

Now let's dig a little deeper to learn about some more blocks to healing. First, I want to talk about the blocks to our healing that can come from dysfunctional relationships. I want to point out how sickness and disease can be caused by dysfunctions in one or more of three areas of relationships that we have. I believe you might hear from God about these three areas. What are the three relationships? First we have a relationship with God. Second we have a relationship with others. Right? And the third is one that's not often considered—another area of relationship. Can you guess what it is? Yes! We have a relationship with ourselves.

So, let's just talk a little bit about how dysfunction in those three areas of relationships can cause health problems or be blocks to our healing. The first is that sin causes separation from God. We know that. Sin also causes separation from others and from ourselves, but primarily from God.

Isaiah 59:2 (NKJV) *Your iniquities have separated you from your God and your sins have hidden His face from you so that He will not hear.*

So sin is the primary cause of separation from God. Therefore, the first step of healing is to become a child of God through the new birth that Yeshua offers to us. The greatest affect of us trusting in Yeshua is that it opens us up to have a relationship with God. So He whom we were separated from, we can now have a relationship with because He has taken our sin.

Now, here's where this goes, though. Many of us say we believe, that we are citizens of the Kingdom, that we're children of God, that we know our sins are forgiven. Yet I know, because I talk to people, that you might be one who has a dysfunctional relationship with God. You don't really believe He loves you. Deep down, you don't really have that assurance. It might be because of a dysfunctional relationship with your earthly father. When you think of relating to an authority figure like a father, you can't do it because the authority figure in your life beat you or neglected you or put you down all the time. So that's what you expect from God. Many of us are missing a very basic component in our hearts—this deep sense within us that we are loved, that we are accepted, that God has a plan for us, that God is working for our good. That's the dysfunctional part of our relationship.

Now another dysfunctional part of our relationship with God has to do with knowing the Word and receiving from it. I see two extremes of this. First there are the people who are ignorant of the Bible. If you are from this group, when you hear people teaching from the Bible or talking about it, you just can't relate to it because you don't know the stories. When somebody refers to David, you wonder, "Who's David? I don't know what David did." This ignorance is very easily remedied. You just have to get into the Bible and read!

The other extreme of this problem are people who are so immersed in the doctrines they've learned over the years that they don't grasp what they're reading. I see this often when I'm teaching. In my Messianic Judaism classes, I often teach through questions. We'll have a question. Then we'll read a Scripture that answers that question. And it amazes me. It absolutely amazes me how often many people will read a Scripture, but not really see what it says. I'll ask a question that that Scripture answered. My whole point is that I'm trying to show them that maybe something they've learned before is incorrect. Yet the people will answer with how they learned it rather than with what we just read. It's like they didn't even hear the actual words. It's the Bible but they didn't even hear it! It just went in one ear and out the other. It's like all the doctrines that we've learned—all the previous teachings—block us from hearing it!

And it so blesses me when somebody finally gets it and realizes, "All I've got to do is look at what it says, and I'll know how to answer the question!" I have the privilege of witnessing that sometimes. But before they get there oftentimes they will come out with great, eloquent answers that they've heard great teachers teach, but it isn't the answer to the question which was answered by the verse right there! I have to believe that this is what happens all the time when they read the Bible, not just when they answer my questions. What that says to me is that they're not really getting it. They're reading it and it's so familiar and they've heard so many teachings on it that they don't see what it really says. They need to say, "Lord, help me look at what it really says. Please speak to me about what You are saying here, so that I can receive it."

Another thing that separates us from God, I would say, is religion. Many of us were raised in a religion which taught that we have a wrathful God who is there to strike us with bolts of lightning when we get out of line. But the Bible says that we're His children. I love this verse in Luke that says, *Fear not little flock, your Father has resolved to give you the Kingdom* (Luke 12:32).

That's one end of the spectrum on religion. The reverse of that is where religion has taught us that we have such a permissive God who loves us so much that no matter what we do, it's not wrong. We can go do anything. All we have to do is come back and just apologize and everything will be fine and there will be no affect of that sin in our lives. So, we have these two extremes. We have the wrathful God that I don't even want to hear from because I'm afraid He's going to zap me. And we have the God that's just a big sugar daddy.

Well, sickness and disease, I believe, are connected to our relationship with God, with the One, True God who is neither of those extremes. Sickness and disease is specifically connected to our obedience of God. Read Deuteronomy 28. It is an incredible chapter speaking of the blessings of obedience and the curses of disobedience.

The second relationship area that we have dysfunction in is one I touched on a little before. It is our relationship with ourselves. Many people who I talk to suffer from self hatred, low self-esteem, guilt, condemnation, and shame that they are not living up to the standards they think they should be living up to. They have not fully received all the power of Yeshua's redemption. It's very hard to hear God saying, "I love you" when we hate ourselves!

Now, let me just say what the Bible says about this. If God says He loves us, what right do we have to not love ourselves? God tells us to obey His commands, right? And His command is to love one another. Doesn't that include ourselves? I don't see you nodding your heads on this. Is my logic going too fast for you? We are told to love one another. Does that include myself? Yes, it includes ourselves.

Now, how about this? We say we love God. God commands us to love Him and we say, "Yes, I love God!" This same God whom we love says that we are made in His image. So, if we love Him how can we hate His image, namely, ourselves? See, it's like we are saying that we hate God, if we do that. We are denying His statement of love and the enemy is very happy to agree with us about that. You can get tremendous agreement from the enemy if you want to have him agree with you that God doesn't love you. The adversary is all too eager to agree with that.

Now, here's an interesting thing I learned. In doing this series, I studied some authors that are making these connections based on medical research. Here's something that makes so much sense to me. Doctors have now found a connection between problems of poor self image or self-hatred or low self-esteem and diseases of the immune system. Now, doesn't that make sense? If you hate yourself, then your immune system that is designed to attack things that can hurt you is instead attacking what you hate. Some of these diseases of the immune system are absolutely incredible because instead of fighting off bacteria and viruses and things like that, the immune system turns on the body and begins to destroy different parts of the body—the nerves or the blood-manufacturing organs, etc. Some of these immune diseases are Lupus, Crohn's Disease, Diabetes, Rheumatoid Arthritis, and Multiple Sclerosis. Those are all auto-immune diseases where the immune system has gotten out of whack and is attacking the very body it's supposed to be protecting. Well, the connection, I think, is amazing. Many of the people who have one of these diseases, as noted, are people who also have self-hatred. Their immune system is responding to that.

The third area of dysfunctional relationships is in relating to each other. Remember, I'm going through these things because I'm expecting you to be listening to God about your own relationships and your own health. So, in the area of relationships with others, we have a long list of problems: unforgiveness, envy, bitterness, competition, hatred, anger, etc.

Here's an interesting thing about such feelings that I'm starting to understand now. As believers we often struggle with our feelings. We have strong feelings and then we read the Bible and we begin to understand that we're not supposed to go by our feelings. We're not supposed to do things just because we have feelings about them. We're supposed to go by the Word of God. If I have a very strong feeling of hatred for someone, I'm not supposed to obey that and kill them! The Bible tells me not to. I've had people come to me—even believers—(not about murder, but something else) and say, "I felt so strongly about it. I had to do it!" Well, I don't think that's the Spirit of God.

But I've been wondering, "Well, then why did you give us feelings, God?" I think I really see a key in this right here. Have you ever had someone that you were in conflict with that has hurt you so deeply and every time you think about them, you get this knot in the pit of your stomach? Yea? Okay. It's a feeling! And I believe this is how God wants us to use our feelings. He wants us to be aware of our feelings, to not hide from them, but to let them show us something. When we have a strong thing going on with someone, particularly in the area of relationships where every time we see a certain person's face, we fly into a rage, or every time we think of them, we get depressed, we should be able to conclude that there's something wrong here that we need to deal with. We need to deal with it through the Spirit of God. So, feelings are useful in these things. They're given by God.

Now, when we have feelings like this, we need to understand that it's not the other person's problem. It's our problem because it's having an affect on us. You'll see this a little bit in a scientific experiment later. In the New Covenant there are ways given to deal with those things that we have suffered when people have hurt us. Not that we will erase the memory of them and what they did, but we don't have to carry the thoughts of hatred and bitterness with us. The Spirit of God and true forgiveness can remove those harmful thoughts and heal that pain from those experiences. The reason we need to do this is because otherwise they can continue to affect our lives in very significant ways.

Something else that we might hear about from God that greatly affects our relationships is the power of our tongue. Our words can widen the gap in a broken relationship or our words can bring healing. We can say things that bring curses on ourselves or on other people. Or we can say things that help bring blessings. Other people can say things about us that can severely affect us negatively or that greatly affect us positively. This is a huge topic that would take another whole book to talk about. Suffice it to say that we do have the power to deal with the negative affect of words spoken to us or about us. However, we have to be aware of it being a problem in order to deal with it.

There's another area of relationship we don't usually think about. We have a relationship with our ancestors which could be causing a blockage to our health. Some things are handed down through the generations. You may have a disease or problem that your great, great grandmother or father or a great aunt suffered from. But that doesn't have to be the end of it because often times by the power of the Spirit of God, that can be broken. But you've got to be aware of it. Making a family tree can be a good thing to do to help you understand what the different people in your ancestry did and what they passed down to you or your relatives.

Let me just give you a little example of a Biblical insight here about this connection, not between generations, but between what's going on inside of us and sickness. In Luke 21: 25-26, Yeshua is predicting what is going to happen in the future, and He says, *"There will be signs in the sun and in the moon and in the stars and on the earth, distress of nations with perplexity, the sea and the waves roaring* (pretty much predicting what's gone on with the tsunami and hurricane Katrina, etc., right?) *men's hearts failing them from fear and the expectation of those things which are coming forth on the earth, for the powers of the heavens will be shaken.*

Does anybody see a connection here between fear and some kind of problem? Yes, heart disease! Fear is a major source of heart disease. How do we deal with fear? It's spiritually rooted. As I pointed out before, the root of fear is lack of trust in God! You may know this verse as a song—

Isaiah 43:1 *Fear not for I have redeemed you, I have called you by name.*

Do you realize that it's an imperative? Do you know what an imperative is? It is a command! See, God is saying, "Fear not." He's commanding that to us! It's a commandment! Fear is the opposite of faith and trust. And when we're in fear we're not trusting. So, what is that? It's disobedience. It's sin. And, it opens the door to the power of the evil one. How can you tell if you're disobeying it? Well, I think all of us recognize the feeling of fear. It's a very important feeling that God gave us because it protects us when we're in dangerous situations. We get afraid and we run away or we do something that keeps us safe, which is good. But day to day fear is not good. We can tell when we're walking in fear.

Fear has subcategories. The most obvious one is panic. Everybody can relate to panic—that "Oh, no!" feeling. We know when that's going on. But Philippians 4 says *"Be anxious for nothing."* Again, it's an imperative. Anxiety is just another form of fear. It's less intense than panic, but it's more ongoing. You don't get panic attacks that last for months, but you do get anxiety that lasts that long. Another word for that anxiety is worry. Actually, in the King James, it says, *"Be careful for nothing"* which is an Old English way of saying it, but it is very descriptive. God is commanding us, "Don't be full of cares for anything."

And there's a word that we throw around in our culture that refers to many of those things. It's the word "stress." How many of us say, "Oh, I'm stressed out. This is stressing me and that is stressing me." Well, why are we being stressed? It's really rooted in fear that we won't succeed, that this person will be mad at us, or that we will lose our job, etc. All of these things are stress. So, what diseases have doctors found are related to stress, anxiety, worry, and panic? Well, angina, high blood pressure, arrhythmias (irregular heart beat), immune system malfunction—all related to stress. I'd like to show you something from page 134 of Henry Wright's book, *A More Excellent Way* (Whitiker House, 2009). He's quoting here from an article in the "Health and Science" section of the *Dallas Morning News* (November 16, 1996). This is amazing. The article is titled, "Hormonal Reaction to Stress is Tied to Disease."

> Stress sends emergency hormones flowing into the bloodstream and it may cause brittle bones in women, infections, and even cancers, researchers say. A natural flight or fight reflex that gives humans the speed and endurance to escape dangers is triggered daily in many modern people, keeping the hormones in a constant hyper-readiness. In many people, these hormones (the name of the hormone here, is called Cortisol) turn on and stay on for a long time, Dr. Phillip Gold of the National Institute of Mental Health says. If you're in danger, Cortizol is good for you. It makes you able to get away! But if it becomes unregulated, it can produce disease. In extreme cases this hormonal state destroys appetite, cripples the immune system, shuts down processes that repair tissues, blocks sleep, and even breaks down bone.

So, what he's saying here is that we are designed by God to have this hormone released when there's great danger so we can get away from it. But if we're constantly in a state of stress, that hormone is constantly being released and it's not good for us. Here's another thing in this article—an amazing study at Ohio State University. It showed that routine marital disagreements can cause the fight or flight hormone reaction. "Dr. Janice KeKoth Glazer, a psychologist, said a study of ninety newly-wed couples showed that marriage arguments were particularly damaging to women. [This is amazing.] In the study, couples were put in a room together with blood-sampling needles in their arms. [Now, right away that would give me stress! But they managed to adjust to that.] Blood samples could be taken at intervals without the subjects knowing it."

So, they tested these men and women before they started this test. "A researcher then interviewed the couples and intentionally promoted discussion that aroused disagreement and argument between them." Okay? Now the couples were newly-weds! So, they should be getting along well at this point. There shouldn't have been a lot of hostility! This is what the doctor was saying. "Yet the samples taken during the disagreements showed that the women experienced sudden and high levels of stress hormones, just as if they were in a fight or flight situation of great danger. The women also had steeper increases than the men." So, men got them, too, but women had them more. "The test continued throughout an overnight hospital stay and more samples were taken just before discharge. For the men, the blood hormonal levels went back to normal, but the women still had high levels even when they were discharged."

Isn't that amazing? Now, I have to say, I have such a respect for some of the things women can do. I visited a young mother in the hospital just after her baby was born. She'd been in labor for something like a day and a half and finally had a caesarean. And she was happy and chipper! It's amazing what women can handle! But yet in other ways there are things women don't handle so well.

But what these studies are showing is that women are wired differently from men and there's an affect of stress on them. So now you can understand why God gave us Ephesians 4:26—this verse has been very important in my marriage—*Be angry but don't sin. Don't let the sun go down on your anger.* Do you see the wisdom of God in that? Do you see the power in that? When you're angry, those kinds of hormones start flowing through your body and God says, "Don't let it last because it's harmful to you." If you don't get these things cleared up, the levels stay high and this can breed all kinds of health problems.

So, medical science is confirming this connection. God knows what He is talking about. He tells us in Romans 12:18 to *"if possible, and to the extent it depends on you, live in peace"* because lack of peace creates stress in our lives. Let me just give you the last part of this article here. "People with such high levels of stress hormones are at a much greater risk of getting sick, said Dr. Ronald Glazer, an Ohio State Virologist and the husband of the doctor who did the study. "If the hormonal levels stay up longer than they should, there is a real risk of infectious disease." Amazing!

I just want to take a minute here now to look at another Scripture on fear. This verse has been foundational to me in dealing with my fears. I'm going to read it in the New King James version because David Stern in the *Complete Jewish Bible* does a little bit different thing with it. I'd like to go through this verse as we're winding up here. It's a wonderful verse and there's so much in it that relates to dealing with fear, anxiety, and stress.

I John 4:18 (NKJV) *There is no fear in love. But perfect love casts out fear because fear involves torment. But he who fears has not been made perfect in love.*

"There is no fear in love." This is saying that fear and love cannot exist in the same place. They cannot be together. In other words, when we're walking in the Love of God, and we fully grasp it—the way God wants us to grasp it—how much He loves us, there's no place for fear!

I can personally tell you that I have experienced this. I can even remember when this Scripture first became a revelation to me. You know how sometimes you remember where you were when certain important things happened to you? I was driving out of the parking lot at Building 147 at Xerox and I was somehow thinking on this Scripture, *There is no FEAR in love.* It was probably because I was afraid of something at the time. And that Scripture just became alive to me and the fear left.

Now let's look at the end of that verse.

But he who fears has not been made perfect in love.

In other words, if there is fear, there is something missing in what you could call our love covering. If there is fear, love has not accomplished what it's supposed to do, which is to eliminate fear because where there is perfect love, there is no fear.

Now, I'd like you to consider this just for a moment, just in terms of human relationships. When we know someone loves us with all their heart, can we fear them? No! Because we know they love us! Right?

But if we know someone who is a good person—we know for a fact that they are good, let's say—but we don't know that they love us. We have to have some fear of them, because no matter how good they are, if they don't love us, we don't quite trust them. Do you see that? In fact, the real issue that comes up with a nice person is, "What happens if I do something bad? How will this person react to that, if they don't really love me?" Because we fear they'll reject us for that. So, that's why love is a key issue in our personal, human relationships.

So, if we struggle with fear, it means there's a breach in one or more of our circles of relationships. And the real healing of this spiritual root, I believe, is to get our relationship of God right, first. Then if there's a breach in a relationship with someone else, it's easy to detect. You don't feel safe with that person.

The verse also says *fear involves torment*. And here's where we get to this being a source of a lot of things that we struggle with. "Torment" speaks of the realm of the enemy here, where he can put things on us. So, what's the way to get rid of that torment? What's the way to be delivered of this? Perfect love casts it out! So, the beginning of healing is reconciliation with God, with His Love, with His Fatherhood, making peace with Him. Then what follows is making peace with ourselves and making peace with others in our lives.

So, that's how we can walk in health, by walking in His perfect love and shalom. That is actually the answer to our last question, "How can we walk in health? When we stay close to Him in His Perfect Love and spend time there, meditating on His Word and listening to Him, we will be allowing Him to always point out the things that are blocking good health. He will show us any negative emotions, like anger or resentment or pride that are creeping up on us. He will show us where our relationships are slipping. He will show us where we are letting fear or anxiety sneak in. And He will convict us when we are letting our tongue lead us into sin. He will show us anything we are doing that is causing a big enough crack for the enemy to get in and get a hook on us. In other words, Yeshua will keep us walking in righteousness and in perfect shalom (peace) which will definitely maintain spiritual health, but will also help maintain good, physical and emotional health. He says He is our Healer. He is the source of our health. Spending time with Him; staying near Him, being open to Him, I'm convinced, brings health, unless He has a reason, as He did for the blind man and for Lazarus, for taking us through a trial of health trouble.

Now, there are other topics on staying healthy that we could delve into, like eating foods that build up our bodies rather than tear our bodies down, etc., but I'm going to end here. And I want to encourage you to be in prayer and not just praying, but being alone with God between now and Yom Kippur. Let me say this again. I believe that there's a special grace during these Ten Days for times of introspection, for asking God to show us the things within us that we need to deal with because they could be causing us problems.

Let's pray together.

Father, we thank You for these Appointed Times that You've shown us have a special purpose for us to deal with things during this time. And, Lord, I just pray for all of us today, that we would all have contrite hearts, that we would be willing to let Your Spirit reveal to us the things that need to change. And I also pray for each of us to have the ability and the discipline to hear from You; to take that time to be alone and to just be quiet and hear what You would say to us. And, Lord, I believe that You're going to say some significant things that are the truth and as You say in Your Word, it will set us free.

I pray, Father, that You would help us with this discipline of being quiet. Give us ears to hear what You are saying about our relationship with You. If there's something where we are not lined up with Your Word, if we're not truly trusting You, help us to change. Give us ears to hear about our relationship with ourselves, about what we think about ourselves. And help us, Lord, to overcome.

And give us insights into our relationships with each other. If there's someone that we're holding something against, if there's someone that we are bitter against, if there's unforgiveness, if there's envy—all these things—I just pray that You will reveal them.

And also in the area of our tongues, things that we've said against ourselves or against others, or the things that have been said against us, I pray You will reveal those things.

Also, reveal the affects of others on our lives going back generations and what affects are still lingering on us today. So, Lord, this is a big thing that we're asking here, but I believe that this is the time to be asking it. So we pray for You to give that revelation. In the Name of Yeshua. Amen. Amen.

CHAPTER 16

A KINGDOM OF COHANIM

So, we are still using our creativity a lot in celebrating this holiday. We understand that it is a Zih-kh'ron Teruah—a memorial of sounding of Shofars and shouting for joy. But, we keep wondering what it is exactly that we're supposed to remember at this time. I have pondered this for years, "What did God have in mind when he told Moses to remember something? What was it that He wanted Moses and the Israelites to remember?"

Now as soon as you bring up the idea of the Shofar, it, of course, brings to mind the things in the Bible that we've looked at already:

Jericho, where they blew the Shofar and the walls came tumbling down; and Gideon, when his tiny army blew the Shofars, lit the torches, and routed their enemies.

Those could be what we are supposed to remember, but you know what? They both happened after Moses wrote this! So, it couldn't have been those things.

Now the folks who created the traditional reading schedule—what we call the Parashah—decided what we should read on Rosh Hashanah. In case you aren't familiar with this, in synagogues all around the world, the same passages of Scripture are read each week. The entire five books of Moses are gone through in one year. And when they got to Rosh Hashanah, those who created the original reading schedule, chose to read the story in Genesis chapter 22 called the Akida—the story where Abraham was told to sacrifice Isaac. Of course, the story ends on a happy note when a ram is found. The association between the Shofar and the ram is why we read the story of the Akida.

Now, it's a great story. There's a lot to focus on—a lot to learn—in that story. But as I've prayed about this, I think that all three of these events are really not even near the magnitude, the importance of another event associated with the Shofar that nobody has even mentioned yet. It's something in the past. What is it? Mount Sinai!! Was Mt. Sinai important? Yes!

So, we're going to look at Mt. Sinai starting in Exodus 19. And just to catch you up on the story here, the Israelites after 430 years of being in Egypt, and the last bunch of those years being in slavery, were delivered from that slavery. They crossed the Red Sea, Pharaoh's army was wiped out, and they came to Sinai. I'm going to pick up the story in verse five where God makes a promise to the people.

Exodus 19:5-6 *Now if you will pay careful attention to what I say and keep My covenant, then you will be My own treasure from among all the peoples, for all the earth is Mine; 6 and you will be a kingdom of cohanim for Me, a nation set apart. These are the words you are to speak to the people of Isra'el.*

So we have here a promise. It's a conditional promise. "*If you obey My voice and keep My covenant ....*" But the promise is that the people will be a special treasure, a kingdom of cohanim (priests), and a holy nation. In Hebrew that "special treasure" is "s'gulah mee-kol ha-amim," "*a special people.*" The "kingdom of cohanim" is "mah-m'leh-khet cohanim." Then, of course, "and a holy nation" is "v'goy kadosh." We all recognize the word "kadosh." We sing it in songs, "Holy."

So, the people would be this kingdom of cohanim. We need to first make sure we understand what a cohanim is. As we learned before, it's plural in Hebrew. The singular is cohane. What does a cohane do? When I first started to read the Bible, (long before we had the *Complete Jewish Bible*) the word "priest" in there—as soon as any good Jewish boy reads the word "priest," it conjures up images of Catholic churches. Right? Maybe that's what it does for you. But, here you see that this is a word that Moses used. So, there were cohanim and they played a huge role in our history from the time of Moses.

So what did they do? Well, we can break down what they did to just a few things. They heard *from the people* and interceded for them *to God.* They made sacrifices and they prayed for the people. And also, very importantly, they heard *from God* and communicated it *to the people.* So, they spoke for God to the people. I think what God was promising here is that they would be a kingdom of cohanim to the rest of the world—that Israel would be a kingdom of cohanim to all the nations. And, of course, we read that there was a condition attached there. And the condition was what? Can you remember without looking back? *"Obey My voice and keep My covenant."*

So, let's move on.

Exodus 19:7-8 *Moshe* (Moses) *came, summoned the leaders of the people and presented them with all these words which ADONAI had ordered him to say. 8 All the people answered as one, "Everything ADONAI has said, we will do." Moshe reported the words of the people to ADONAI.*

Now this is awesome. This is wonderful. *"All the people answered as one,"* it says. They were in unity. And they were pledging obedience. They were pledging to listen to the voice of the Lord. They were pledging to keep the Covenant. And they were committing themselves to be *a kingdom of cohanim and a holy nation.* They would all be cohanim. So what an awesome moment this was in history. This was a turning point—a great expectation. Then in verse nine to sixteen, God gives some further instructions of what they are to do so they can hear His voice. It had to do with consecrating or cleansing themselves. Then marvelous things began to happen.

Exodus 19:17-18 *Moshe brought the people out of the camp to meet God; they stood near the base of the mountain. 18 Mount Sinai was enveloped in smoke, because ADONAI descended onto it in fire—its smoke went up like the smoke from a furnace, and the whole mountain shook violently.*

So, this, I believe, is what we are to be remembering—what happened next here.

Exodus 19:19-20 *As the sound of the shofar grew louder and louder, Moshe spoke; and God answered him with a voice. 20 ADONAI came down onto Mount Sinai, to the top of the mountain; then ADONAI called Moshe to the top of the mountain; and Moshe went up.*

If you listened to it in Hebrew, you would hear "v'yahee kol haShofar," "and when the voice of the Shofar" sounded long and became louder. It actually says, "khazak meh-ode" "became stronger and stronger." Moses spoke and God answered him "b'kol," "by voice." As I pointed out in the chapter on the Shofar, because of this—this word play, the "kol Shofar" and the "kol' of Adonai, the Shofar is associated with the voice of God. We think of wanting to hear the voice of God. The Shofar is like that voice. So, remember that for later.

The second verse that we just read was:

Exodus 19:20 *ADONAI came down onto Mount Sinai, to the top of the mountain; then ADONAI called Moshe to the top of the mountain; and Moshe went up.*

What follows in Scripture is the most important document or part of a document that has ever been written. It's the Ten Commandments! Yet some people think, "Well they're just a bunch of commandments written on stone tablets." But you know what they were? They were the beginning of the revelation of the Bible. They were the beginning of God giving us His Word!

So, I think that God meant for Yom Teruah (Rosh Hashanah) to be a memorial of remembering the sounding of the Shofar on the mountain when He gave us His Word, the Bible.

Now, one interesting question would be, "Was Yom Teruah remembered in this way in the Bible?" Do we have any example of it? And you know what? We do! We have an example in Ezra when the Israelites came back from Babylonian captivity.

Nehemiah 8:2 *Ezra the cohane brought the Torah before the assembly, which consisted of men, women and all children old enough to understand. It was the <u>first day of the seventh month</u>.*

So, Ezra did choose, for some reason, on that day, Yom Teruah, to read the Word to the people.

I'd like to focus now on a kind of soul-searching for today. It's actually in the same flow of Scripture because it happens immediately after the Ten Commandments. You must understand that the giving of the Ten Commandments was an incredible turning point in the history of the world. It was one of the most significant things. Think about the influence that this Book, the Bible, has had over the centuries. Not only on those who directly follow it, but understand that Islam came out of this book. Did you know that? Mohammed copied many things from this book. He twisted them a little (or a lot sometimes) but still they were from the Bible. So, if you consider all Christianity, all Judaism, and all of Islam—all of them—came out of this book! Incredible influence!

At this moment, at this incredible turning point—a moment in time when the entire world is hanging in the balance, if you will—what is called a Kairos moment—look what happened. The Ten Commandments had been given. God is there on this mountain. It's shaking. The Shofar has blasted. Moses has told the people what God said. The people agreed to follow God's Covenant. Then listen to what happens.

Exodus 20:18 *All the people experienced the thunder, the lightning, the sound of the shofar, and the mountain smoking. When the people saw it, they trembled. Standing at a distance,*

It was an awesome, frightening sight, so they stood afar off. That's bad enough! But, here's the awful part.

Verse 19 *They said to Moshe, "You, speak with us; and we will listen. But don't let God speak with us, or we will die."*

Now, this may not sound that important to you, but I believe what is happening here is that the people are backing out of the promise that they had made just before. Remember?

Exodus 19:5-6 *... Now if you will pay careful attention to what I say and keep My covenant, then you will be My own treasure from among all the peoples .... and you will be a kingdom of cohanim for Me, a nation set apart ....*

Instead of obeying this, I want you to grasp what they are saying here. They're saying, "Moses you be our cohane." Do you see that? "We'll listen to you!" I believe the people at this point were backing out— breaking their promise. The promise there of being a special treasure, a royal priesthood, and a holy nation was broken because they didn't want to come near and hear God. Now listen to Moses' response.

Exodus 20:20 *Moshe answered the people, "Don't be afraid, because God has come only to test you and make you fear him, so that you won't commit sins."*

So, Moses makes one last appeal, saying, "No, no!! Don't pull back!"

Exodus 20:21 *So the people stood at a distance, but Moshe approached the thick darkness where God was.*

So, I see this as a very sad ending to the story—the people are standing afar off not willing as individuals to directly interact with God. Now, lest you think this is a weird Messianic Jewish teaching, traditional Judaism also teaches this. If you know Orthodox traditions, you are aware that there is something called the Tikkun La'il Shavuot that happens at the time of Shavuot or Pentecost in the spring. It's an all-night prayer vigil that is kept before that holiday. The reason it's kept is because the Jewish scholars recognize that our ancestors were not prepared to meet with God at Mt. Sinai. So they stay up all night before Shavuot which is actually the day this happened. They pray that they will be ready to meet God. So they acknowledge that this is exactly what happened.

So, here's what I think. Because of the people's refusal, God chose the descendants of Aaron to be the cohanim. So Israel became a kingdom with cohanim—with priests—instead of a kingdom of cohanim. That's a huge difference. All the difference in the world. And perhaps this bittersweet part to the story is why in the reading plan, Akida is read instead of this passage because it's not really a victory. It's a tragedy. It was a great moment, the Word of God was given, but the people backed out on the covenant.

So, today we can look back on this from our perspective of having received the New Covenant, and we can say, "How could they have done that? We wouldn't have drawn back!" Right? We would've been right in there wanting to meet with God. We would've wanted to be this s'gulah mee-kol ha-amim, this special treasure! We would've wanted to be mah-m'leh-khet cohanim. Wouldn't you want to be a royal priest? We would've wanted to be a holy nation—goy kadosh, wouldn't we? Well, before we get too high minded, let's look at this from their perspective.

Why did they draw back? On the surface, when I first looked at it, I said, "Well, it was just because they were afraid of these awesome signs that God was doing." And I thought, "Lord, why did You have to be so theatrical? Did You really need all the thunder and lightning? You scared the people! If You hadn't done that, they would've been right there."

But, you know, as I studied further, Moses says what? "He's testing you." And I started to see that the problem was not the frightening manifestations. The problem was that they didn't want to meet with God as individuals. In defense of this, lest we get a little bit prideful, understand where we are in history at this time. At that point in time when this happened, the sacrificial system had not even been put in place. So, the idea that a person could have their sins cleansed wasn't there. The laws concerning sacrifices for atonement had not yet been given. And certainly the sacrifice of Yeshua had not happened. So I can understand a little bit of fear—of being afraid to go into the presence of God.

Just think how frightening it would be, meeting God with no assurance of forgiveness like we have today, or even like they had a few days later. There was no invitation to come boldly to the throne of grace! Can you understand that fear with me? I mean they didn't really know what was going to happen.

On the other hand, maybe the people didn't really want to be a *holy* nation. Maybe they wanted to continue to live with the pleasures of sin. Maybe they understood that being pure would be a sacrifice.

There is yet another side to this. If we study about the Levitical priesthood, we find out that there's a huge responsibility on the cohanim. What's the responsibility? There's the responsibility to pray and intercede for people. There's the responsibility to listen to God and to speak to the people, sometimes words the people don't want to hear. And there's a need to be holy. There's a need to live your life pure and without sin. And finally, for cohanim, their life is not their own. A cohane's life is dedicated to the Lord. They serve the Lord all of their life. That's their main thing to do. So for all of these reasons, the fear of the responsibility, the not wanting to be pure and holy, and maybe just laziness, not wanting to take this on, they backed away.

So, this is why the creators of the reading plan didn't want to read this story at this time. But I believe the Lord wants us to remember this event. If you read the rest of Moses' writings, the rest of the five books—if you read them with this in mind, you can see the high price that Moses had to pay because the people did not do what they were supposed to do at this time. What was his biggest problem over the next forty years? The people!! Right? It was the people doing their own thing, not listening to God. He had the burden—the responsibility—of carrying them. If you read through those first five books, it's amazing how many times Moses was at the end of his wits, saying, "God, I can't handle this."

Well, today we remember this event with a bit of a different perspective because we have the New Covenant. But I think the New Covenant tells us that we are to remember this event. Why is that? Let me show you.

1 Peter 2:9 *But you are a chosen people (*s'gulah mee-kol ha-amim - His treasured possession*), the King's cohanim (*mah-m'leh-khet cohanim - a royal priesthood*), a holy nation* (goy kadosh), *a people for God to possess!*

Do you see what's happening here? Peter is quoting the promise in Exodus 19:5-6. And he's saying, "You—you followers of Yeshua, you *are* what they were supposed to become!" So the Lord has called all Yeshua's followers to be cohanim—to be priests. And what would that make His Kingdom? It would make it a kingdom of cohanim, mahm'leh-khet cohanim. But here's the problem. That's what we're called to be, but we're all faced with the same choice as our forefathers! See, we have free-will. We're faced with that same choice of stepping in or stepping back.

Why have we been called? Well, Peter goes on. It's very clear.

1 Peter 2:9b *In order for you to declare the praises of the One who called you out of darkness into his wonderful light.*

That's really the same reason Israel was called way back then, 3500 years ago. Our forefather's were called to the nations to show forth God's light.

So, the question I want to challenge you with for these next Ten Days is, "Will you stand afar off or will you step forward and draw near the thick darkness where God is, as Moses did?"

Now, before you run away in fear, and, of course, nobody's going to say they're running away in fear, but you might be doing that in your mind, let's understand that Yeshua's life and work make a huge difference in how we see this calling and how we are equipped for responding to this calling. I'd like to read to you a few verses that tell us how we are equipped. First of all we are promised victory over sin.

Romans 6:14 *For sin will not have authority over you; because you are not under legalism but under grace.*

We're going to have victory over sin. We can live holy lives.

1 Corinthians 1:30 *It is His doing that you are united with the Messiah Yeshua. He has become wisdom for us from God, and righteousness and holiness and redemption as well!*

He is our righteousness. It's not our own ability to be right before God, but because of what Yeshua did, God sees us as right. Righteous means "right standing." And then He promises us that we can all hear His voice.

John 10:27 *My sheep hear My voice, I recognize them, they follow Me ….*

And finally, in this cohane role, we're supposed to speak something.

Acts 1:8 *But you will receive power when the Ruach HaKodesh comes upon you; you will be My witnesses both in Yerushalayim*

(Jerusalem) *and in all Y'hudah* (Judea) *and Shomron* (Samaria), *indeed to the ends of the earth!"*

So by the power of His Spirit in us, we will be able to speak for Him. We will be able to speak His Word. By the power of His Spirit within us, we will be able to overcome sin, we'll be able to hear from Him, and we'll be able to speak for Him.

But unfortunately, not all His followers have stepped forward to this calling to be royal cohanim. If we think about the history of the followers of Yeshua, for many centuries, I look at it and I can see that they adopted the same system that the Israelites adopted! For instance, we know that in the Catholic Church, what are the leaders called? Priests. Now, they didn't make up the term, they got it from Moses, but if you know something about the Catholics, not so much today, but over the past 15 centuries there was a very strong, clear distinction between the priests and the people. In fact, the priest was the only one who could read and interpret the Word! The priest was the only one who could administer the sacraments, the Lord's supper.

So, there was this division made, and what affect does that kind of thing have on all the people? Well, we as the people, we don't feel like we're cohanim! He's the cohane. I go to him to hear from God. He intercedes. I don't do those things.

Well, as the Bible became more available, 500 years or so ago, the power of the Word began to break this stronghold, and we see the Reformation happening. In the Reformation there was a big change. They stopped calling their leaders priests. Instead they called them ministers, reverends, and pastors. But in many, many places there's still a strong division between the clergy and the laity. The continuing of this discourages the people from fulfilling this calling. For centuries and even today, most people who are part of Protestant denominations all over the world, work a job, you know, they go out and work in the world. They give their offerings and the minister does the serving of God.

Now, praise God in the Messianic Movement we're beyond that problem!! Or are we? Now I am thankful that many in my congregation are beyond that problem. And I want to give thanks to God for that! What do I mean they are beyond this problem? They see that the primary purpose of their lives is to serve God—to intercede, to speak to God for the people, to speak from God to people, and to serve Him by advancing His Kingdom. But, you might not be quite in that place yet. And here are some of the reasons I hear people give for that.

- I don't think I'm qualified.
- I have so many problems. I can't help.

- I have this besetting sin that I can't get rid of, so I can't be a servant of God.

And then the one that nobody would admit, of course, is, "I like the pleasures of this world too much to put them aside." And some people who genuinely want this are not hearing from God. So they say, "What would I have to say? I don't have anything to say." Of course, they're not reading the Word very much and they're not praying very much.

So my job, and the leadership's job in your congregation, is to get you to that place. Not to see someone else as your cohane, but to be a cohane yourself. You see the Lord wants each of us to be a cohane. He wants each of us to live a holy life. He wants each of us interceding. He wants each of us hearing from Him and communicating to the people; serving Him. Now let me temper this a little bit. That doesn't mean that everyone is going to get up and go start a congregation. Okay? Or quit their job and go into full-time ministry. If you look at the Levites, they all had different functions. They served at different times and different places. There was only one High Priest—only one Cohane HaGadol, but the others made sacrifices, carried wood. They sang. They cleaned. They did all kinds of things—all about serving.

Another critical thing to understand about the Levites is that the Bible says they had no property. The land that was divided up for the rest of the Israelites was not given to the Levites, because the Lord said, "I am your property—your inheritance." So they forsook that and dedicated themselves to the Lord. Serving God was their identity.

So, I'm going to end here by asking the question that maybe is on your heart right now, "Where am I at? Have I stepped into that role? Have I stepped forward into that place of meeting God? Or have I stepped back?" Well, let me give you some test questions here and you will know.

Do you have a burden for people—especially those who don't know the Lord? Do you find yourself crying out for them and praying for them, and risking being rejected to share with them about the Truth?

Do you hear from God? Again, there are three ways to hear from God: through His Word, through listening, and through being alone with Him. He wants you to hear His voice every day, all year.

And do you have a desire to serve? Do you have a willingness to humble yourself to serve? You know some of those priests, they took out the ashes. And they took out the "ofel." Do you know what that is? It's the excrement of the animals that were going to be sacrificed. They served in lowly ways. Some of them served in very exalted ways, but others served in very lowly ways. So is there a willingness to humble yourself to serve?

Well, the key is if you're thinking, "Well, I don't know if I'm in the right place in all these things," to then let these next Ten Days be a time to seek the Lord for what the obstacle is.

- Is it that you have a besetting sin that you need to be set free from?
- Is it that you just don't want to give up the pleasures of this world?
- Is it that there are so many cares—so many troubles in your life that you have to deal with, that you don't have time to serve God?

Or is it that you don't know how to hear from Him? Because once you begin hearing His voice, He will tell you that He has a plan for your life. I don't have to tell you. He'll tell you—a plan for your good, a plan that brings fulfillment, a plan for which you can bear fruit and accomplish things beyond your dreams, according to His dreams.

So, I want to leave you with that challenge: If you are a follower of Yeshua, I challenge you to accept the call on your life to be a cohane, and to begin to pray to fulfill that call. Turn away from the cares and pleasures of this world to this calling.

Now these Days of Awe are days for t'shuvah which can also be thought of as breaking up the fallow ground of our hearts. To prepare ourselves for our role as royal cohanim, we need to each start looking at our hearts. I can't look at your heart. Each of us has to look at our own heart. And that's the beauty of God giving us this time. He says to do this every year. He knows we need a time to examine our hearts every year.

On Yom Kippur we will read through the traditional list of sins, called the "Al Khet." But we need to do more than read through that list of sins. We need to examine our hearts and find out what's holding us back. So, I want to encourage you to draw your attention away from other things during these Ten Days, and look at the state of your heart. Consider your motives—why you're doing things—your character, your actions. Look over your past. Remember your sins and repent of them.

I was given an article, written by Charles Finney, edited by Keith and Melody Green and published in their "Last Days Newsletter." It is eight pages long. It's really a very powerful article to help you break up the fallow ground. I want to encourage you to read it. Reading it will help you break up your fallow ground whether you're already serving the Lord as a cohane or you're just now considering drawing near the thick darkness where God is, as Moses did. So that's my encouragement to you.

Let's Pray.

Lord, we thank You for Your Yom Teruah and the Days of Awe to follow. And I just thank You, Lord, that every person who has prayed and committed themselves to follow You, is called to be a special treasure, a royal cohane, and part of this holy nation. And so I just pray right now that Your Spirit would impart an understanding that this is the Truth, that You have really called us to be these things.

[If you have any doubt that you're called, just raise up your hands to the Lord and say, "Lord, show me. Lord, I need assurance that I'm called to be a cohane in Your royal Kingdom. Give me assurance of that."]

And Father, we thank You for enabling us to fulfill this calling. We repent of standing afar off, backing away, expecting others to go close to You for us. Give us courage to draw near the thick darkness where You are. In reality it's not such a thick darkness. It's really a beautiful place where You welcome us. Give us a burden for the lost, for the hurting, for the hungry. Give us a desire to hear from You, O Lord, to be in Your Word. Give us a desire to be holy before You, to be people that are kadosh. And as we enter into these Ten Days, O Lord, we pray that You would, by Your Spirit, reveal to us the things that are holding us back. And I pray, Lord, for each person, that these Ten Days would not just be another ten days, but they would truly make an effort to be alone with You, to hear Your voice, and to seek You for that revelation of the things that need to change in their lives. And we ask these things in the mighty Name of Yeshua. Amen. And amen.

Breaking Up The Fallow Ground Handout
An Outline For Repentance.

Charles G. Finney
Edited and paraphrased by Keith & Melody Green
Further edited and paraphrased by Jim Appel

Charles Finney saw countless tens of thousands come to the Lord and all before the days of radio, TV, mass publications, or internet! We thank God for continuing to anoint and use his writings. Many thousands have been helped by this handout to break through to God's precious forgiveness. Remember one thing as you read this—God loves you so much, and is waiting for you to be thoroughly cleansed by His grace through repentance.

Hosea 10:12 (KJV) *"Break up your fallow ground: for it is time to seek the Lord, till He come and rain righteousness upon you...."*

Fallow ground is ground which has once been tilled, but has gotten hard and now lies wasted. It needs to be broken up and made soft again before it is ready to receive seed. If you mean to break up the fallow ground of your heart, you must begin by looking at your heart—examine carefully the state of your mind and see where you are. Many people never even seem to think about doing this. They pay no attention to their own hearts, and never know whether they are doing well in their walk with the Lord or not—whether they are bearing fruit or are totally barren. But God has set an Appointed Time each year for doing this. Now is the time. You must draw off your attention from all other things and look into this right now! Make a business of it. Do not be in a hurry.

Examining ourselves and breaking up the fallow ground doesn't mean that we just take a casual glance at our past life, see that it has been full of sin, and then go to God and make a sort of general confession asking for forgiveness. General confessions of sin are not good enough. Why? Our sins were committed one by one; and as much as we are able, we ought to review and repent of them one by one! It's a good idea to carry around pen and some paper as you go over them, and write them down as they come to mind.

Go over them as carefully as a businessman goes over his books; as often as a sin comes to your memory, write it down! To help us we have this list. What this list is going to do is remind us of what the Word of God says is sin.

Now, if you find you have committed a fault against anyone, and that person is within your reach, go and confess it immediately and get that out of the way. If they are too far away for you to go and see them, sit down and write them a letter (or better yet call them) and confess the injury you have committed against them. If you have defrauded anybody, send the money, the full amount and the interest.

As you go over the catalogue of your sins, be sure to resolve them for immediate and entire reformation. Wherever you find anything wrong, commit yourself at once in the strength of God, to sin no more in that way. It will be of no benefit to examine ourselves unless we determine to change what we find wrong in heart, our temper, or our conduct. Do not put it off – this is what the Ten Days of Awe are for!

Go to work! Be thorough! Don't think about getting off easy by going around the stumbling blocks. Take them up out of the way! In breaking up our fallow ground, we must remove every obstacle. Things may be left that you may think are little things. Then you may wonder why you don't have your peace with God. The reason is your proud and carnal mind has covered up something God has required you to confess and remove. Unless you take up your sins in this way, and consider them in detail, one by one, you can form no idea of the amount or weight of them.

You should go over the list as thoroughly and as carefully and as solemnly as if you were preparing yourself for the Judgment!

I Corinthians 11:31 (KJV) *For if we would judge ourselves, we should not be judged.*

Sins of Omission

These are things we didn't do that we should have! These often stem from our iniquity, our carnal, fleshly nature.

Lack of Love for God

Mark 12:30 *And you are to love ADONAI your God with all your heart, with all your soul, with all your understanding and with all your strength.'*

Matt. 22:37-38 *You are to love ADONAI your God with all your heart and with all your soul and with all your strength. This is the greatest and most important mitzvah* (commandment).

Think how grieved and alarmed you'd be if you suddenly realized a great lack of affection for you in your wife, husband, or children, if you saw that someone else had captured their hearts, thoughts, and time. Perhaps in such a case you would almost die with a just and holy jealousy. God calls Himself a jealous God. Have you given your heart to other loves and offended Him? Lack of love for God is idolatry.

Ingratitude (Un-thankfulness)

Write down all the times you can remember when you have received great blessings and favors from God for which you have never given thanks. How many cases can you remember? Some remarkable protection where your life was spared, some wonderful turn of events that saved you from ruin. Write down the instances of God's goodness to you when you were still in sin, before your conversion, for which you have never been half-thankful enough - and the uncountable mercies you have received since. How long is the list of times where your ingratitude has been so black that you are forced to hide your face in shame?! Get on your knees and confess them one by one to God, and ask Him to forgive you. As you're confessing these, they will immediately remind you of others . . . write them down too. Go over them three or four times in this way, and see what an incredible number of times God has given you mercy for which you have never thanked Him!

Neglect of the Bible

Put down the cases when perhaps for weeks or longer God's Word was not a pleasure to you. Some people, indeed, read over whole chapters in such a way that afterwards they could not tell you what they had been reading. If that is so with you, no wonder your life has no direction, and your relationship with God is in such a miserable state.

Unbelief.

Recall the instances in which you have virtually charged the God of truth with lying, by your unbelief of His express promises and declarations. If you have not believed or expected to receive the blessings which God has clearly promised, you have called Him a liar.

Lack of Prayer

Think of all the times you have neglected private prayer, family prayer, and group prayer meetings; or you've prayed in such a way as to grieve and offend God more than if you hadn't prayed at all.

Neglect of Fellowship

Have you allowed yourself to make small and foolish excuses that have prevented you from attending meetings? Have you ever neglected and poured contempt upon the gathering of the saints merely because you "didn't like church"?!

The Manner in which You have Performed Spiritual Duties
Think of all the times when you have spoken about God with such a lack of feeling and faith, in such a worldly frame of mind, that your words were nothing more than the mere chattering of a wretch who didn't deserve that God should listen to him at all. Or think of when you have prayed in such an unfeeling and careless way that if you had been put under oath five minutes later, you could not say what you had been praying for.

Lack of Love for Souls
Look around at all your friends and relatives, and think of how little compassion you have felt for them. You have stood by and seen them going straight to hell, and it seems as though you didn't even care! How many days have there been when you have failed to make their wretched condition the subject of even one single fervent prayer, or to prove any real desire for their salvation?

Lack of Care for the Poor and Lost in Foreign Lands
Perhaps you have not cared enough about them to even attempt to learn of their condition. Do you avoid mission's magazines? Or mission websites? How much do you really know or care about the unconverted masses of the world? Measure your desire for their salvation by the self-denial you practice in giving from your substance to send them the Gospel. Do you deny yourself even the hurtful excesses of life, such as tobacco or alcohol? Do you defend your standard of living? Will you not suffer yourself any inconvenience to save them? Do you daily pray for them in private? Are you setting aside funds to put into the treasury of the Lord when you go up to pray? (As in the story of the widow's mite - Mark 12:41-44.) If your soul is not agonized for the poor and lost of this world, then why are you such a hypocrite as to pretend to be a follower of Yeshua? (See Matt. 25:31-46.)

Robbing God
Think of all the instances in which you have totally misspent your time, squandering the hours which God gave you to serve Him, and save souls. Precious time wasted in vain amusement or worthless conversation, in reading worldly novels, or even doing nothing; cases where you have misused your talents and ability to think. Think of how you have squandered God's money on your lusts, or spent it for things which you really didn't need, which did not contribute to your health, comfort, or usefulness. Think of a professing believer using God's money to poison himself with tobacco or intoxicating drink!

Misusing God's Name

Exodus 20:7 *"You are not to use lightly the name of ADONAI your God, because ADONAI will not leave unpunished someone who uses His name lightly."*

This is talking about using the God's Name or His Son's Name as a curse word. But how about claiming we have heard His voice when we are really not sure?

Not Keeping the Sabbath

Exodus 20:8-11 *"Remember the day, Shabbat, to set it apart for God. You have six days to labor and do all your work, but the seventh day is a Shabbat for ADONAI your God. On it, you are not to do any kind of work -not you, your son or your daughter, not your male or female slave, not your livestock, and not the foreigner staying with you inside the gates to your property. For in six days, ADONAI made heaven and earth, the sea and everything in them; but on the seventh day he rested. This is why ADONAI blessed the day, Shabbat, and separated it for himself.*

This is letting other things be our priority on the day devoted to Him, whether as a Jew on Saturday or as a Gentile on another day.

Not Honoring Our Parents

Exodus 20:12 *"Honor your father and mother, so that you may live long in the land which ADONAI your God is giving you.*

Speaking poorly of them, or criticizing them, contending with them is dishonoring them.

Sins of Commission

Envy

Have you been jealous of those in a higher position? Have you envied those more talented or more useful than yourself? The sign of envy is that it has caused you pain to hear them praised. Has it pleased you more to dwell on the faults of others rather than on their virtues, on their failures rather than their successes?

Bitterness

Are you harboring a grudge or a bitter spirit toward anyone? When people mistreat us, we find it hard to forgive. We nurse the pain, keeping the wound open. This is sin! To get rid of this sin we must spend as much time as needed with the Lord until we can forgive every offense, until every last root of anger and resentment is gone, until God heals the wound, until it doesn't hurt anymore, until we can love that person enough to sincerely pray for them.

Slander (Gossip)

Think of all the times we have spoken behind people's backs of faults (real or supposed) unnecessarily and without cause. Love "hopes all things," but we sometimes give no benefit of the doubt and suspect or accuse of the worst. This is slander. We need not lie to be guilty of slander. To tell the truth with the intent to injure is slander.

Cheating

God has said that we should treat all men in the same manner we would like to be treated (Matt. 7:12). Not that you should do what you would expect them to do. If that were the rule it would allow for all kinds of evil. When you don't treat people right, in business deals, etc., you are cheating them of what God intended for them!

Have you cheated the government? In other words, have you accepted unemployment insurance, welfare, food stamps, social security, student loans, etc., gained by fraud?

Lying

Any form of designed deception is lying. If we purpose to make an impression other than naked truth, we lie. Think of all your words, looks, and actions designed to make an impression on others contrary to the truth, for selfish reasons.

Hypocrisy.

For examples of hypocrisy, think of all the times you prayed for things you didn't really care about or confessed sins that you never intended to stop doing.

Love of Things and Possessions

What has been state of our hearts concerning our earthly possessions? Have we looked at them as really ours as if we had a right to use or dispose of them as our own? If we have loved property and sought after it for its own sake or to gratify ambition, we have sinned and must repent.

Vanity

How many times have you spent more time decorating your body to go to a meeting, than you have in preparing your heart and mind for the worship of God? You have cared more about how you appeared outwardly to men than how your soul appeared in the sight of God. You sought to draw off the attention of God's people to look at your pretty appearance. And you pretend that you do not care anything about having people look at you? Be honest about it! Would you take all this pain about your looks if every person were blind?

Levity (A spirit of excessive, inappropriate or ungodly humor)

How often have you joked before God, as you would not have dared in the presence of an earthly dignitary or important official? You have either been an atheist and forgotten that God exists, or you have had less respect for Him and His presence (which is everywhere) than you would have had for a mere judge on earth.

Bad Temper

Perhaps you have been irritable towards, or angry at, or have even mistreated, or worse yet—actually abused, verbally, mentally, or physically, your wife, husband, children, parents, siblings, neighbors, employees, co-workers, or fellow Believers. Write it all down! Get free of this stronghold from the enemy!

Exodus 20:12 *Do not murder.*

Yeshua said if we nurse anger against our brother or call him a fool it's as bad as murdering him. We could gather all the sins against other people and place them in this category. Let's repent of our murderous anger and rage and be set free from it.

Worship of Idols and Other Religions

(Note from Keith Green: *I found as I was sitting down to write out my sins, that there were whole categories of sins that are common today, that would never even have been spoken of to the congregations in Finney's day. Some of these include drugs, sexual sins, and the whole area of idolatry and witchcraft.*)

False peace induced by drugs; the occult involvement, including astrology, witchcraft, meditation, yoga, and the whole gamut of Eastern religions and philosophies, including New Age. These are all grave sins and must be completely forsaken.

Idolatry

Exodus 20:2-5 *"I am the Lord your God, who brought you out of the land of Egypt, out of the house of bondage. You shall have no other gods before Me.* "You shall not make for yourself a carved image, or any likeness of anything that is in heaven above, or that is in the earth beneath, or that is in the water under the earth; you shall not bow down to them nor serve them. For I, the Lord your God, am a jealous God,*

If anything in your life is more important to you than the Lord, if anything is taking away your time, your energy, or your focus from Him, that is idolatry.

Sexual Sin

Yeshua said that to look upon a woman (we would say, or a man) with lust is as bad as committing adultery. This sin is possibly also committed when we dress in a way as to cause someone to lust after us.

Conclusion

Now, after truly repenting, you should feel free and light, as if burdens have been lifted off your heart, as if you are walking without gravity. There should be a new sense of joy that is pushing a smile onto your lips. If you don't feel this, then perhaps you haven't pressed all the way through to receiving God's forgiveness. Perhaps you are still stuck in the place of feeling guilty and condemned for all the sins God revealed. Or perhaps you are still feeling shocked to find yourself such a sinner, and shame has taken over. Shame and condemnation are not from God. The Ruakh HaKodesh convicts us to repentance. He does not condemn us.

Romans 8:1 (KJV) *There is therefore now no condemnation to them which are in Christ Jesus, who walk not after the flesh, but after the Spirit.*

Repeat this verse aloud over and over until you can feel God's forgiveness and Love soothing your spirit with the full realization of Him now being pleased with you.

CHAPTER 17

THE ONE WHO IS
FORGIVEN MUCH, LOVES MUCH

Leviticus 23:24-25 *"Tell the people of Isra'el, 'In the seventh month, the first of the month is to be for you a day of complete rest for remembering, a holy convocation announced with blasts on the shofar.*

Leviticus 23:2 *"Tell the people of Isra'el: 'The designated times of ADONAI which you are to proclaim as holy convocations are my designated times. Do not do any kind of ordinary work, and bring an offering made by fire to ADONAI.' "*

In Hebrew, the word that the *Complete Jewish Bible* translates here as "designated times" is "Moadim." The NIV uses the term "appointed feasts", the KJV and the NKJV use the term "feasts of the Lord." As I said at the beginning of this book, I like the term the New American Standard Bible (NASB) uses, which is "appointed times of the Lord."

So, the Lord has made an appointment with us on these days. He has set the agenda for us.

Well, I pray about this every time we come around to this time of year to try to understand it. And this year what came to me was this.

God's calendar laid out in Leviticus 23 for the whole year, is a carefully constructed calendar with a purpose—a very clear, strong purpose. He wants us to experience something. He wants to do something in our lives through the times He has appointed.

So, if we look at that calendar, we find that Rosh Hashanah or Yom Teruah comes ten days before Yom Kippur. Yom Kippur is the day that atonement was made for the nation of Israel. We think of atonement as sacrifice for forgiveness of sin and that's about it. But really it is that and so much more! You might be thinking what can be more than that. But there is more than that in the Day of Atonement.

Why was a Day of Atonement needed in ancient Israel? Well, the Bible teaches us that God is omnipresent. God is here with us right now and God is in the farthest reaches of the universe right now. But at times God makes Himself known in a way we can experience with our human perception, whether it's with our natural senses or our spiritual sense. Somehow, probably most of you have experienced this, you have this awesome moment and you say, "God is with us." You say, "I was in God's presence. It was awesome! I experienced it!" Have you ever experienced that?

We call this a "manifestation of the presence of God." Now, the principle to understand, though, is that in the Scriptures the most often mentioned description of God is that He is Kadosh. He is Holy. In Hebrew that word, "kadosh" means "separate." He is separate from evil. He is separate from sin. He is holy. He is pure. Sin and evil cannot dwell in the presence of God. So, the principle that we have is that the greater the manifestation of our Holy God, the greater the need for the people in the presence of that holy manifestation to also be holy.

So, on Yom Kippur atonement was necessary not just for the forgiveness of sin, but it was necessary so that the manifest presence of the Holy God of Israel could dwell in the Temple among the Israelites. And that happened first in Moses' Tabernacle in the desert, and then in the Temple Solomon built which Ezra and Nehemiah rebuilt.

Here's how I understand this. You can argue with me about this, but here's how I understand it. God is Holy, so, if we have sin or evil in us, we cannot survive in the presence of God. So, without atonement, God's presence would have consumed the people. Nobody could have been close to that place. I get this from a verse in Exodus. It's a very interesting verse. What's happening here is that the Israelites have sinned terribly with the golden calf and God tells them, "Okay, go up and take the Land, but I'm not going to go with you." And Moses begins to plead with God, saying, "Please go with us."

Exodus 33:3 (NKJV) *Go up to a land flowing with milk and honey; for I will not go up in your midst, lest I consume you on the way, for you are a stiff-necked people.*"

What God was saying was that your sin is so great that if I would come down into your midst to be with you, you would just burn up. You would vaporize. That's the awesomeness of the true manifestation of the presence of God.

So, following this, to prevent the people from being consumed, atonement was made and God's presence was able to come. Then after that, once per year atonement was made on Yom Kippur for the entire nation of Israel. Understand that atonement was made whether the person was there sacrificing or not. It was made by the cohanim. It was made for everybody so God could dwell with them. Atonement was made by the sacrifice of two animals: one for sin and one for iniquity (described in Leviticus 16). This enabled the presence of God to dwell amongst the people of Israel.

I'd like you to grasp the great importance this held for the people. Here's a way of thinking of it. Suppose there was a manifestation of God's presence in Washington D.C. Okay? Now, the first thing people say is that there wouldn't be any politicians there. They'd all be consumed, right? Well, let's say the manifest presence of God lived in Washington D.C. How would we feel about that? Would we be afraid that any enemy could ever attack us? No, because the presence of God is in our nation! Would we be afraid that there would be a plague or a famine? No, because the presence of God is there! So, understand that to the people in ancient Israel, to have the presence of God in their midst was the most important thing in their national life! That was what it was all about! God's presence protected them and caused them to be blessed. Enemies couldn't attack them; their crops were plentiful; they had joy, health, and justice. God's presence was everything to them.

So, from ancient Jewish sources, because it was so important, we understand that Yom Teruah began the Ten Days of Awe. It was to prepare for the making of atonement so that God's presence could remain for another year. Why did that need preparation? Well, imagine if the atonement was made and nobody cared! Could you imagine what that would be like? I mean God would not be pleased! If they made the atonement and people's attitude was, "Oh yeah. They made the atonement again. Big deal!" That would be awful. And I don't think the atonement would have worked, do you? How could if work if the people weren't repentant?

So God set up this calendar with these Ten Days before the Atonement and said, "I want you to start meditating on My holiness. I want you to start meditating on My awesomeness. I want you to start meditating on your own sin and your own unworthiness and how much you need to have a day of atonement so that My presence can dwell in your midst." This is why Yom Teruah comes ten days before Yom Kippur. The people sought God, and repented for themselves so that when atonement was made they would appreciate it! They would have their sinfulness revealed by the Spirit of God during those Ten Days and then when atonement was made there would be this joyous cry of gratitude. They would have soft hearts and thanksgiving and overflowing of joy would be there. This would really be like a personal revival once a year. The Ten Days of Awe would lead to this.

And then, that's not the end of this particular calendar period. Four days later we have the most joyous of Jewish holidays, Sukkot, the Feast of Tabernacles! What's the joy all about? The atonement has been made! We have God's presence in our midst! We're thanking Him for that and for the harvest. The joy is overflowing! That's how I understand it went in ancient Israel and when the Temple was still standing.

Traditional Jewish people still do some of that today. They remember the blessings of God over the past year. They also remember that our future is in God's hands. Both are good things to do. They do observe the Ten Days of Awe by doing personal repentance and soul searching and resolving to change for the better which is also good.

The Shofar plays a big part in all of this process for them and for us. The sounding of the Shofar is a powerful, loud sound that wakes us up and makes us remember how awesome and Holy our God is and how sinful we are. It reminds us of our need to repent and change. It helps us remember His Laws and to realize how we've broken His Laws. So like Jews everywhere right now, we should be remembering our past year, and our iniquity, sin and transgressions.

So, for Yom Teruah and the Days of Awe the practices of the Jewish community are all pretty similar today to how things were in Biblical times. But Yom Kippur, the day the Ten Days lead to, is very different today. Even though there has been a nation of Israel for the past sixty years. What's missing? The Temple. Today there is still no Temple. The Temple was destroyed by Rome thirty-seven years after Yeshua's crucifixion. And according to Leviticus 17:1-9, sacrifices can only be made at the Temple. So, ever since the year 70 CE, there has been no animal sacrificing. So, atonement has not been made for 1937 years!

You are aware that there are groups in Israel who are seeking to rebuild the Temple. I believe it's going to happen. And they are planning to re-institute the sacrifices. Now, I don't know how long the Lord will allow them to actually make animal sacrifices. But, as for now without the Temple they can't even start them.

So, if you ask traditional Jewish people, "When you go to the synagogue on Yom Kippur and after you spend a whole day there fasting and praying, has atonement been made for you?" They would answer, "Well, I don't know." Today there's no faith in an atonement for the nation because it is not Biblically supported. There's no expectation for atonement. They only have a hope that God will forgive personal sin. And what about the manifest presence of God coming? Well, forget about that. There's certainly no expectation of God's manifest presence dwelling in the Land or coming to the Temple Mount! Believe me! Nobody is anticipating that to happen on Yom Kippur. It would be awesome if it did, but no one is expecting it.

So that's modern Judaism, but how are we—those who have the Brit Hadashah, the New Covenant—supposed to keep these Moadim in light of the revelation in the Brit Hadashah? For many, many centuries, the church has said, "Well, that revelation says you're not supposed to keep these holidays." But you are reading this book because you believe like I do that there is something about these days—that God gave them and He said to observe them forever and so they've got to have some kind of meaning. So, let's talk about what the meaning is in the light of the revelation we have today. Read this verse with me. Yeshua said:

Matthew 5:17 *"I came not to destroy the Torah but to fulfill it."*

So, how did He fulfill this particular part of the Torah, this instruction that God has given us? Well, if you think about it a little, it becomes very clear. His atoning sacrifice on the cross fulfilled the Yom Kippur sacrifices. Through Yeshua there is atoning for sin and iniquity for all who will receive Him as Messiah and Lord. Let me just explain a little bit more about sin and iniquity. Yeshua fulfilled the Yom Kippur sacrifices of the two goats. One goat was sacrificed humanely. That was for sin. The other goat, the scapegoat, actually suffered a painful death being thrown off a very high cliff and dying as it hit the rocks at the bottom. That goat, the Scriptures tell us, died for iniquity.

Well do you remember what the difference is between sin and iniquity? I know when I first read it in Scripture, I thought they were just synonyms for the same thing. Well, according to the Hebrew, sin is missing the mark, not living up to God's standard for behavior or speech. It is a violation of God's laws. So, it's an act—something we do. Iniquity is not that. Iniquity is our inclination to evil.

Yeshua's sacrifice actually atoned for both of these things. It's amazing how the prophet Isaiah in chapter 53 addresses this where he says "He was wounded for our transgressions and He was bruised for our iniquity."

Now, remember, the Yom Kippur atoning sacrifices in the Temple did more than atone for sin and iniquity. What did they do? It allowed what? Yes, it allowed the manifest presence of God to dwell in the Temple. Our bodies are called what? They are called temples of the Holy Spirit. So, Yeshua's atoning did more than bring us forgiveness of sin. What else did it do for His followers? It allowed the presence of God to dwell in this fleshly Temple. So, you see, without His sacrifice, we could not have the Holy Spirit of God dwelling within us. The Spirit dwelling in you and I is a manifestation of the presence of God!! It's the greatest manifestation of the presence of God—that the Spirit of God dwells in you and you know it. Do you know that the Holy Spirit dwells in you? That's an incredible thing!

But what about Yom Teruah (Rosh Hashanah)? What is the significance to followers of Yeshua today who have that atoning sacrifice? When I first came to believe, I brought some of these things up to a pastor in our church, and he said, "Well, you don't need to keep these holidays because He has already made the atonement." He was thinking we wanted to go out and make the atonement again. But obviously we're not supposed to do that because in Hebrews it says this speaking about Yeshua:

Hebrews 9:12 *He (Yeshua) entered the Holiest Place once and for all. And he entered not by means of the blood of goats and calves, but by means of his own blood, thus setting people free forever.*

The author of Hebrews here is not talking about Passover. On Passover nobody went into the Holiest Place. He's talking about Yom Kippur when the High Priest, the Cohane HaGadol, went into the Holy of Holies, and Yeshua fulfilling that. So, because Yeshua did it once and for all, and it doesn't have to be done over and over every year, we should be <u>even more grateful</u> than the ancient Israelites were.

But here's the question. I want you to be honest with me. Do you live in a continual state of gratitude for that sacrifice and a continual state of awareness of how unworthy you are of receiving the Spirit within you, and that need you have for atonement? Because I don't. I slip away from that. I need to be refreshed in that. Are you honest enough to say that's you, too; that you need that refreshing periodically?

So, here's what I see. This refreshing is all the more difficult because it's done forever. It doesn't happen once a year. So, God gave Yom Teruah in the calendar, I believe, to give us an annual day to restore that attitude of gratitude that we're supposed to have, that thankfulness, that soft heart to the Lord. I believe that it was always God's plan that followers of Yeshua, like the early Jewish followers who were the entire early church, would keep these Ten Days of introspection, of soul-searching, of seeking the Ruakh HaKodesh (Holy Spirit) for a fresh revelation of God's holiness; and of our own sin and iniquity. And I believe the early followers did that year after year to remind themselves of what He had done.

We need to do the same today, just like we did in the last chapter in "breaking up the fallow ground" of our hearts. This helps to strengthen our faith and remain grateful for and rejoice in His once-and-for all atonement. It will "restore the joy of our salvation" (Psalm 51:12) Then when Yom Kippur comes we will appreciate Yeshua's work in the way it deserves.

So, I'd like to now go to a story in one of the Gospels—one of my favorite stories. Yeshua taught us something about the need to have this attitude in such a powerful way. It always touches my heart and I hope it will touch yours, too.

Luke 7:36-37 *One of the P'rushim* (Pharisees) *invited Yeshua to eat with him, and He went into the home of the Parush* (Pharisee) *and took His place at the table. A woman who lived in that town, a sinner, who was aware that He was eating in the home of the Parush, brought an alabaster box of very expensive perfume ....*

Now, let's think a little bit about this woman. She was publicly known as a sinner. I mean the only thing I can think of is that she must have been a prostitute. I don't know who else would be publicly known as a sinner. I believe this was actually Miryam (Mary) from Magdala. You might know her as Mary Magdalene. We are not sure, but her identity is not important to the story. She comes in. Obviously, she was not invited to this home, but she sneaks in.

Luke 7:38 ... (she) *stood behind Yeshua at His feet and wept until her tears began to wet His feet. Then she wiped His feet with her own hair, kissed His feet and poured the perfume on them.*

Now, I don't know about you, but it's hard to imagine this actually happening. Could you imagine yourself sitting there and someone coming and doing this? I mean, it would be embarrassing. It would be almost frightening. It was such an intense, emotional moment. But, what about the other side? Can you imagine yourself doing what this woman did? Kind of busting into this home of an important person in town and coming up behind Yeshua, and just weeping and pouring your tears on His feet, and pouring this perfume on Him. Just think about where she was emotionally to do that? I once heard a definition of someone who was a "Jesus freak," a term that was used in the sixties and seventies. The definition was, it is somebody who loves Jesus more than you do. I think this woman fits in that category. I believe all of us would say, "Whew! This woman really loved the Lord to have done that!!"

Luke 7:39 *When the Parush* (Pharisee) *who had invited Him saw what was going on, he said to himself, "If this man were really a prophet, He would have known who is touching Him and what sort of woman she is, that she is a sinner."*

Now, you have to understand the culture of that time. The Pharisees' understanding was that if you were touched by a sinner, it made you unclean. You were then not clean enough to go into the Temple to worship. You would have to go through an extensive purifying process to be declared clean again. So, you never wanted anyone you knew was a sinner to touch you. And he thought, "This guy is supposed to be a prophet! He should know this. He shouldn't let this person touch him."

Luke 7:40 *Yeshua answered, "Shim'on,* (Simon) *I have something to say to you." "Say it, Rabbi," he replied.*

Yeshua knew what Shimon was thinking. We call this a word of knowledge. We saw this before in the story of the man whose friends let him down through the roof. Yeshua knows our thoughts. Shimon was soon to become aware of this.

Luke 7:41-44 *"A certain creditor had two debtors; the one owed ten times as much as the other. When they were unable to pay him back, he canceled both their debts. Now which of them will love him more?" Shim'on answered, "I suppose the one for whom he canceled the larger debt." "Your judgment is right," Yeshua said to him. Then, turning to the woman, He said to Shim'on, "Do you see this woman? I came into your house—you didn't give me water for My feet, but this woman has washed My feet with her tears and dried them with her hair!*

Now culturally understand that washing a guest's feet was part of the common customs of the day because they walked on the dusty roads and they wore sandals. So, it was the custom to wash feet, especially for an honored guest.

Luke 7:45 *You didn't give me a kiss; but from the time I arrived, this woman has not stopped kissing my feet!*

Again, this was a common custom. When an honored guest arrived, the host kissed them on the cheek.

Luke 7:46 *You didn't put oil on My head, but this woman poured perfume on My feet!*

Anointing the head with oil was another common custom of honoring a guest.

Luke 7:47-49 *Because of this, I tell you that her sins—which are many!—have been forgiven, because she loved much. But someone who has been forgiven only a little loves only a little." Then He said to her, "Your sins have been forgiven." At this, those eating with Him began saying among themselves, "Who is this fellow that presumes to forgive sins?" But He said to the woman, "Your trust* (or your faith) *has saved you; go in peace."*

Isn't that an amazing story? Powerful, powerful story! But there is an important principle here that I think many people miss when they read this story. Which debtor loved the forgiving creditor more? The one that owed more!

Why did the sinful woman show greater love for Yeshua than the Pharisee? Because she was forgiven more! It's very simple! She was a bigger sinner than he. Now, the thing that I think confuses some people is that the way it is actually written in English it sounds like she was forgiven because she loved much. But that's not what He's saying at all here. He's saying, she was demonstrating such intense love <u>because</u> she knew she was forgiven of so much. Do you see that? She was the one with the ten times bigger debt. That's why she was so loving. It's very important to see that. The wording can fool you because it sounds like it is the other way around, "Oh, she was forgiven much because she loved so much." No! She was forgiven of much because she repented. Then she showed great love because she knew how great her sin was. She was crying tears of gratitude because she knew how much she had been forgiven. She was so thankful. And Yeshua says, not only was she forgiven, but her trust or faith in His forgiving power has saved her. The way I understand that is that she was not going to be a sinner anymore. She was going to walk with Him the rest of her life. And if she really was Miryam of Magdala that's what happened.

On the first level, we understand this. She was forgiven more because she was a bigger sinner! She was a prostitute and Shimon was a pious, religious man. Obviously, she was a bigger sinner than him. So, on the first level, it seems clear. But there's a deeper level. Why did Yeshua choose to share this with Shimon? The whole dialogue was with him. Yeshua wasn't saying it for the woman's sake. He was saying it for Shimon! Well, I believe it is because Shimon had no intense emotional demonstration of love for Yeshua.

Why didn't he? I think it was because he had not repented at all! He hadn't been forgiven of anything! He didn't even know he was a sinner! He didn't think he needed forgiveness. So, he had no gratitude! He had no love for Yeshua! You can't be forgiven unless you repent. And repentance starts with recognizing your own sinfulness. He was a Pharisee who was trying to keep the Law and thinking he was doing well! So, he was really in a place of self-righteousness, not at all repentant.

So, I believe Yeshua shared this with Shimon to bring him to conviction—to bring him to repentance. We don't know whether it worked or not. He was trying to show him that he, too, had a debt. It might not have been as big as this woman's, but maybe it was. As a Pharisee he was following all the Laws of Moses or so he thought. But did he really keep all the Laws?

How about the law recited in the synagogue every Shabbat? *You shall love the Lord Your God with all your heart, all your soul and all your strength.* How was he disobeying that commandment? I see it. Do you see how he was disobeying that command? Well, think about it a minute. The Lord his God Himself was sitting at his dinner table! Was he loving Him? So, what do you think? Is that a sin? Yea! It's a HUGE sin! He didn't even show Him the customary courtesy of washing His feet, or giving Him a kiss, or anointing His head with oil, much less declaring his love for Him.

He was probably among those who "*began saying among themselves, 'Who is this fellow that presumes to forgive sins?' "*

So, which one was really the bigger sinner, the repentant prostitute or the Pharisee? He was the bigger sinner. She was at least repentant! He was self-righteous, which is much more dangerous. Notice that because Shimon was totally unrepentant, Yeshua says nothing to him about salvation. He doesn't say he's saved. He just says, "Look at this woman. She's saved."

How does this apply to Yom Teruah (Rosh Hashanah)?

Well, would you like the flame of your love for the Lord in your heart to burn stronger and brighter? I hope you are nodding your head because it can always burn brighter for all of us! Do you remember a time in your life when it did burn brighter? Like when you first came to the Lord and it consumed you and you could do nothing but tell other people about it and just rejoice? It was so strong it influenced everything you did? I can remember that time. And you know, I know it's almost impossible to stay in that place, but we can surely get back there every once in awhile. Now, if you went through that whole list of sins in the "Breaking Up the Fallow Ground" section, then you are most likely at that rejoicing place already.

I believe this story gives the key to getting back to that place because the point of this story is that when we can recognize our own sin, and we can remember what we used to be like, and we can remember the things we still fall in, like the previous few chapters have been helping us do, we will love our Savior, Yeshua, more. I actually fell into a couple of sins the other day while driving down the road when a couple people cut me off. You know, the flesh is still with us. We need that atonement covering so that the presence of God can dwell in us because we're still fighting iniquity!

So, I want to challenge you, if you didn't stop and take any time yet after reading the previous chapter, do it now. Take time each day. Get alone with God. Shut off the TV, the radio, the i-pod, the computer, the cell phone and get alone with the Lord for awhile. And here's what to do. Open your heart and ask the Ruakh HaKodesh (Holy Spirit) to reveal, first of all, the awesomeness of God, the Holiness of God. And then ask the Holy Spirit to reveal to you, to me, (I'm going to be asking this, too.) to us our own iniquity and sinfulness and unworthiness. Reveal how much we need the atonement in our lives. Reveal it to the point where we'll be so grateful again for what Yeshua did that we could be like that woman. We could walk into the house of our local attorney or doctor, or some important official and if Yeshua was there, come up behind Him and weep at His feet and kiss them. That's how strong the love would be in us. I believe it's a remembrance that we need because, you know, we could remember our sin. We just tend to purposefully forget it. "Oh, that's been atoned for already, so I don't need to remember that. It's in the past." Or, "Okay, it happened yesterday, but I asked forgiveness for it." The point is not to become depressed with our own sin, but the point is the more we are aware of our own sinfulness and unworthiness, the more we'll appreciate Yeshua's atoning sacrifice.

So, then when you celebrate Yom Kippur and focus on Yeshua's atoning sacrifice, you'll be in a place of such gratitude, such thanksgiving that there will be a flame burning in your heart, there will be tears in your eyes. We'll be restored to the place David called—*the joy of our salvation.* Remember, the more you grasp His holiness and your unworthiness, the more thankful and grateful you'll be for what Yeshua did and the more you'll love Him.

So, with that we're going to end with the sounding of the Shofar again. Its powerful, loud sound will wake us up and make us remember how awesome our God is and our own unworthiness.

First, let's say the blessing again over the Shofar.

Blessed are You, Lord our God, Ruler of the universe, who has sanctified us with His commandments and commanded us to hear the sound of the Shofar.

So, when we get to the shouting, I'd like you to shout something different this time. David says in one of his Psalms, "Praise the Lord, O my soul." You know what he's doing? His spirit is speaking to his soul, telling it to praise the Lord. So, what I want you to do is to shout at your soul. I want your spirit to shout at your soul and say, "Wake up!! Wake up, soul! Wake up to God's awesome holiness! Wake up to the Ruakh HaKodesh's revelations in these Ten Days. Wake up to this understanding of who God is and who we are, and to Yeshua's atoning sacrifice." And if you have not received that sacrifice yet, all you have to do is go through these days of repentance saying, "Lord, forgive me. I'm a sinner. I need Your atoning sacrifice. I receive you as my Lord and my Messiah" and you will have that atonement sacrifice for yourself.

Alright, now, blow your Shofar or play the recording.

(Shofar blasts.)

Hallelujah! Wake up, soul. Wake up to the Lord! Wake up! Wake up! Awake! Hallelujah! Awaken me. Awaken me. Hallelujah! Awaken me, Lord! HALLELUJAH! Yes, awake! Hallelujah! We praise You, Lord!

CHAPTER 18

SHOUT FOR JOY
FOR FUTURE EVENTS

You should know by heart by now that Rosh Hashanah is a Shabbaton Zih-kh'ron Teruah—a Sabbath of remembrance with the blowing of Shofars and shouting for joy. So what more can we remember and shout for joy about? Well, I thought of a few more things.

One of the most precious things, I think, that we can remember with shouts of joy is this. In the past few decades, we Messianic Jews, Y'hudim Mishikhim and those of you who have joined with us, you Gerim Mishikhim, have had the privilege of being able to worship God on His Appointed Times. Remember that this wasn't allowed for literally thousands of years. It was a law within the church that nobody who was a part of the church could do anything that smacked of Judaism. And it's only been in the last thirty years or so that we've had this privilege of worshipping God on His Appointed Times. So that, I believe, is something to shout for joy about. I rejoice that I'm born at this time, because if not I wouldn't even know about these things.

So, we are going to do what God has commanded. We are going to blow our Shofars and as we listen to their sound, we are going to shout for joy! What you shout when we blow the Shofars is up to you. But the important thing is to exercise your vocal chords, because that's what is commanded for this day. You know, one time another minister and I were in an African-American church and they really knew how to shout!! Whoohoo! Do they shout! So today is a day for shouting and for blowing of Shofars. Tradition says it's important to *hear* the Shofars and to shout.

First, let's say the blessing over the blowing of the Shofar:

> Blessed are You, Lord our God, Ruler of the universe, who has sanctified us with His commandments and commanded us to hear the sound of the Shofar.

Now, Blow your Shofar and shout.

Hallelujah! Lord we praise You! Yeshua Adonai we worship You! We worship You. We give You honor. We lift up Your Name! We thank you that You have brought us to this day when we can celebrate Your Appointed Times. Thank You for Your mercy to us. Thank You for Your awesome blessings! Thank You for giving us Appointed Times to rest and to celebrate in joy! Thank You for Your provision of so many holidays for us! Thank You! Thank You!

Okay! Now let's think about this a minute. Why are we to have this memorial day of remembering once a year? Is it just for fun? Well, it is joyful and fun, but it is for so much more than that as we've been learning. What is one of the main reasons? Yes! It's because God knows that, for our own good, we need to remember what He has done and who He is, so that our faith will be strengthened. Psalm 136 says over and over, *"He is good and His mercy endures forever"* after repeating His great deeds.

You know for sure, by now, that Yom Teruah points us to Yom Kippur. And you know that since God gave us Yeshua and the New Covenant (the B'rit Hadasha) there is no need for the Yom Kippur sacrifices. Yet God did not rescind Yom Kippur for us Mishikhim (Messianic Believers). Concerning Yom Kippur God says:

Leviticus 23:31-32 (NKJV) *"You shall do no manner of work; it shall be a statute <u>forever </u>throughout your generations in all your dwellings. "It shall be to you a Sabbath of solemn rest, and you shall afflict your souls;*

As you've heard over and over now, Yom Teruah is the beginning for the Ten Days of preparation leading to this day of *"afflicting our souls."* "Afflict" here, "anah" in Hebrew, means *to abase self, chasten self, deal hardly with, humble.* Again we get back to the need for a contrite heart to participate in these Ten Days.

Isaiah 66:2 (NKJV). *"But on this one will I look: On him who is poor and of a contrite spirit, And who <u>trembles</u> at My word.*

As we learned before, the Hebrew word for "trembles" there is "kharade" which means *trembles, fearful, reverential, afraid.* This is the attitude God loves to see toward His Word. This is the kind of person who will have the right attitude during these Ten Days. If we are not in a place where we can truly "afflict our souls," Yom Kippur is of no value to us. So what does God want us to remember with the sounding of the Shofar and shouting for <u>joy</u> to prepare us to "afflict our souls" so that Yom Kippur will be valuable to us?

Well, a few chapters ago, we looked at times in the past in Scripture where there was shouting for joy. Now we will look at things in the present and in the future. We can remember things in the future because the Bible is a book that predicts the future! We can remember His promises that are being fulfilled in the present. And we can remember His promises for the future and, in faith, rejoice in them. So, do you still have your Shofar with you? Here we go.

First we are going to look at some things in the past, when the Shofars were blown, to help us be thankful for the things in the present.

The dedication of Solomon's Temple

2 Chronicles 5:12 *Also the L'vi'im (Levites) who were the singers, all of them—Asaf, Heman, Y'dutun and their sons and relatives—dressed in fine linen, with cymbals, lutes and lyres, stood on the east side of the altar; and with them 120 cohanim sounding trumpets),*

They were blowing trumpets because God chose the Temple in Jerusalem as the dwelling place for His manifest presence. We know that the Temple was destroyed and the one Nehemiah built to replace it was also destroyed. Not much to shout for joy about there.

But now, let's look at the <u>present</u> and see if there's something to shout for joy in the remembrance of the Temple.

1 Corinthians 3:16 (NKJV) *Do you not know that you are the temple of God and that the Spirit of God dwells in you?*

Who is being referred to here? Right! Followers of Messiah! He dwells in us now! So, let's sound the Shofar and shout for joy that we are the Temple of His Ruakh HaKodesh.

Blow your Shofar.

Thank You Lord that You have chosen to come and dwell in us. Thank You that You sent Your Ruakh to be with us every day. Thank You that You love us so much to send Yeshua to sacrifice Himself so that You can come and make Your home with us. Thank You that we can be in Yeshua and Yeshua in us. Thank You that You have not left us alone. Thank You. Thank You.

Jubilee

Leviticus 25:8-9   " ' *You are to count seven Shabbats of years, seven times seven years, that is, forty-nine years. 9 Then, on the tenth day of the seventh month, on Yom-Kippur, you are to sound a blast on the shofar; you are to sound the shofar all through your land;*

Let's remember that our God has given us a Jubilee. We have been honored to celebrate the Jubilee in our days. God ordained it to be a day for canceling of debts, setting slaves free, restoration of inheritance. Let's shout for joy that God has canceled our debt of sin and has set us free from slavery to sin, that we have an eternal Jubilee!

Blow your Shofar again.

Thank You, Yeshua, that You paid the debt we could not pay. Thank You that through the Power of Your Blood, we are set free from sin and from all slavery to sin. Thank You that You set us free from all bondage. Thank You that You have brought us out of the kingdom of darkness into Your marvelous Light. Thank You that we can live forever in Your Jubilee. Thank You. Thank You.

Jericho

Joshua 6:20 *When the people heard the sound of the shofars, the people let out a great shout; and the wall fell down flat; so that the people went up into the city, each one straight ahead of him; and they captured the city.*

The sound of the trumpets with the shouts of joy knocked down the walls at Jericho. This is ridiculous in the natural. So, let's remember that our God gives strategies to overcome the obstacles in our lives, and to knock down walls between Jewish and Gentile believers, between denominations, between unbelieving Jewish people and the Gospel.

He also knocks down the strongholds in our own minds. Let's shout together about those things.

Blow the Shofar.

Thank You, Adonai, that Your Power is greater than any force in our lives, greater than any stronghold no matter how looming. Thank You that by the Power of Your Blood we can totally defeat the enemy in our life. Thank You that by the Power of Your Name and by Your divine strategy we can knock down all walls and every obstacle that hinders our victory in You. Thank You that through You there can be unity and Power against the enemy here on earth. Thank You. Thank You. Praise Your Name.

Gideon

Judges 7:20-21 *All three companies blew the shofars, broke the pitchers and held the torches in their left hands, keeping their right hands free for the shofars they were blowing; and they shouted, "The sword for ADONAI and for Gid'on* (Gideon)*!" Then, as every man stood still in place around the camp, the whole camp was thrown into panic, with everyone screaming and trying to escape.*

This is about Shofars, torches and jars or pitchers. Let's remember that our God can give us victory even in the midst of overwhelming odds as He did Gideon.

Sound the Shofar and shout for joy

Oh, Almighty God that You are so great—so awesome. You are above all. You are the Creator of the universe. Thank You that in You, we never need to fear anything that comes against us. Thank You that we don't need to depend on might in numbers or in our own strength or in our own plans. Thank You that when we have You, we have everything we need to fight against anything in our lives. There is no power greater than You. There is no force mightier than You. Thank you for victory! Thank You in Yeshua, we can conquer all. In Yeshua, we have complete victory. Hallelujah! Thank You!

Gathering in of the Exiles

Isaiah 27:12-13 ... *and you will be gathered, one by one, people of Isra'el! On that day a great shofar will sound. Those lost in the land of Ashur will come, also those scattered through the land of Egypt; and they will worship ADONAI on the holy mountain in Yerushalayim* (Jerusalem).

This is a metaphorical Shofar. Let's be thankful we have heard this Shofar sound. Let's sound the Shofar and shout for joy that He is gathering together the exiles of Israel and that we are alive to see and participate in this fulfillment of this prophecy!

Sound your Shofar.

Oh Yeshua Adonai, we are so grateful to be alive to see this great day, to see You bringing Your scattered people back to their Land. Thank You for bringing them back, Lord. And thank You that they are having the opportunity to hear Your Word and so many of them are receiving You as their Messiah. We give You praise. Thank You. Thank You.

Bringing up the Ark to Jerusalem

2 Samuel 6:14-15 *Then David danced and spun around with abandon before ADONAI, wearing a linen ritual vest. So David and all the house of Isra'el brought up the ark of ADONAI with shouting and the sound of the shofar.*

Let's remember that Adonai chose to live among the Israelites in His manifest presence over the Ark. And let's shout for joy as we thank Him that today He chooses to dwell within each of us!!

Blow it again!

Oh Adonai how can we ever thank You enough that You love us so much You come to dwell within us? Thank You! Thank You! Thank You for not leaving us orphaned. Thank You for not leaving us to fend for ourselves. Thank You for coming into our hearts, for showering Your love upon us, for speaking to us, for guiding us, for teaching us, and for doing Your Kingdom work through us. Oh how we thank You. We thank You from the bottom of our hearts. THANK YOU!

*   *   *

Future Events

Now let's look at some promises for the future.

Daniel 9:27 *He will make a strong covenant with leaders for one week [of years]. For half of the week he will put a stop to the sacrifice and the grain offering. On the wing of detestable things the desolator will come and continue until the already decreed destruction is poured out on the desolator.*

The "he" Dani'el (Daniel) is referring to here is the anti-Messiah or anti-Christ. The anti-Messiah will make a seven-year covenant. This is known as the Tribulation period, or the time of Jacob's trouble.

Some of these terrible things are predicted in Revelations where they are connected with Shofars or trumpets. They are judgments of God and they are definitely not things to shout for joy about.

Revelation 8:7-13 *The first one sounded his shofar; and there came hail and fire mingled with blood, and it was thrown down upon the earth. A third of the earth was burned up, a third of the trees were burned up, and all green grass was burned up. The second angel sounded his shofar, and what looked like an enormous blazing mountain was hurled into the sea. A third of the sea turned to blood, a third of the living creatures in the sea died, and a third of the ships were destroyed. The third angel sounded his shofar; and a great star, blazing like a torch, fell from the sky onto a third of the rivers and onto the springs of water. The name of the star was "Bitterness", and a third of the water became bitter, and many people died from the water that had been turned bitter. The fourth angel sounded his shofar; and a third of the sun was struck, also a third of the moon and a third of the stars; so that a third of them were darkened, the day had a third less light, and the night likewise....*

Revelation 9:1-3 *The fifth angel sounded his shofar; .... Then out of the smoke onto the earth came locusts, and they were given power like the power scorpions have on earth. ... to inflict pain on them for five months; and the pain they caused was like the pain of a scorpion sting.*

Revelation 9:13-15 *The sixth angel sounded his shofar,... four angels had been kept ready for this moment, for this day and month and year, to kill a third of mankind;*

Again, nothing to shout for joy about.

Revelation 9:20-21 *The rest of mankind, those who were not killed by these plagues, even then did not turn from what they had made with their own hands—they did not stop worshipping demons and idols made of gold, silver, bronze, stone and wood, which cannot see or hear or walk. Nor did they turn from their murdering, their misuse of drugs in connection with the occult, their sexual immorality or their stealing.*

But, we see that these coming judgments have a purpose.

Revelation 10:7 *... in the days of the sound from the seventh angel when he sounds his shofar, the hidden plan of God will be brought to completion, the Good News as He proclaimed it to His servants the prophets."*

At the sounding of the seventh Shofar God's plan will be brought to completion. Now that's something to shout about!

Sound and shout!

We thank You, Yeshua our Messiah, that someday Your judgments will be finished and complete. We thank You that someday You will reign as King and all evil will be removed and gone. Thank You that You will conquer the enemy with the sword from Your mouth. Thank You that we will be able to reign with You in peace, in Your complete, wonderful, glorious shalom when there will be no sin, no evil, nothing to defile all the beauty around us. Thank You!

Let's look at another future thing to shout about.

Dani'el talked about the seven-year covenant the Anti-Messiah will make. In the middle of the seven years, after three and a half years, he will stop the sacrifices and guilt offerings, and he will set up an "abomination that causes desolation" in the Temple. This *implies* that the Temple in Jerusalem will have been rebuilt and animal sacrifices resumed! We know the control of the Temple Mount is the biggest issue in the Middle East peace process! So how this will happen, we don't know, but Yeshua confirmed this prophesy and its connection to a rebuilt Temple.

Matthew 24:15 *"So when you see the abomination that causes devastation spoken about through the prophet Dani'el standing <u>in the Holy Place</u>" (let the reader understand the allusion),*

Yeshua refers to the Holy Place which is in the Temple; so therefore, the Temple has to be in existence! Dani'el wrote his prophecy around 600 BCE. Some scholars have interpreted Dani'el's prophesy to refer to the defiling of the Temple by Antiochus Epiphanes in 150 BCE when he sacrificed a pig on the altar and poured pigs blood all around it. But, Yeshua's refers to this in the year 33 CE as a future event. When Yeshua spoke of it, this Antiochus Epiphanes event was 180 years in the past already!! So, the abomination that Yeshua is talking about is not caused by Antiochus Epiphanes.

We also know that the destruction of the Temple in 70 CE was by fire and that no abomination was set up, so, we can deduce that the Temple will be rebuilt and animal sacrifices resumed. But, Yeshua goes on to say more about this time.

Matthew 24:21-22 *For there will be trouble then worse than there has ever been from the beginning of the world until now and there will be nothing like it again! Indeed, if the length of this time had not been limited, no one would survive; …*

Not much to shout for joy about here. But, let's go back to the prophecy in Dani'el that Yeshua referred to, and look at the person mentioned there.

Daniel 9: 27(NIV) *"He will confirm a covenant with many for one 'seven.' In the middle of the 'seven' he will put an end to sacrifice and offering. And on a wing of the temple he will set up an abomination that causes desolation, until the end that is decreed is poured out on him."*

A few years ago, before 9-11, I read the book *Left Behind* by Tim Lahaye. It is the first of a series of seven novels about the End Times. You probably read it. It describes how the anti-Messiah comes to power at the gathering of the world's religious and political leaders at the UN. In August of 2000, after just finishing that book, I received a notice from a prayer group in New York City that Millennium Year meetings of the world's religious and political leaders were planned for September. Many of you saw news reports on them as they occurred. Many of us were in prayer. Everybody who had read *Left Behind*, including me, thought the anti-Messiah could actually come to power at those gatherings. Then I remembered the following Scripture which tells when the anti-Messiah will actually come forth.

2 Thessalonians 2:1-3 (NKJV) *Concerning the coming of our Lord Jesus Christ* (Yeshua Ha Mashiakh, the Messiah) *and our being gathered to Him, we ask you, brothers, not to become easily unsettled or alarmed by some prophecy, report or letter supposed to have come from us, saying that the day of the Lord has already come. Don't let anyone deceive you in any way, for that day will not come until the rebellion occurs and the man of lawlessness is revealed, the man doomed to destruction.*

This man of lawlessness is the anti-Messiah.

2 Thessalonians 2:4 (NKJV) *He will oppose and will exalt himself over everything that is called God or is worshipped, so that he sets himself up in God's temple, proclaiming himself to be God.*

This is the abomination of desolation (referred to by Yeshua and Dani'el) that the anti-Messiah sets up in the restored Temple in Jerusalem.

2 Thessalonians 2:5-6 (NKJV) *Don't you remember that when I was with you I used to tell you these things? And now you know what is holding him back, so that he may be revealed at the proper time.*

Something is "holding him back," preventing the "Man of Lawlessness" or "Man of Sin" from being revealed or coming to power.

2 Thessalonians 2:7-8 (NKJV) *For the secret power of lawlessness is already at work; but <u>the one who now holds it back</u> will continue to do so <u>till he is taken out of the way</u>. And then the lawless one will be revealed, whom the Lord Yeshua will overthrow with the breath of His mouth and destroy by the splendor of His coming.*

Notice, that the something "holding it back," preventing the "lawless one" from being revealed is referred to in a personal way: the "one who now holds it back," not "that which holds it back" "till <u>he</u>," (the one who holds it back) is taken away. Who is the one who now holds it back? Do you have any idea? Yes, the Ruakh HaKodesh! Where did we learn the Ruakh HaKodesh dwells? That's right! In God's people! In us! When will the Ruakh HaKodesh be taken out of the way? When the believers leave, since He dwells in us, right? Think about it for a minute. If He is dwelling in us, He can't leave until we leave! Do you see that now?!

Now, remember all the terrible things that will happen on the earth following the anti-Messiah's takeover? Let's read that again.

Matthew 24:21-22 *For there will be trouble then worse than there has ever been from the beginning of the world until now and there will be nothing like it again! Indeed, if the length of this time had not been limited, no one would survive;*

Now remember, those of us who have the Ruakh HaKodesh within us won't be here when the anti-Messiah comes to power, right? We will already have departed! So, I think we have something we can shout for joy and blow Shofars about, don't you?

How will we be taken away?

1 Thessalonians 4:16-17 *For the Lord himself will come down from heaven with a rousing cry, with a call from one of the ruling angels, and with <u>God's shofar</u>; those who died united with the Messiah will be the first to rise; then we who are left still alive will be caught up with them in the clouds to meet the Lord in the air; and thus we will always be with the Lord.*

A rousing cry, a call from one of the ruling angels, and God's Shofar will cause us to meet the Lord in the air! So, there's the proof. Those who have His Ruakh will be taken away before the Man of Lawlessness or Sin is revealed, before all the terrible things described in Matthew 24 happen. This event is commonly called the Rapture, although the word "rapture" doesn't actually appear in the Bible. When will it happen? Many of us believe it will happen on some future Rosh Hashanah! Why do we believe that? For two reasons. (I mentioned the reasons before in this book, but it bears noting them again here.)

1. There are two other references in the B'rit Hadashah to this event besides the one in 1 Thessalonians. They are Matthew 24:31 and 1 Corinthians 15:51-52. All three refer to the blowing of a Shofar when this happens. Yom Teruah (Rosh Hashanah) is the Appointed Time for blowing the Shofar.

2. We know the great events in the ministry of the Messiah all happened on the four Appointed Times in the spring. Therefore we believe that the next great event will happen on the next Appointed Time in the fall, namely, Yom Teruah!

Now that's something to shout for joy and blow the Shofar in remembrance about, right? But, you can only shout for joy about this if you are sure you'll be gathered in, if you're alive at that time, or if you've already died by then, that you'll be resurrected. If you're not sure, then you can't shout for joy over this promise. If you're not sure, but you'd like to have that assurance, you can receive it right now.

It comes when the Ruakh HaKodesh begins to live within you. But, the Ruakh HaKodesh is a Holy Spirit. "Holy" in Hebrew is "kadosh" which means "separate from sin." The Ruakh HaKodesh can only dwell within you when your sins have been atoned for, taken away by the sacrifice of Messiah on the cross. To find out how to accept the Messiah's sacrifice right now, turn to pages 30-31.

For those of us who are sure we have received His Ruakh dwelling in us, we're going to hear the Shofar blow and shout for joy in remembrance of His promise to raise us up to meet with Him in the air to be with Him forever!!

Sound your Shofar and shout for joy!!

O Lord we praise You! We rejoice in Your soon return! We rejoice that You are coming soon!! Come Yeshua Adonai. Come quickly. Come and save us from the coming troubles and tribulations. Thank You that You plan to come! Thank You that You long to come! Words cannot express how excited we are about it. We are exuberant! We are bursting with joy! Hallelujah! HALLELUJAH!! COME YESHUA! COME ON THIS ROSH HASHANAH! THIS YOM TERUAH!! COME TODAY!

CHAPTER 19

THE MESSAGE OF AKIDA (THE BINDING OF ISAAC)

Genesis 22:1 *After these things, God tested Avraham (Abraham). He said to him, "Avraham!" and he answered, "Here I am."*

This is the beginning of the Parashah reading which is read in synagogues all over the world every year on Yom Teruah (Rosh Hashanah). The traditional connection between this passage and this holiday is the ram, as you'll see later.

This is a very powerful story. I believe the Lord has a very simple, yet very profound message for each of us in this story.

The Hebrew word that is translated "tested," is not always translated as "tested." In the King James Version it says, "God tempted Abraham." But we know according to Apostle James that God cannot tempt anyone. The word is "nih-sah" and it means "to test or prove or try." Let's see how Avraham (Abraham) is tested.

Avraham answered God, "Heneni." In other words, "I'm here." "I'm ready. What do You have to say to me? I'm ready to obey and serve."

Genesis 22:2 *He said, "Take your son, your only son, whom you love, Yitz'chak (Isaac); and go to the land of Moriyah (Moriah). There you are to offer him as a burnt offering on a mountain that I will point out to you."*

Now first of all, Yitz'khak (Isaac) wasn't Avraham's (Abraham's) only son. If you've read the book of Genesis, you know that he had another son, Yishma'el (Ishmael). But it's interesting that because Yitz'khak (Isaac) was the son of promise, God doesn't even consider Yishma'el to be a son. He calls Yitz'khak "your only son" because he's the one for the promises. And the promises that God made to be fulfilled through Yitz'khak are in the just preceding chapter, Genesis 21. It's the promise of multiplication and blessing. Yitz'khak was the seed through whom the blessing was supposed to come. He was to receive the blessing and pass it on down. So, this is a very strange thing that God is telling Avraham to do.

In addition to that, we know from previous chapters that Yitz'khak (Isaac) is Avraham's greatest love. Avraham had longed for a son for many, many years. He was almost a hundred years old by this time. Finally he had a son through Hagar, the handmaid of his wife, Sarah. But that wasn't the right son. Thirteen years later Avraham and Sara finally had the son that God had promised them. So if you can just imagine how this son was the fulfillment of so many years of prayer and such longing. And now God says, "You are to sacrifice this son."

I want to point out to you some foreshadowings here, or parallels of the account of the Messiah that we read especially in the latter part of the Gospels. The first is that the Gospels say that Yeshua is God's only son. The second is that God's greatest love was His only son. So here we have a parallel that's happening in the life of Avraham.

God told Avraham to offer Yitz'khak as a burnt offering. You know in our day and age if God were somehow to speak that to us, we would be sure it was NOT God because there are commandments in the Bible that say not to do that. But we need to understand that in those days, those commandments had not been given yet, and the people that were all around Avraham—all the pagans people groups around him—practiced human sacrifice regularly. They sacrificed their children. (See 2 Kings 16:3.) God's commandments against this were given much later. That's why Avraham didn't say, "Oh, that can't be God." He heard God and he knew it was God.

Avraham was to offer Yitz'khak as a sacrifice. God offered His Son, Yeshua, as a sacrifice. That's the second foreshadowing.

The next interesting thing here is the place where God tells him to make this sacrifice. It's at the mountain called Moriah.

2 Chronicles 3:1 *Then Shlomo (Solomon) began to build the house of ADONAI in Yerushalayim on Mount Moriyah, where ADONAI had appeared to David his father.*

So, Mt. Moriah is where the Temple was built. So the third foreshadowing is that the place where God told Avraham to sacrifice Yitz'khak is the exact same mountain where God's Son was sacrificed more than 2000 years later.

Genesis 22:3 *Avraham got up early in the morning, saddled his donkey, and took two of his young men with him, together with Yitz'chak his son. He cut the wood for the burnt offering, departed and went toward the place God had told him about.*

If you've read the book of Genesis, you have to see that this is totally out of character for Avraham. Avraham had a history of bargaining; of arguing; of coming up with excuses; of doing things differently. He bargained with Lot over who would get the land. He bargained with his allies. When he defeated their enemies, he said, "No, I don't want to take any payment from you." He bargained with Avimalek (Abimilech). The final bargaining which is the most famous was when he did intercessory bargaining with God about Sodom. "Will you not save the city if there are forty righteous men?" "How about 30?" "How about 20?" "How about 10?" So, for Avraham to hear this new instruction from God that was so radical and to not even comment—to just get up the next morning and cut the wood and saddle the donkey was really amazingly out of character. There's no mention of any objection from him.

So, I believe this was much more than, "Oh, I heard the voice of God in my head." "You know, I sense that God was telling me this." I believe this was a very strong manifestation of God to Avraham. There was no doubt that this was God. There was no question that this was what God was telling him to do. It was a clear command directly from the Lord because he immediately got up and went to do what he was called to do.

Genesis 22: 4-5 *On the third day, Avraham raised his eyes and saw the place in the distance. 5 Avraham said to his young men, "Stay here with the donkey. I and the boy will go there, worship and return to you."*

Now, here we seem to get back to the Avraham who's a little shifty. Remember when he lied to the king of Egypt about who his wife was? So, what is this all about? "We will come back to you"? Yitz'khak is supposed to be a burnt offering. Burnt offerings don't come back. So, what is this all about? Well, in the Book of Hebrews there is actually a comment on this that explains it in a very amazing way.

Hebrews 11:17-19 *By trusting, Avraham, when he was put to the test, offered up Yitz'chak as a sacrifice. Yes, he offered up his only son, he who had received the promises, 18 to whom it had been said, "What is called your 'seed' will be in Yitz'chak." 19 For he had concluded that God could even raise people from the dead! And, figuratively speaking, he did so receive him.*

So, the author of Hebrews has pondered this Genesis passage and by revelation he has come to the conclusion that Avraham was really trusting that God would raise Yitz'khak from the dead. I believe it was because he had this contradiction going on. "God promised to multiply my descendants through Yitz'khak. So, if I sacrifice Yitz'khak, he's got to come back to life because God has to keep His promises." But even so, as you can imagine, this still must have been very hard for him. So, the fifth foreshadow of the Messiah is that Yitz'khak's father knew that when he died he would rise from the dead. And we see that in the sacrifice of Messiah Yeshua.

Genesis 22:6 *Avraham took the wood for the burnt offering and laid it on Yitz'chak his son. Then he took in his hand the fire and the knife, and they both went on together.*

Now here's a little bit of information that we can glean from this. We know that Avraham was well over 100 years old at this time. From this verse we can understand that Yitz'khak was old enough to carry the wood up the mountain. So he had to be at least a teenager to be able to do that. So, here's the sixth foreshadow. I don't know if you've ever seen this before. I actually never saw it before. The son had to carry the wood of his sacrifice. Yeshua carried the wood of his sacrifice—the cross. Isn't that amazing?!

Genesis 22:7 *Yitz'chak spoke to Avraham his father: "My father?" He answered, "Here I am, my son." He said, "I see the fire and the wood, but where is the lamb for a burnt offering?"*

So, we have a little bit of a problem here. Yitz'khak's getting suspicious. "What's going on here?" And Avraham has to deal with it.

Genesis 22:8 *Avraham replied, "God will provide himself the lamb for a burnt offering, my son"; and they both went on together.*

Evidently this satisfied Yitz'khak. But this is an interesting statement because it sounds like it might be a half truth. How did Avraham know that God was going to provide a lamb? But it's really a statement of faith because the way this is worded it actually is Elohim yireh Lo ha-say. Literally in Hebrew it is "God will see for Himself for the lamb" or "God will provide for Himself the lamb" or "God will provide Himself a lamb." It's interesting that every English translation has this strange construct. It isn't ever in any translation simply "God will provide the lamb." It's always "God will provide *Himself* the lamb" or "God will provide the lamb Himself."

There are two ways you can understand this. One way is that God Himself will provide a lamb. The other way is, "God will provide the lamb. It will be Himself." Now we see the seventh foreshadow of Messiah's sacrifice because when He sacrificed Himself or allowed Himself to be sacrificed, the way we understand the New Covenant is that the Messiah was God Himself come as a man. So, God Himself was sacrificing Himself fulfilling this amazingly. Actually I saw two foreshadows in this. God provided the Lamb—He provided Messiah Yeshua—but in true sense it was God Himself.

Also, we need to just think about this—about how strange this statement is. The whole point of sacrifice is that men make it to God. Right? All the sacrifices in the Bible are men making them to God. But here somehow God is going to make the sacrifice. Why is that? Well, in Hebrews it tells us that the sacrifices that were in the Tanakh—in the Old Covenant—the blood of bulls and goats—made *atonement* for people. We have to understand that the word "atonement" in Hebrew is "kippur." The word "kippa" comes from the same root meaning "covering." So the animal sacrifices that were made covered the people's sins. The author of Hebrews refers to this.

Hebrews 10: 4 *For it is impossible that the blood of bulls and goats should take away sins.*

Do you see that? They covered sins but they didn't take them away.

Hebrews 10:5 *This is why, on coming into the world, he says, "It has not been your will to have an animal sacrifice and a meal offering; rather, you have prepared for me a body.*

This has always been interpreted as the Messiah talking. This is a quote from the Psalms. The Messiah is saying, "You have prepared for Me a body, not an animal, not a meal (grain) sacrifice, but a body so that sins could actually be taken away not just covered over." It took a greater sacrifice to take away sins.

Genesis 22:9 *They came to the place God had told him about; and Avraham built the altar there, set the wood in order, bound Yitz'chak his son and laid him on the altar, on the wood.*

This is where the name of this passage comes from. The Hebrew word used here for bound is "ah-kode." Another form of that word is "Akida" which this passage is called. Yitz'khak had carried the wood. So we know he was big enough and strong enough to resist his father who was more than 100 years old, but evidently he didn't. Why would Yitz'khak have allowed himself to be bound this way? Well, I believe he had so much trust in his father and was so obedient that he did what his father asked. That's the ninth foreshadow because Messiah Yeshua allowed his Father to sacrifice Him as that terrible sacrifice.

Genesis 22:10 *Then Avraham put out his hand and took the knife to kill his son.*

This is an incredible thing that Avraham was willing to take out the knife and get ready to slay his son even though somehow he knew that his son was to be this blessing for the world. I saw something very significant in this, that it is kind of a challenge for all of us. When God answers our years of prayers and gives us something, we then tend to think it's all over. But sometimes it's just the beginning of things! And now we have to be obedient for what God has given us to be a blessing. I learned that when I became a rabbi. Ever since I came to the Lord, I had prayed to be in full time ministry. It took nineteen years. And when it happened miraculously, I was just so thrilled and excited about it, but I also realized that it was a call to greater obedience. If I didn't walk out the blessing in obedience, it would become a curse instead of a blessing.

Genesis 22:11-12 *But the angel of ADONAI called to him out of heaven: "Avraham? Avraham!" He answered, "Here I am." 12 He said, "Don't lay your hand on the boy! Don't do anything to him! For now I know that you are a man who fears God, because you have not withheld your son, your only son, from me."*

In this verse, we get the answer to the question of why God told Avraham to do this. God was testing Avraham to know his level of commitment. And as we can see here, our level of commitment is a function of our fear of God. "I know that you fear Me—that you respect Me."

Genesis 22:13-14 *Avraham raised his eyes and looked, and there behind him was a ram caught in the bushes by its horns. Avraham went and took the ram and offered it up as a burnt offering in place of his son. 14 Avraham called the place ADONAI Yir'eh [ADONAI will see (to it), ADONAI provides]—as it is said to this day, "On the mountain ADONAI is seen."*

Now this is a familiar phrase to some of you because you've heard the song: "Jehovah Jireh." Well, that's the way a non-Hebrew speaker would say it. In Hebrew there is no "J" sound. A Hebrew speaker couldn't say that because they have trouble pronouncing the "J's." The Hebrew way to say this is "Adonai Yeereh." Oftentimes when we read this or hear that phrase we think of God providing physically for us. We think He's going to provide finances or something that we need. But actually what He provided was the ram for the sacrifice. He provided the sacrifice. And that is a foreshadowing. God provided the sacrifice at the time of Messiah.

Genesis 22:15-18 *The angel of ADONAI called to Avraham a second time out of heaven. 16 He said, "I have sworn by myself—says ADONAI—that because you have done this, because you haven't withheld your son, your only son, 17 I will most certainly bless you; and I will most certainly increase your descendants to as many as there are stars in the sky or grains of sand on the seashore. Your descendants will possess the cities of their enemies, 18 and by your descendants all the nations of the earth will be blessed—because you obeyed my order."*

So, Avraham's obedience to this brought something incredible. It brought this promise of God. And there is something there that you might not have caught. The Book of Hebrews (below) explains that verse 16 in Genesis 22 (above) is saying something really special.

Hebrews 6:13 *For when God made his promise to Avraham, he swore an oath to do what he had promised; and since there was no one greater than himself for him to swear by, he swore by himself....*

Verses 17-18 *Therefore, when God wanted to demonstrate still more convincingly the unchangeable character of his intentions to those who were to receive what he had promised, he added an oath to the promise; 18 so that through two unchangeable things, in neither of which God could lie, we, who have fled to take a firm hold on the hope set before us, would be strongly encouraged.*

So what is this all about? Well, in Genesis 22:16 God tells Avraham, "I have sworn by Myself." The writer of Hebrews is saying this is extraordinary that He would not just swear, but would swear by Himself. It's extraordinary because it gives added weight to the promises. And what are the promises here? They are that the descendants of Avraham would be a blessing to all the nations. Of course we know that's the Messiah. It is also that Avraham's descendants would be blessed. They would be a blessing and would be blessed.

So that's the amazing story of the Akida. Now let's just take a few minutes here. What does this say to us? What are the applications to our lives? The first one is very simple. It is that God's ways are not our ways. His thoughts are not our thoughts. He can tell us to do things completely out-of-the-box. This was the most out-of-the-box thing that anybody had ever been told to do by God. The second thing is that God will test us. He will put us in trying circumstances. It's the devil who tempts us. But God tests us for our good and for the good of the Kingdom.

I want to just give a little more insight on that. We think of testing as an academic thing because we get tested in school. We take tests with a pen or pencil and paper. But here's the thing. What is the purpose for a test? In our experience here in America, the test is usually for someone else's benefit. It's not for our benefit. We are given a test so the teacher will know if we've learned the material—so she can give us a grade. Right? We're given a test so the administrators can know whether they can promote us to the next class. How about this one? How about a driving test? Why do you take that one? Well, it's to keep the other people on the road safe. Right? It's not for your benefit. It's so we know that you're safe and are not going to kill other people on the road. So the tests we've taken were for someone else: the teacher, the administrators, the other drivers.

But we need to understand that tests can be for our good. And when you think about it, our tests really were for our good. What happens when you are facing a test in school? What do you do? You study! You study more than you would have if there weren't a test. So you learn more! When we take mid-terms or finals or SAT's they force us to apply ourselves in a more dedicated way. And when we face that driving test, what do we do? We pray!! Yes, but we also go get someone to teach us. We practice and practice. It makes us work at it. So, we really do benefit from tests. We don't think of it that way. We think of them as nuisances and difficult things, but tests really are important.

Now God's tests are more clearly benefits for us. God's testing is somewhat like sports, if you watch sports. It's like the time trials in track and field. When there's going to be a big race, they don't just gather the top 6 or 7 runners and let them race. The day before they have maybe 30 runners who all race in time trials. Then they pick out the top 6 or 7 for the actual race. What happens sometimes is the runners have been practicing on their own against the clock, and working out, etc., but they haven't been running in a real race. When they actually run against someone, the adrenalin kicks in and they do better than they've done before. So, they reach a new level in these trials.

Similarly for us, tests develop us. They develop us physically, mentally, and emotionally. God's testing is more like athletic training than academic testing. If you've done any athletic training, you know that the human body becomes stronger when it exercises. This is actually a miracle of God. You take those barbells, you lift them for awhile and your muscles become stronger. If you took your car and drove it really fast for several days would it become any faster? No! It would probably break down. But our human bodies are amazing! When they are worked, they become stronger.

So when God tests us, we are stretched and strengthened. Our spirit-man becomes stronger. Our soul-man that opposes our spirit-man becomes weaker. And we become more mature. As we exert ourselves, we go further than we thought we could in the testing. We overcome an obstacle. We gain confidence in things we couldn't do before. This is the great value of testing in the Kingdom of God. We actually qualify for higher responsibilities and more difficult assignments by passing the testing God puts us through.

And finally, one more thing about testing, we are supposed to follow the example of Yeshua.

Hebrews 5:8 *Even though he was the Son, he learned obedience through his sufferings ...* Verse 14 *But solid food is for the mature, for those whose faculties have been trained by continuous exercise to distinguish good from evil.*

Now the main application I want to leave you with is this. I want to go back to what we recite every Shabbat, the Vehahavta. "Vehahavta" is the first word in the passage, "and you shall love." "Ahava" is love. Here's the beginning of the Vehahavta.

Deuteronomy 6:5 *You shall love the Lord your God with all your heart, with all your soul, and with all your strength....*

So, what does it mean to love the Lord with all your heart? In Hebrew it's "kol levavkhah." "Lev" is the heart. "Kol" means "whole" or "all" or "every way." Love Him in every way, in all manner, all together, with everything, wholly. It's just all out. So we see that God is commanding us to love Him more than we love what? Anything! Everything!

And later in the New Covenant, Yeshua is asked, "What is the greatest commandment?" What does He quote? He quotes this. "You shall love the Lord your God with all your heart...." So, if this is the greatest commandment, how do we walk it out? How do we demonstrate that we love the Lord? How do we live a life of loving the Lord?

Well, as this story of Avraham and Yitz'khak presents, love can never be proven by just words. It's always demonstrated by sacrifice, by giving, by helping. That's how love is expressed.

As I was thinking about this, I realized that how we show love, how we offer that sacrifice, differs depending on who we love—depending on who that person is. Let's say it's a baby. How do we show love to an infant? Well, we sacrifice time. We sacrifice money, right? We give lots of affection. We provide protection and provision. Those are the ways we love a baby. But once that baby has grown up a bit, we change the way we love them. We still give affection and sacrifice to provide and protect, but we're really not loving that baby as he grows up to be a small child unless we give what? Discipline! Discipline and teaching.

I just saw this the other day with a young father in our congregation. He came to the office with his little girl and it was the first time I saw him have to discipline her. She is now at that age where she needs discipline. We discussed discipline a little bit afterwards. Now, if he and his wife weren't disciplining her, would they be loving her? No! It's terrible if we don't discipline them.

Then what happens when they become teenagers? Oh, boy. We still have to provide for them. We still have to show affection. But here's what I've found we have to do. We have to begin to show trust. We have to begin to respect them when they want to do something. We have to encourage them to do the things that they want to do—the things that are good that they want to get involved in. So, it's a whole new thing. We have to kind of push them out of the nest and let their wings flap a little bit and not hold them back. So, that's a different type of love.

Then think about the love of a peer. You probably don't need to provide for or protect your friend. Affection? Yes, shake hands or give them a hug maybe, but it's not like it is for a baby. But what about if people start coming against that friend? How about the story of Jonathan and David in the Bible? Who came against David? Jonathan's father. And what did Jonathan do? He stood by David even though it was his father. So that's love for a peer.

Then, finally, how do we show love for a parent? Now I'm not talking about an aging parent who needs care and decisions made. I'm talking about a parent who is still your parent. You're a teenager or a young adult maybe but your parent is still your parent. How do you show love for a parent who is still in charge? Respect. Honor. How about trust? How about obedience? I saw this in Yitz'khak. Why was he willing to be bound? Because he trusted his father. Because he was being obedient. So, this is a picture of the kind of love that God wants from us. This is what He's saying when He says, "You shall love the Lord your God...."

It's not like loving a baby or a child. It's loving a father—showing Him respect (That's the fear of God.)—trusting Him (That's called faith), and being obedient (doing the things that you normally wouldn't think you could do).

I believe this is what the Lord wants to ask us right now. I want you to take this very personally. Do you love God the way He commands you? With all your heart and all your soul? It's a command! And do you demonstrate that love by respect and trust and obedience—doing things that you maybe don't want to do, that He is asking you to do? To be obedient, we need to diligently seek what God's will is. How can we be obedient if we don't know our loving Father's will—if we don't know what He wants us to do? Well, He has given us the Scriptures that tell us His will in many, many ways. So we need to search it out. But there are many specific things that He would have us do that aren't in here. "I want you to visit Joe next week and help him fix his car." It's not in the Bible, but God can say that to us. So we need to do two things. We need to know the Word so we know what He says in the Bible, but we also need to cultivate our communication skills so we can hear from God. How can we obey Him if we don't hear what He's saying?

So, this is a life-long thing. If we're not fully obeying Him then we're not fully loving Him. If we love Him more than anything else, we will give His will higher priority than anything or anyone else no matter how much we love them. Right? That's hard, but that's how it is.

So, as we enter this time of examining ourselves, I challenge you to ask yourself if you really love God with all your being. And if you do, He will ask you to demonstrate it. You can say it all you want, but that doesn't really count for beans. "Oh yes, I love you, Lord! I love you with all my heart, soul, mind and strength." And He says, "Will you.....?" And we say, "Oh no, Lord, I can't do that." That's where the rubber hits the road.

He might ask you to give up something you love more than Him! He's a jealous God. He doesn't want us to love *anything* more than we love Him! For me, it was my independence. I wanted to make up my own mind about what I was doing. Many people love money more than they love God. Or it might be another person. So, they will follow that other person even if that person is leading them away from God. It might be fame or reputation. "I don't want to go out and witness to somebody. I might make a fool of myself. People might think ill of me. So I'm not going to do what He's told us to do, to go out into all the world." Sad to say, but we can love ministry more than we love God. Really! You can love serving God more than God himself! You can spend so much time working for God that you don't have time to spend with Him! You can love yourself more than God. You can love your art or talent, your painting or your music. Those are some of the things we can love more than God. Well, I believe God is going to put His finger on what it is that you love more in these next Ten Days, if you will pray the prayer below. God is telling us that the best thing for us is to love Him more than anything and to live like we love Him more.

So, I hope you are willing to pray this prayer with me.

Lord, we thank You for Avraham and Yitz'khak's incredible example for us. We thank You for Yeshua's willingness to go to His sacrifice just like Yitz'khak was. God show me if there's something that I love more than You. Show me if there is something that I'm not willing to sacrifice to You.

[If the Lord is showing you something right now, just lay it before the Lord.]

Lord, we just lay these things at Your feet. We ask You to send fire from heaven and just consume this sacrifice right now. We want our love for You to be pure. We ask this in Yeshua's Name. Amen.

Appendix I

Rosh Khodesh
The Biblical New Moon Celebration

Rosh Hashanah is also a Rosh Khodesh festival day. What is Rosh Khodesh—also spelled Hodesh or Chodesh? The term is Hebrew for "The Head of the Month." In most translations of the Bible it is referred to as the "New Moon." It marks the beginning of each month of the Jewish lunar calendar. The Biblical calendar is a lunar calendar, not a solar one to which we are accustomed. The lunar month starts with the re-appearance of the moon. The Jewish people used to have men watching for this nightly after the moon disappeared. When they saw the first new sliver appear, they lit fires on hilltops to announce that Rosh Khodesh—the new month had come.

The sounding of the silver trumpets was commanded for the Rosh Khodesh celebration.

Numbers 10:10 *Also on your days of rejoicing, at your designated times and on Rosh-Hodesh, you are to sound the trumpets over your burnt offerings and over the sacrifices of your peace offerings; these will be your reminder before your God. I am ADONAI your God.*

Yom Teruah (Rosh Hashanah) is the biggest Rosh Khodesh festival day. The two Appointed Times have similar offerings. Here are the offerings God required for Rosh Khodesh.

Numbers 28:11-15 *At each Rosh-Hodesh of yours, you are to present a burnt offering to ADONAI consisting of two young bulls, one ram and seven male lambs in their first year and without defect; 12 with six quarts of fine flour mixed with olive oil as a grain offering for the one ram; 13 and two quarts of fine flour mixed with olive oil as a grain offering for each lamb. This will be the burnt offering giving a fragrant aroma, an offering made by fire for ADONAI. 14 Their drink offerings will be two quarts of wine for a bull, one-and-one-third quarts for the ram, and one quart for each lamb. This is the burnt offering for every Rosh-Hodesh throughout the months of the year. 15 Also a male goat is to be offered as a sin offering to ADONAI, in addition to the regular burnt offering and its drink offering.*

And here are the offerings God commanded for Yom Teruah (Rosh Hashanah).

Numbers 29:1-6 *In the seventh month, on the first day of the month, you are to have a holy convocation; do not do any kind of ordinary work; it is a day of blowing the shofar for you. 2 Prepare a burnt offering* to make a fragrant aroma for ADONAI—*one young bull*, one ram and seven male lambs in their first year and without defect—3 with their grain offering, consisting of fine flour mixed with olive oil—six quarts for the bull, four quarts for the ram, 4 and two quarts for each of the seven lambs—5 also one male goat as a sin offering to make atonement for you. 6 This is to be *in addition to the burnt offering for Rosh-Hodesh* with its grain offering, the regular burnt offering with its grain offering, and their drink offerings ...; this will be a fragrant aroma ... to ADONAI.

So, in addition to the Rosh Khodesh offerings, the offerings required for Yom Teruah (Rosh Hashanah) are the same as the Rosh Khodesh offerings except *only one bull* is required instead of two and *no drink offerings* are required.

Here are accounts of keeping Rosh Khodesh:

I Chronicles 23:31 *They were to be present regularly before ADONAI whenever burnt offerings were offered to ADONAI on Shabbat, at Rosh-Hodesh, and at the other designated times, in the numbers required by the rules for sacrifices.*

II Chronicles 8:12-13 *Then Shlomo (Solomon) offered burnt offerings to ADONAI ... according to the mitzvah of Moshe on Shabbats, at Rosh-Hodesh and at the designated times ....*

Here's a Rosh Khodesh cleansing commanded in Ezekiel.

Ezekiel 45:18-19 *Adonai ELOHIM says this: On the first day of the first month you are to take a young bull without defect and purify the sanctuary. 19 The cohen (priest) will take some of the blood from the sin offering and put it on the door-frames of the house, on the four corners of the altar's ledge and on the supports of the gate of the inner courtyard.*

Here's a record of the Israelites keeping both Yom Teruah and Rosh Khodesh when they returned from exile in Ezra and Nehemiah's day.

Ezra 3:1-6 *When the seventh month arrived, after the people of Isra'el had resettled in the towns, the people gathered with one accord in Yerushalayim (Jerusalem). 2 Then ... cohanim (priests), and Z'rubavel (Zerubbabel) ... with his kinsmen, organized rebuilding the altar of the God of Isra'el; so that they could offer burnt offerings on it, as is written in the Torah of Moshe the man of God. 3 ... Despite feeling threatened by the peoples of the [surrounding] countries; they offered on it burnt offerings to ADONAI, the morning and evening burnt offerings. ... 5 and afterwards the regular burnt offering, the offerings for Rosh-Hodesh and those for all the designated times set apart for ADONAI, ... even though the foundation of ADONAI's temple had not yet been laid.*

Rosh Khodesh Being Revived

In Acts 3:21 Kefa (Peter) teaches that *The Messiah ... has to remain in heaven until the time comes for restoring everything, as God said long ago, when He spoke through the holy prophets.*

We are in this time of restoration. We have witnessed Israel being restored to the land. Messianic Jews are being restored to their place in the body of the Messiah through Messianic Judaism. The gifts of the Holy Spirit are being reactivated in the body of the Messiah. And among Y'hudim Mishikhim (Messianics), the Holy Days of Leviticus 23 are being observed again.

This Appointed Time of Rosh Khodesh is also being restored. But, how should we celebrate it? What is the meaning in keeping it? Is there any special significance to it? These are questions to which the right answers are being found.

The Scriptures are filled with warnings about worshiping the moon. Needless to say: we do not worship the moon. What we do is worship the Creator at the divinely appointed time of the New Moon.

Celebrating Rosh Khodesh

As noted earlier, God appointed Rosh Khodesh to be a Feast Day or holiday. This is underscored by Amos 8:5 where it is reflected as a Sabbath day wherein there is no buying, nor selling: *You say, "When will Rosh-Khodesh be over, so we can market our grain? and Shabbat, so we can sell wheat?"*

How should this Appointed Time be celebrated today? To answer this question, let's look at how it was observed in the Tanakh (Old Testament).

First, it was a time to seek the Lord.

II Kings 4: 22-23 *She called to her husband and said, "Please send me one of the servants with a donkey. I must get <u>to the man of God</u> as fast as I can; I'll come straight back."*

He asked, "Why are you going to him today? It isn't <u>Rosh-Hodesh</u> and it isn't Shabbat."

She said, "It's all right."

Second, it was a time for blowing the Shofar. Psalm 81:3 tells us to: *Sound the shofar at <u>Rosh-Hodesh</u> ....*

It was a time dedicated to worshiping God in His presence at the gate to the inner court of the Temple.

Ezekiel 46:1-3 *This is what Adonai ELOHIM says: The east gate of the inner courtyard is to be shut on the six working days, but on Shabbat it is to be opened, and on <u>Rosh-Hodesh</u> it is to be opened. 2 The* *prince is to enter by way of the outer vestibule of the gate and stand by the support of the gate. The cohanim are to prepare his burnt offering and peace offerings. Then he is to* prostrate himself in worship *at the threshold of the gate, after which he is to leave; but the gate is not to be shut until evening. 3 The people of the land are also to* prostrate themselves in worship before ADONAI *at the entrance to that gate on Shabbat and on* Rosh-Hodesh. And in Ezekiel 40:44 we learn: *Outside the inner gate, in the inner courtyard, were rooms for the singers ....*

The leaders and people worshiped and the singers sang. It was also a time of burning sweet incense before the Lord as shown here.

II Chronicles 2:4 *"Here, I am about to build a house for the name of ADONAI my God, to dedicate it to him, and to burn before Him* incense made of sweet spices; *the house will also be for the continuing show-bread and for the burnt offerings presented every morning and evening, on the Shabbats, at every* Rosh-Hodesh, *and at the designated times of ADONAI our God. This is a perpetual regulation for Isra'el."*

It was also a time to give a freewill (voluntary) offering.

Ezra 3:5 *... and afterwards the regular burnt offering, the offerings for* Rosh-Hodesh *and those for all the designated times set apart for ADONAI, as well as those of everyone who volunteered a* voluntary offering *to ADONAI.*

It was also a time to make reconciliation before God for the House of Israel.

Ezekiel 45:17 *The prince's obligation will be to present the burnt offerings, grain offerings and drink offerings at the feasts, on* Rosh-Hodesh, *and on Shabbat—at all the designated times of the house of Isra'el. He is to prepare the sin offerings, grain offerings, burnt offerings and peace offerings* to make atonement for the house of Isra'el.

II Chronicles 31:1-3 *After all this was over, all Isra'el who were there went out to the cities of Y'hudah and smashed the standing-stones, chopped down the sacred poles, and broke down the high places and altars, ... 2 Hizkiyahu (Hezekiah) re-established the divisions of the cohanim and L'vi'im .... 3 He determined a portion of the king's property to be given for the burnt offerings, that is, for the morning and evening burnt offerings and for burnt offerings on Shabbats,* Rosh-Hodesh *and the designated times, as prescribed by the Torah of ADONAI.*

Nehemiah 10: 32-33 *We will impose on ourselves a yearly tax ... for the service of the house of our God, 33 for the showbread, for the regular grain offering, for the regular burnt offering, for [the offerings] on Shabbat, on* Rosh-Hodesh, *at the designated times and at other holy times ....*

Rosh Khodesh was memorialized by gathering with family.

I Samuel 20:5-6 *David answered Y'honatan* (Jonathan), *"Look, tomorrow is* <u>Rosh-Hodesh</u>, *and I ought to be dining with the king. Instead, let me go and hide myself in the countryside until evening of the third day. 6 If your father misses me at all, say, 'David begged me to let him hurry to Beit-Lechem* (Bethlehem), *his city; because it's the annual sacrifice there for his whole family.'"*

And with all this, Hosea 2:11 hints that it was also a time of mirth. The passage infers it: *"I will end her happiness, her festivals, Rosh-Hodesh, and Shabbats ...."* (A temporary cessation due to judgment, since II Chronicles 2:4 states that this is an *"ordinance forever to Israel"* and because Yeshua said in Matthew 5:17-18 *"Don't think that I have come to abolish the Torah or the Prophets. I have come not to abolish but to complete. 18 Yes indeed! I tell you that until heaven and earth pass away, not so much as a yud or a stroke will pass from the Torah— not until everything that must happen has happened."*)

So in looking at how the time of the New Moon was observed, we see the following major themes:

- seeking God
- blowing of the Shofar
- worshiping and singing
- sweet incense
- free will offering
- reconciliation for the House of Israel
- family gatherings
- mirth

It is clear from Isaiah 66:22-23 that celebrating Rosh Khodesh is appropriate for Believers today and even during the Millennial reign of our Messiah: *"For just as the new heavens and the new earth that I am making will continue in my presence,"* says ADONAI, *"so will your descendants and your name continue. 23 Every month on Rosh-Hodesh and every week on Shabbat, everyone living will come to worship in my presence,"* says ADONAI.

Paul mentions that Rosh Khodesh is a shadow of things to come.

Colossians 2:16-17 *So don't let anyone pass judgment on you in connection with eating and drinking, or in regard to a Jewish festival or* <u>Rosh-Hodesh</u> *or Shabbat. 17 These are a shadow of things that are coming, but the body is of the Messiah.*

So, how should Believers celebrate Rosh Khodesh?   Let us reexamine the list above.

Meeting with the Lord and seeking Him is eternally beneficial, especially on a day He has designated specifically for that purpose.

Blowing of the Shofar is important because this has an effect in the spirit realm by way of spiritual warfare, whose benefits ought to be pursued.

Sweet incense is a type for petitional prayer! We see this here.

Revelation 5:8 (NKJV) *Now when He had taken the scroll, the four living creatures and the twenty-four elders fell down before the Lamb, each having a harp, and golden bowls full of incense, which are the prayers of the saints.*

A freewill offering today can be money, but it can also be an offering of thanksgiving or praise to go along with the time of worship. It can be an offering of a vow (but vows have to be kept, otherwise they are displeasing), or it can be an offering of our personal time.

Reconciliation for the House of Israel can be made by way of intercession which is different from petition prayer in that intercession is not for yourself. It is on behalf of someone else. And intercession includes identifying with those being interceded for, and travailing for them, and thereby coming to a place of authority before God on their behalf. That is what Yeshua is doing in heaven for us right now (see I John 2:1-2).

Of course, Yeshua is our sacrifice and our offering. So burnt offerings, drink offerings, meat offerings, peace offerings, and sin offerings are now replaced by a time of personal repentance and confession of sin.

Gathering with family for the purpose of focusing on the Lord is always a good thing.

As for mirth, going into the House of the Lord with other Believers and worshiping and praising is really a celebration. During these times, Israel was commanded to rejoice and be glad before the Lord. It is a command!

Psalm 100:2 *Serve ADONAI with gladness. Enter his presence with joyful songs.*

The Significance of Rosh Khodesh

As mentioned earlier, the Biblical lunar calendar begins when the first sliver of light appears after the moon has been in total darkness. At first glance, it may appear strange that the time of the New Moon (Rosh Khodesh) begins when the moon is basically in darkness. But when we consider the operation of God, it is not quite so strange. The creation of the universe began with total darkness.

Genesis 1:2-3 ... *darkness was on the face of the deep, ... 3 Then God said, "Let there be light"; and there was light.*

Later on, the creation of the first day began with the evening.

Genesis 1:5 *So there was evening and there was morning, one day.* (This verse is why the Hebrew day lasts from sunset to sunset.)

Furthermore, Isaiah 60:2 (KJV) reads, ... *darkness shall cover the earth, and gross darkness the people, but the Lord shall arise upon thee, and his glory shall be seen upon thee.*

We see that in God's economy, we move from darkness to light—and then from *"glory to glory"*—greater light to greater light (II Corinthians 3:18). Rosh Khodesh starts out with a dark moon. After that the first sliver of light is seen. Then it moves into full light. It's prophetic. We are in darkness now, but we are moving into His Glorious Light.

In the book of Ezekiel, there is an awesome revelation about the time of the New Moon.

Ezekiel 46:1 (KJV) *Thus saith The Lord God; The gate of the inner court that looketh toward the east shall be shut six working days; but on the Sabbath it shall be opened, and in the day of the <u>new moon</u> it shall be opened.*

Now the prophet Ezekiel was speaking of what he was seeing in his day in the natural. But we know that the patterns that we see here on earth are types of the real (the heavenly). Moses was to follow the patterns given to him precisely.

Hebrews 8:5 *But what they are serving is only a copy and shadow of the heavenly original; for when Moshe (Moses) was about to erect the Tent, God warned him, "See to it that you make everything according to the pattern you were shown on the mountain."*

Hebrews 9:24 (KJV) *For [Messiah] is not entered into the holy places made with hands, which are figures of the true; but into heaven itself, now to appear in the presence of God for us.*

This then is the awesome revelation of Ezekiel: that the gates of the inner court of heaven are open at Rosh Khodesh!

What is the deeper meaning of this? For one thing, it speaks of favor with God. It is a time of divine invitation. In the book of Esther, one quickly grasps what a difference the favor of the king makes! Now, what about the favor of the King of Kings and Lord of Lords?

Esther 4:11 *"All the king's officials, as well as the people in the royal provinces, know that if anyone, man or woman, approaches the king in the inner courtyard without being summoned, there is just one law—he must be put to death—unless the king holds out the gold scepter for him to remain alive ...."*

Esther 5:1-2 *On the third day, Ester* (Esther) *put on her royal robes and stood in the inner courtyard of the king's palace, opposite the king's hall. The king was sitting on his royal throne in the king's hall, across from the entrance to the hall. 2 When the king saw Ester the queen standing in the courtyard, she won his favor; so the king extended the gold scepter in his hand toward Ester. Ester approached and touched the tip of the scepter.*

On the day of Rosh Khodesh, we have favor; the heavenly gate of the inner court is open unto us and we can enter in. We have a royal invitation to do so. We need to grasp this one thing: as New Covenant Believers we have access to God at any time we choose to seek Him. But in the time of the New Moon, God is specifically seeking to have access to us!

The inner court is no ordinary place. It is a place of glory! It is a place of divine visitation! Look at this Scripture.

Ezekiel 10:3-4 *Now the k'ruvim* (cheribum) *were standing to the right of the house when the man entered, and the cloud filled the inner courtyard. 4 The glory of ADONAI rose from above the keruv* (cherub) *to the threshold of the house, leaving the house filled with the cloud and the courtyard full of the brilliance of ADONAI's glory.*

I asked the Lord to give me one more thing to share about Rosh Khodesh, and I heard the Spirit say, "If you love Me, I will manifest Myself to you." You see at this Appointed Time, you are not necessarily required to meet with God, though He has ordained this time to meet with you. You will meet with Him at this time for only one reason: that you love Him.

Appendix II
The Two Silver Trumpets

Community Assembling
Numbers 10:2-3 *Make two trumpets; make them of hammered silver. Use them for summoning the community and for sounding the call to break camp and move on. When they are sounded, the entire community is to assemble before you at the entrance to the tent of meeting.*

Leaders Assembling
Numbers 10:4 *If only one is sounded, then just the leaders, the heads of the clans of Isra'el (Israel), are to assemble before you.*

Marching (the silver trumpets)
Numbers 10:5-8 *When you sound an alarm, the camps to the east will commence traveling. 6 When you sound a second alarm, the camps to the south will set out; they will sound alarms to announce when to travel. 7 However, when the community is to be assembled, you are to sound; but don't sound an alarm. 8 It will be the sons of Aharon (Aaron), the cohanim (priests), who are to sound the trumpets; this will be a permanent regulation for you through all your generations.*

Battle in the Land Against an Oppressing Enemy
Numbers 10:9 *When you go to war in your land against an adversary who is oppressing you, you are to sound an alarm with the trumpets; then you will be remembered before ADONAI your God, and you will be saved from your enemies.*

Rejoicing, Appointed Times, offerings
Numbers 10:10 *Also on your days of rejoicing, at your designated times and on Rosh-Hodesh, you are to sound the trumpets over your burnt offerings and over the sacrifices of your peace offerings; ...*

A Memorial
Numbers 10:10 *... these will be your reminder before your God. I am ADONAI your God.*

Appendix III
Biblical Uses of the Shofar

Exodus 19:16,19 To meet God and hear His voice*
Leviticus 25:8-10 To proclaim the year of Jubilee on Yom Kippur
Joshua 6 In warfare—prior to shouting—against Jericho*
Judges 3:27 To assemble the people for war
Judges 7 In warfare—after shouting—by Gideon*
I Samuel 13:3 Communicating
II Samuel 2:28 Halting hostilities
II Samuel 6:15 and I Chronicles 15:24,28 Bringing the Ark of God*
II Samuel 15:10 and I Kings 1:34 Announcing a new king
II Chronicles 15:14 Entering into covenant with the Lord
Nehemiah 4:18-20 To gather against an attack*
Psalms 81:3-4 New Moon and Pesakh
Jeremiah 4:5 Warning to flee because destruction is coming
Isaiah 58:1 To consecrate a fast
Hosea 5:8 and 8:1 A rebuke from God
Joel 2:15-17 Proclaiming a fast to avert judgment
Amos 2:2 Judgment of God
Zephaniah 1:14-16 The Day of the Lord
Psalms 98:6 and 150:3 To praise God in worship*
Matthew 24:31 & I Thessalonians 4:16-17 To announce the Rapture*
Revelation 8:6 The judgments of the seven "trumpets"

To Meet God and Hear His Voice
Exodus 19:16,19 *On the morning of the third day, there was thunder, lightning and a thick cloud on the mountain. Then a shofar blast sounded so loudly that all the people in the camp trembled. 19 As the sound of the shofar grew louder and louder, Moshe (Moses) spoke; and God answered him with a voice.*

To Proclaim the Year of Jubilee
Leviticus 25:8-10 *You are to count seven Shabbats (Sabbaths) of years, seven times seven years, that is, forty-nine years. 9 Then, on the tenth day of the seventh month, on Yom-Kippur, you are to sound a blast on the shofar; you are to sound the shofar all through your land; 10 and you are to consecrate the fiftieth year, proclaiming freedom throughout the land to all its inhabitants. It will be a yovel (Jubilee) for you; you will return everyone to the land he owns, and everyone is to return to his family.*

* highlighted in Chapter 6 "The Shofar" pp. 71-90

To Assemble for War

Judges 3:27 *Upon arrival in the hills of Efrayim (Ephraim), he began sounding the call on the shofar; and the people of Isra'el (Israel) went down with him from the hill-country; he himself took the lead. 28 He said to them: "Follow me, because ADONAI has given your enemy Mo'av (Moab) into your hands.*

In Warfare

Joshua 6:4-5 *Seven cohanim (Priests) are to carry seven shofars in front of the ark. On the seventh day you are to march around the city seven times, and the cohanim will blow the shofars. 5 Then they are to blow a long blast on the shofar. On hearing the sound of the shofar, all the people are to shout as loudly as they can; and the wall of the city will fall down flat.*

Judges 7:20 *All three companies blew the shofars, broke the pitchers and held the torches in their left hands, keeping their right hands free for the shofars they were blowing; and they shouted, "The sword for ADONAI and for Gid'on (Gideon)!"*

Communicating

I Samuel 13:3 *Y'honatan (Jonathan) assassinated the governor of the P'lishtim (Philistines) in Geva (Geba). The P'lishtim heard of it; so Sha'ul had the shofar sounded throughout the land, saying, "Let the Hebrews hear!"*

Halting Hostilities

II Samuel 2:28 *Then Yo'av (Joab) sounded the shofar, and with that the people halted. They stopped pursuing Isra'el, and they stopped fighting.*

Bringing the Ark of God

I Chronicles 15:24, 28 *... the cohanim (priests) blew the trumpets in front of the ark of God. ... 28 So all Isra'el brought up the ark for the covenant of ADONAI with shouting; blowing on shofars and trumpets; ....*

Announcing a New King

I Kings 1:34 *There Tzadok (Zadok) the cohen (priest) and Natan (Nathan) the prophet are to anoint him king over Isra'el. Sound the shofar and say, "Long live King Shlomo (Solomon)!*

Entering into Covenant with the Lord

II Chronicles 15:12-14 *... and they entered into a covenant to seek ADONAI, the God of their ancestors, with all their heart and with all their being; 13 [they also agreed] that whoever refused to seek ADONAI the God of Isra'el should be put to death, whether small or great, man or woman. 14 They swore this to ADONAI in a loud voice, with shouting and blowing of trumpets and shofars.*

To Gather Against an Attack

Nehemiah 4:18-20 *As for the construction-workers, each one had his sword sheathed at his side; that is how they built. The man to sound the alarm on the shofar stayed with me. 19 I said to the nobles, the leaders and the rest of the people, "This is a great work, and it is spread out; we are separated on the wall, one far from another. 20 But wherever you are, when you hear the sound of the shofar, come to that place, to us. Our God will fight for us!"*

For New Moon and Pesakh

Psalms 81:3-4 *Sound the shofar at Rosh-Hodesh* (New Moon) *and at full moon for the pilgrim feast, 4 because this is a law for Isra'el, a ruling of the God of Ya'akov* (Jacob).

Warning to Flee to the City for Destruction is Coming

Jeremiah 4:5 *Announce in Y'hudah* (Judah), *proclaim in Yeru-shalayim* (Jerusalem); *say: "Blow the shofar in the land!" Shout the message aloud: "Assemble! Let us go to the fortified cities!"*

To Consecrate a Fast

Isaiah 58:1,4,6 *Shout out loud! Don't hold back! Raise your voice like a shofar! Proclaim to my people what rebels they are, to the house of Ya'akov* (Jacob) *their sins. ... 4 Your fasts lead to quarreling and fighting, ... Fasting like yours will not make your voice heard on high. ... 6 "Here is the sort of fast I want—releasing those unjustly bound, untying the thongs of the yoke, letting the oppressed go free, breaking every yoke ....*

A Rebuke from God

Hosea 5:8 *Blow the shofar in Giv'ah* (Gibeah), *a trumpet at Ramah; sound an alarm .... 9 Efrayim* (Ephraim) *will be laid waste when the day for punishment comes; I am announcing to the tribes of Isra'el what will surely happen.*

Hosea 8:1 *Put the shofar to your lips! Like a vulture [he swoops down] on the house of ADONAI, because they have violated my covenant and sinned intentionally against my Torah.*

Proclaiming a Fast to Avert Judgment

Joel 2:15-17 *"Blow the shofar in Tziyon* (Zion)! *Proclaim a holy fast, call for a solemn assembly." 16 Gather the people; consecrate the congregation; assemble the leaders; gather the children, even infants sucking at the breast; let the bridegroom leave his room and the bride the bridal chamber. 17 Let the cohanim* (priests), *who serve ADONAI, stand weeping between the vestibule and the altar. Let them say, "Spare your people, ADONAI!*

Judgment of God
Amos 2:2 *I will send fire on Mo'av (Moab), and it will consume the palaces of K'riot (Kerioth). Mo'av will die with turmoil and shouting, along with the sound of the shofar.*

The Day of the Lord
Zephaniah 1:14-16 *The great Day of ADONAI is near, near and coming very quickly; Hear the sound of the Day of ADONAI! When it's here, even a warrior will cry bitterly. 15 That Day is a Day of fury, a Day of trouble and distress, a Day of waste and desolation, a Day of darkness and gloom, a Day of clouds and thick fog, 16 a Day of the shofar and battle-cry against the fortified cities and against the high towers [on the city walls].*

Worship
Psalm 98:5-6 *Sing praises to ADONAI with the lyre, with the lyre and melodious music! 6 With trumpets and the sound of the shofar, shout for joy before the king, ADONAI!*
Psalm 150:3 *Praise him with a blast on the shofar!*

Gathering in of the Exiles
Isaiah 27:12-13 *On that day ... you will be gathered, one by one, people of Isra'el (Israel)! 13 On that day a great shofar will sound. Those lost in the land of Ashur (Assyria) will come, also those scattered through the land of Egypt; and they will worship ADONAI on the holy mountain in Yerushalayim (Jerusalem).*

The Rapture
Matthew 24:31 *He will send out his angels with a great shofar; and they will gather together his chosen people from the four winds, from one end of heaven to the other.*
I Thessalonians 4:16-17 *For the Lord himself will come down from heaven with a rousing cry, with a call from one of the ruling angels, and with God's shofar; those who died united with the Messiah will be the first to rise; 17 then we who are left still alive will be caught up with them in the clouds to meet the Lord in the air; and thus we will always be with the Lord.*

The Judgments of the Seven "Trumpets"
Revelation 8:6 *Now the seven angels with the seven shofars prepared to sound them.*

Appendix IV
Dates of the Original Teachings

Pronunciation Key

' (an apostrophe) - a very short vowel called a guttural stop

ai - pronounced like "igh" in light.

i - ee

kh - a guttural sound pronounced like the "ch" in Bach
(Spelled "ch" in most sources.)

Glossary

[Key: term (Strong's number) - *actual meaning;* English equivalent]

(All terms are Hebrew unless otherwise noted.)

[Some spellings are different from the Complete Jewish Bible (CJB) for pronunciation clarity.]

(In Hebrew, adjectives are placed *after* the nouns they modify.)

(Plural Hebrew words end in -im or -ot, not in -s or -es.)

avone - *inclination to evil;* iniquity (p. 162)

ADONAI Yireh (pronounced yeereh) - *the LORD provides;* Jehovah Jireh (pp. 244-245 spelled Yir'eh)

ah-kode (a form of H6123) - *bound* (top of p. 244)

ahava - *love* (p. 247)

Akida - *binding* (noun, a form of ah-kode); the name given to the Parshah reading of the story of Abraham almost sacrificing Isaac (chapter 19, p. 139)

Al Khet - *for sin;* short for: "for the sin which we have committed"; the list of sins read as confession on Yom Kippur (p. 203) (Traditionally spelled "Al Chet")

anah (H6031) - *to afflict, to chasten* [or] *... to humble one's self. (p. 59)*

Ani ADONAI roph-eh-khah - *I am the LORD who heals you* (p. 153)

Aseret Yemai T'shuva - *Ten Days of Repentance;* what the ten days between Rosh Hashanah and Yom Kippur are sometimes called (p. 99)

Avraham - *father of a multitude;* Abraham

BCE - Before the Common Era (same as B.C.)

b'kol - *by voice* (p. 73 and 196) (Also can mean *in the whole*)

b'rit - *covenant*

B'rit Hadashah - *New Covenant;* New Testament

b'rit milah - *covenant of circumcision*

CE - Common Era (same as A.D.)

cohane - *priest* (singular noun) (spelled "cohen" in CJB)

Cohane HaGadol - *The High Priest*

cohanim - *priests* (plural of "cohane")

Diaspora - (Greek) *dispersion;* referring to the history of the Jewish people being banished from Israel and scattered among the nations (pp. 18 and 23)

eklectos (Greek) - *chosen, favored* (p. 26)

Elisheva - *my God is my oath* (or *sustenance);* Elizabeth

Elohim yireh Lo ha-say - *God will provide for Himself the lamb.* (p. 243)

Elul (Aramaic) - *search;* the Hebrew month before Rosh Hashanah
(p. 122)

erev - *evening or eve* (as in New Year's *eve)*

Etz Khaiyim Hee - *Tree of Life;* referring to a Hebrew prayer song
(p. 133)

Ger - A Gentile who has chosen to live among the Children of Israel
like Ruth did.

Ger Mishikhi - *Anointed Ger* (singular noun and adjective); A Messianic
Gentile who has chosen to live among the Children of Israel.

Gerim - (plural of Ger) Gentiles who have chosen to live among the
Children of Israel.

Gerim Mishikhim - *Anointed Gerim* (plural of Ger Mishikhi); Messianic
Gentiles called this because they have chosen to live and worship
among the Children of Israel. (This term solves the problem of wondering what to call Gentiles who join the Messianic Movement aside
from calling them "Ruths.")

Gan Eden - *Garden of Eden* (p. 151)

Gid'on - Gideon

Goy - *nation;* Gentile

goy kadosh - *a holy nation* (p. 194, 198, 199)

Goyim - *nations* (plural of Goy)*;* Gentiles

ha - *the*

hagios (Greek, G37) - *set them apart* (p. 172)

ha kol - *everything*

hamartia (Greek, G266) - *sin* (p. 148)

HaMashiakh - *The Anointed One;* The Messiah

ha satan - *the adversary;* satan

heneni - I'm here; *here I am* (p. 240)

kadosh - *holy*

keruv - cherub (p. 258)

ki khed-vat ADONAI he mah-ooz-khem - *for the joy of the LORD is your
defense* (pp. 143-144)

kippa - *covering;* cap worn by Jewish men

Khanukah - *Dedication;* Holiday celebration the retaking of the Temple
by the Maccabees. (spelled many different ways, most traditionally,
Hanukkah or Chanukah) (p. 11)

kha-tso-ts'rah (H2689) - *trumpet* (p. 76)

khatahah - *missing the mark;* unintentional sin (p. 162)

khavarah - *fellowship, friend* (p. 16)

khazak meh-ode - *became stronger and stronger* (p. 196)

kharad (H 2730) - *to tremble, to be fearful, to be reverent* (p. 60)

khet (H2399) - *sin*

kol (H3605, H6963) - *all; the whole; voice*

kol levavkhah - *with all your heart* (p. 247)
kol haShofar - *voice of the Shofar* (p. 73, 196)
kruvim - cherubim (plural of keruv) (p. 258)

L'shanah Tovah Tikkah Tevu - *May your name be inscribed to a good year;* Rosh Hashanah greeting (pp. 99 and 177)
L'shanah Tovah Tikkah Tevu v'Tikkah Temu - *May your name be inscribed and sealed for a good year;* Yom Kippur greeting (p. 177)
L'vi'im - Levites
lev - *heart* (p. 247)

mah-m'leh-khet cohanim - kingdom of priests (pp. 194, 198-200)
Mashiakh (H4899) - *anointed one;* Messiah
Miryam - Mary
mitzvah - *commandment*
mitzvot - *commandments* (plural of mitzvah)
Moad (H4150) - *Appointed Time* (introduced on p. 9)
Moadim - *Appointed Times* (plural of Moad) (introduced on p. 9)
mikveh - ritual bath place (p. 49)
Mishikhi - *anointed* (singular adjective) Messianic
Mishikhim - *anointed* (plural of adjective Mishikhi) Messianic
Mishna - the collections of the Jewish oral traditions (p. 14)
Moshe - Moses

nih-sah - (form of H5254) *to test, to prove, to try* (p. 239)
Nisan (H5212) - *their flight;* first month of the Biblical calendar, the month in which Passover occurs (p. 122)

olam hazeh - *this age* (p. 92)

Parashah - weekly readings from the Torah and the prophets (pp. 194, 239)
Parush - Pharisee ((p. 221, 222)
Pesakh (H6453) - *Passover* (pp. 11, 12, 15, 21, 67, 261)
P'rushim - Pharisees (plural of Parush) (pp. 18, 221)
pasha - *to transgress or rebel* (verb form of pesha)
pesha (H6588) - *intentional sin* (noun); transgression (pp. 153, 169)
Purim - holiday celebrating the time of Esther when she saved her Jewish people

Rabbi Sha'ul - Rabbi - *honored one;* Sha'ul (H7586) *desired; asked for,* Rabbi or Apostle Paul [Jewish Believers in his day would have addressed him as Rabbi. Paul is the Greek translation of Sha'ul (Saul).]
rhema (Greek) - *an utterance; thing said;* the spoken Word of God; a personal Word from God (p. 43)

Rosh Hashanah - *Head of the Year;* Biblical holiday: Feast of Trumpets
Rosh Khodesh (H2320) - *Head of the Month;* New Moon (pp. 251-258)
Ruakh HaKodesh (H7307, H6944) - *The Holy Spirit*

sal-pinx (G4536) - *trumpet;* (p. 74)
Shavuot (H7620) - *weeks, Feast of Weeks;* Biblical holiday, Pentecost
(pp. 11,15,63,198)
s'gulah mee-kol ha-amim (H5459, H3605, H5971) - *special treasured
possession from all the people* (pp. 194,198,199)
slikhot - *forgivenesses;* (also spelled selichot); repentant prayers traditionally recited during the days preceding Rosh Hashanah (p. 15)
Shabbat (H7676, from H7673) - *to cease, to rest;* Sabbath
Shabbaton (H7677) - *Sabbath; a day of rest* (p. 58)
Shalom (H7965) - *completeness, wholeness, well being, peace ...*
Shalu Shalom Yerushalayim - *Pray for the peace (wholeness) of Jerusalem;* (also the title of a song) (p. 116)
Sha'ul (H7586) - *desired; asked for;* Saul [Paul is the Greek translation
of Sha'ul (Saul).]
Shofar (H7782) - *ram's horn trumpet* (detailed explanations on pp. 72,
73)
Shofarot - (plural of Shofar)
shomar (H8104) - *watchman* (p. 119-120)
shomrim - *watchmen* (plural of shomar) (p. 119)
shomrot - *watchwoman* (feminine form of shomar) (p. 119-120)
S'udat Adonai -*The Lord's Supper;* Communion (p. 33)
sukkah - *booth; tent; tabernacle*
Sukkot (also spelled Sukkoth) (plural of sukkah) - Biblical holiday, Feast
of Tabernacles (pp. 11,13,117,150,218,252)

Talmid - *study;* the name of the traditional Jewish Commentary on
Scripture (p. 83)
talmidim - *students, disciples* (p. 155)
Tanakh - Old Testament (also called the Old Covenant) or sometimes
refers to the whole Bible.
Tashlikh (imperfect tense of H7993) - *casting off;* the tradition of casting
bread on flowing water on Rosh Hashanah (pp. 122, 175)
Teruah (H8643) - *sounding the Shofar and shouting for joy* (introduced
on p. 12; further explanation on p. 86)
Tikkun La'il Shavuot - *rectification* or *repairing of the night of Shavuot;*
traditional all night prayer vigil before Shavuot (p. 198)
Torah (H3384) - *instruction, law;* what God gave on Mt. Sinai; refers to
the Five Books of Moses, sometimes to the whole Old Testament
(introduced on p. 45)
t'shuvah (a form of H7725) - *to return, turn back, restore;* repentance
(introduced on p. 99)
tsuris (Yiddish) - *troubles, tribulation* (p. 45)

Tu B'She vat - *15th of Shevat* (a month in the Jewish calendar in January); New Year for Trees (p. 13)
Tikkah Tevu - *may your name be inscribed* (pp. 99 and 177)
Tikkah Temu - *may your name be sealed* (p. 99)
tzedakah - *good deeds* (pp. 135-136)
Tziyon (H6726, H6725) - Zion (pp. 88, 263)
Tishri - *beginning;* seventh month in the Jewish calendar in which Rosh Hashanah occurs (pp. 10, 12)
Theophany (Latin) - an appearance of God in the form of a man (p. 51)

v' - *and*
Vehahavta - *and you shall love* (p. 247)
v'goy kadosh - *and a holy nation* (p. 194)
v'yahee kol haShofar - *and when the voice of the Shofar* (p. 196)

Ya'akov - Jacob, James (pp. 15, 173)
Yarden - Jordan
Yericho - Jericho
Yerushalayim - Jerusalem
Yeshua - *He will save;* Jesus
Yeshua Ha Mashiakh - *Yeshua, the Anointed One;* Jesus, the Messiah
Y'hoshua - Joshua
Y'hudah - *God praiser;* Judah
Y'hudi - *a God praiser* (noun); Jew
Y'hudim - *God praisers* (plural of Y'hudi); Jews
Y'hudi Mishikhi - *Anointed God Praiser* (singular noun and adjective); Messianic Jewish person, called this because of embracing Yeshua (Jesus) as the Messiah
Y'hudim Mishikhim - *Anointed God Praisers* (plural of Yehudi Mishikhi); Messianic Jewish people, called this because of embracing Yeshua (Jesus) as the Messiah
Yitz'khak - Isaac (also spelled Yitz'chak)
yom - *day*
Yom HaShoah - *Day of Calamity;* Holocaust Day (p. 11, 12)
Yom Kippur - *Day of Atonement* (explained in detail on pp. 59-60)
Yomim Norim - *Days of Awe* (introduced on p. 59)
yud - *"y"* the smallest letter of the Hebrew alphabet

zih-kh'ron - *memorial* (intruduced on p. 11)
Zih-kh'ron Teruah - *Memorial for sounding of the Shofar and shouting for joy* (introduced on pp. 11-12)